SOURCES:

STAINED GLASS

Frontispiece. Le Mans Cathedral. Window in south aisle, *c.* 1081, 'The Ascension'.

STAINED GLASS

HISTORY, TECHNOLOGY AND PRACTICE

by

E. LIDDALL ARMITAGE

Foreword by
THE VERY REVEREND RICHARD COOMBS, B.D.

CHARLES T. BRANFORD COMPANY
NEWTON 59, MASSACHUSETTS

TO MY WIFE

ELLEN MARY

IN GRATITUDE FOR ALL HER HELP

Printed in Great Britain

Foreword

It is frightening to realize that our civilization obsessed with the transitory could lose touch with the eternal. It matters not whether the obsession has emerged from a weakness in the character of men and women, from the pressure of impersonal forces, or from a myriad combination of circumstances. The results would be the same. A new civilization would have to rise up to replace what has worn out in order that man's self-realization and God's self-revelation may have opportunity to be expressed.

A book written, a sermon preached, an object of beauty created, which brings man into touch with eternal values, postpones that awful day. But we are foolish if we suppose that all books, all sermons, all of man's creations do this. Some are quite distinctly embedded in the transitory. Our society often makes gross mis-judgements. For at least a century and a half (some would say much longer) we have been mesmerized by man's genius. We have postponed asking for what purpose he is so. The more we exploit the genius, neglecting the purpose, the more we as men become concerned with man, shutting out God. When we recall that man is the personification of the transitory, and God the personification of the eternal, we can perhaps understand what we are doing to ourselves and our civilization.

Here is a book on stained glass. The vast majority of people in our generation will accept it for the curious reason that above all we must maintain our reputation for comprehensiveness, and that even a book on stained glass must be received graciously into our culture. After all, one can find a book on anything, or on nothing, these days! In suggesting that this book, if read and understood by enough people, might help to recapture the lost balance of our age, my own sense of balance might be questioned.

I wish I could write and compile such a book as this. A vast technical knowledge and experience is required, which obviously only a few men possess. But that is not the rarest of the prerequisites. The rarest are the intuition and insight undergirding knowledge by which the artist-author is able to relate his subject to the life and destiny of his fellow human beings. Some men know how to make things. A few also know why they make them. The former deal deftly with the transitory. The latter are also in touch with the eternal.

The author of a book like this one, however, has a distinct advantage. He handles a unique subject. Stained glass is unique because it is created by the few for the many to a degree not even remotely approached by other art forms. A great painting, a

5

glorious symphony, a sweepingly epic poem, all of these can be and often are rejected with the words, 'It means nothing to me.' But this does not happen with a fine window. Stained glass communicates something to everyone.

The stained glass artist, consequently, bears a heavy responsibility. Since he communicates something to everyone he must be careful what he says, careful that he knows himself what he is saying and that it is really what he wants to say. While this may sound simple it is in fact infinitely complex because it involves him morally with himself, his society, and with his God. He works within the confines of rigid disciplines. He may be tempted to discard the disciplines on what seem to be the reasonable grounds of the need for self-expression, the demands of his patron, financial restrictions, or, what is more tragic, on the delusion that he is no longer the servant, but the master, of beauty.

As a layman I would say that there are several ingredients in fine stained glass. One is honesty or the absence of pretence; we should not expect the artist to paint pictures, to arrange flowers, or to imitate a portrait in stained glass, for this is to ask the art form to undertake tasks for which it is singularly inadaptable. Another is harmony or relatedness; a stained glass window is not an abstraction: it rests in some place for some purpose, and it should be related to all that surrounds it. A third is content; a window speaks to all who see it, and since it lives for decades, even centuries, it should speak of things that matter and continue to matter, and thus be ever new. Perhaps the most important is spirituality, or the manner in which the speaking is done. A window should tell of the eternal, not the transitory, qualities of its subject, speaking not of flesh and blood, but of the spirit of man and the Holy Spirit of God.

I am constrained to add a personal word concerning the author of this book, a close and good friend, who has so generously invited me to write this foreword. We initially came to know each other by correspondence across six thousand miles of land and sea. My suspicions that he was a great man were confirmed when first we met. It was my privilege to show him a part of America, a visit which, he has been kind enough to say, assured him concerning the character of people on this side of the Atlantic. It was my further privilege to sit at his feet and hear him speak of art, putting into words all that I had been able until then only inarticulately to feel. Thus was formed a bond which we would both dare to hope might be a symbol of what our two nations can continue to mean to each other in the future as they have in the past.

Edward Armitage has created some fine windows. This is not judgement but merely prophecy. Future generations will make the judgement. As those generations come and go they will look back on us. Amid our monuments to the transitory they will see the work he and his brethren have done. And they will know from their work that our generation did not lose all touch with the eternal.

June, 1958
THE DEANERY
THE CATHEDRAL OF ST. JOHN THE EVANGELIST
SPOKANE, WASHINGTON, U.S.A.

RICHARD COOMBS
Dean of Spokane

Preface

———❧⟨❀⟩⟨❁⟩⟨❁⟩⟨❀⟩⟨❀⟩———

This book is intended as a help to those young students who are trying their hand at the designing of a stained glass window.

As the most intelligent of us are always students I hope that it will be of interest to those of maturer years and experience, people perhaps like myself, who have worked at the problem long enough to realize how little they know, and, though the young rarely appreciate this, there can be no sounder qualification.

Lord Melbourne, man of the world, one of the finest intellects and one of the best read personalities of his time, noted that 'Neither man nor woman can be worth anything until they have discovered that they are fools. This is the first step towards becoming either estimable or agreeable; and until that step is taken there is no hope. The sooner the discovery is made the better, as there is more time and power for taking advantage of it. Sometimes this great truth is found out too late to apply it to any effectual remedy. Sometimes it is never found out at all; and these form the desperate and inveterate causes of folly, self-conceit and impertinence.'

I also include a collation of the views of the best stained glass artists of today, very many of whom I know personally, and with their help hope to provide a broad summary of the principles that guide modern work.

There never has been a wider range of style nor, contrary to the generally accepted view, a finer range of glass available to the artist both as regards colour and quality. A visit to Messrs. James Hetley and Co. Ltd., or Messrs. Miller Beale and Hilder Ltd., or to the Whitefriars Glass Works will amply confirm this truth.

Of course it would be untrue to suggest that the particular tint that the artist desires is always readily available. In fact it would be more true to say that the artists are constantly frustrated by the elusive qualities of the precise colour they find to be urgently necessary. Even at the Whitefriars Studios where we have the unique advantage of making our own glass, the most skilful and experienced technician cannot always be sure that any batch of colour will come out exactly to requirements.

The process of arriving at colour in glass is not the simple one of adding one pigment to another as in oil or water colour painting, where it is possible by combining for example yellow with blue to watch and control the immediate effect until the correct shade is obtained.

With glass, colour depends not only upon the proportion of the chemical ingredients but also on the temperature at which those ingredients are fused, and the duration of the firing. During the firing the glass is a mass of white-hot radiation and it is only after the glass has been taken from the kiln, blown into its particular shape, and annealed by the slow process of cooling, that the actual tint of the glass can be ascertained.

Nevertheless it is still true to say that we have a far wider choice of colour than the medieval craftsmen were able to command. The generally accepted idea that we cannot make such fine glass today as in the Middle Ages is untrue. The real truth is that in the earlier periods they were unable to make aesthetically bad glass whereas today vast quantities of cheap and inferior glass are turned out for commercial purposes.

Any failure to produce fine windows is therefore due not to any lack of superb material but rather to the mental or the psychological outlook of today. I believe it is generally accepted that the best stained glass of the present time is of a better standard than it was half a century ago, and that the craft itself is more virile and full of promise.

The stained glass designer has quite naturally always been influenced by the prevailing art of his day, not always to his advantage. He has always worked within the tradition of the architecture and painting of his period. Today, both in architecture and in painting, there has been an obvious and decided break with tradition, and since glass must generally conform to its architectural setting, to the traditionalist the break is disturbing, but to those of more tolerant outlook, however, this development is not only extremely interesting in itself; it is evidence that the craft is still very much alive today.

There is in consequence a far wider range of style for the student to explore; nevertheless, he should be aware of enthusiasm for modern art unsupported by a sound understanding of traditional design.

In writing this book from the standpoint of the designer, I have tried to demonstrate my strongly held conviction that the earliest stained glass owes its superiority over later achievement to a combination of two important factors: firstly, that early windows were designed as glass with delight in the precious material for its own sake. Secondly, that they were designed with an intense desire to express a deeply felt Christian belief.

The study of glass through the centuries shows the decline of both these attributes until, in the eighteenth century, they completely disappear, with that otherwise fine artist, Reynolds, as the supreme example of futility.

While modern stained glass artists have indeed returned to an appreciation of the material, the more important aspect of the problem remains unsolved, since in general their work is no longer an expression of faith. It is moreover impossible for the individual artist to remedy this deficiency entirely on his own initiative. It is true that every artist inevitably expresses in his own work his own individuality; it is nevertheless equally true that he is profoundly influenced by the prevailing mentality of his time and can only, at best, achieve the highest expression of its highest aspirations.

For example the work of Fra Angelico is undoubtedly individual but no one more definitely expresses the atmosphere of his period. A more contemporary example is William Blake. His work is also highly individual, indeed in his day he was thought to be revolutionary, but it is now seen to be steeped in the idiom of the era into which he was born.

It is therefore my firm belief that, similarly, stained glass windows testify to the cultural and spiritual level of their period.

ACKNOWLEDGEMENTS

It is difficult for me to express adequately my appreciation of all the kindness and help that I have received in attempting to compile this book. My especial thanks are due to Mrs. Frederick Cole and the Rev. Kenneth W. Thornton who have both given me valuable guidance. Without Mrs. Cole's expert criticism and correction, and without Mr. Thornton's wide knowledge and understanding, the limitations of the work would have been even more apparent. It is only fair to state that neither of these kind helpers agrees with every opinion I have expressed, but they have prevented my worst lapses from good taste.

I offer my grateful thanks to Mr. John Betjeman, Mr. T. S. Eliot, Mr. J. A. Knowles, Sir Herbert Read, Dr. Basil Willey and Dr. Christopher Woodforde for allowing me to quote from their books. It was particularly gratifying to find that such distinguished and experienced writers and scholars unhesitatingly gave their help to an unknown like myself.

Mr. H. L. Pawle, the Honorary Librarian of the British Society of Master Glass Painters, has kindly given me every assistance in my researches, and Mr. H. T. Kirkby, the editor of the *Journal*, has also been most co-operative and helpful. Mr. Alfred L. Wilkinson, the Hon. Sec. of our Society has been both patient and generous in giving me the advice I requested on far too many occasions.

I should also like to express my gratitude to Mr. W. J. Wilson, F.S.I.A., the managing director of James Powell and Sons (Whitefriars), Ltd., for his wise counsel and for all his kind help. My brother, H. M. A. Armitage, A.R.I.B.A., has also given me much sound advice and encouragement for which I am grateful.

The task of securing photographs of windows representative of the various periods is not an easy one and I should like to acknowledge with gratitude the kindness and help I have received from Mr. Cecil Farthing and Miss Gladys J. Gardner of the National Buildings Record, Mr. Geoffrey Webb and Mr. Frederick Power of the Royal Commission on Historical Monuments (England), Mr. E. A. Lane of the Victoria and Albert Museum, Miss Judith G. Scott of the Central Council for the Care of Churches, Dr. G. Zarnecki of the Courtauld Institute of Art, Mr. S. E. Dykes Bower, Mr. H. T. Kirkby, Mr. H. L. Pawle and the Very Rev. E. Milner-White, Dean of York.

CONTENTS

Contents

Part III: Modern Practice

LIST OF PLATES

13

PART 1

Historical

B

CHAPTER 1

Historical Introduction

The origins of stained glass are obscure but it seems beyond doubt that the development first began in the Middle East. To allow a certain amount of strong light to enter the building small holes were made in the walls. Craftsmen of aesthetic sensibility later arranged these into various patterns which might be termed the forerunners of the geometrical window. The next step was to fill the small holes with small pieces of coloured glass, a modest foreshadowing of the glories of Chartres.

It must not be imagined that this was an easy and obvious development. Glass was not an everyday material of commonplace utility. In those days it was, in fact, both rare and extremely costly. A piece of ruby glass had the same intrinsic value to the ancient Egyptians as the actual ruby. Glass and precious stones were used indiscriminately in their ornaments and were of similar value. One does not easily contemplate filling even the smallest of window openings with diamonds and rubies.

The use of glass by man had its origin in the stone age. In that period arrowheads and shaving blades were generally made of flint, but for the *élite* obsidian was used. This is a natural glass caused by volcanic action, usually black in colour but sometimes green, red or brown.

The earliest glass-ware of any kind actually made by man was in the form of glazed pottery and beads dating from about 12000 B.C. As regards pure glass, the oldest so far discovered is a moulded amulet of deep lapis-lazuli colour which is dated at about 7000 B.C. The Egyptians must gradually have accumulated an amazing knowledge of metallurgy as shown by their use of tin oxide to make opaque white glass.

This accumulation of knowledge and skill would no doubt be guarded as a trade or professional secret, but nevertheless it must have spread to Phoenicia and later found its way to Greece and Rome. In the excavations at Herculaneum and Pompeii slabs of window glass have been found; these were almost certainly moulded and probably never very transparent. Nevertheless it is certain that at a later date the Romans practised the craft of glass-blowing, because an example of their muff glass has been found at Silchester.

The Romans developed a method of cutting small circular openings in panels of stone and filling them with glass. Another Roman practice was to set pieces of glass

19

in bronze, copper or lead frames. Thus one can catch a glimpse of the development that culminated in medieval glass.

The technique of modern glass can be said to have begun when the Egyptians invented the blowpipe about 300 B.C. This consists of a hollow tube, four or five feet long, with a knob on one end and a mouthpiece on the other. It is still in use today as may be seen by a visit to the Whitefriars Glass Works. Up to this point in history all glass was either coloured, or opaque, but about the beginning of the Christian era, as if pre-ordained, the first relatively transparent glass was made and called crystal glass by obvious analogy. The craft spread to Byzantium, Venice and later to France. There are reports of a colony of Venetian glassmakers settling at Limoges in 959. St. Jerome and St. Chrysostom write of glass windows but these were probably simple mosaics of unpainted glass. It is known that in 1066, the first Benedictine monastery at Monte Cassino had a chapel filled with stained glass windows, and there was a Cistercian interdict which restricted the Order to the use of white glass only.

In dating glass it must be remembered that later windows sometimes incorporated glass of an earlier period because the material was far too precious to be thrown away and wasted. There is comparatively little glass that can be dated indisputably as twelfth century, and 'early medieval glass' is usually understoood to mean that of the thirteenth century. Some authorities have stated that the oldest glass that can be dated with certainty is that in St. Denys of 1108, but unfortunately this has been so much restored that its beauty and value have been largely destroyed.

It should however be noted that many experts assert that the glass in Augsburg Cathedral is the earliest. Dom Charles Norris, O.S.B., writing in the *Buckfast Abbey Chronicle* states that:

> 'The oldest existing stained glass windows are in the clerestory of Augsburg Cathedral. They belong to the year 1065 and are attributed to the monks of Tegernsee.'

Like the Le Mans Ascension window they show marked Byzantine influence, but as Dom Norris points out, whereas the Augsburg windows belong to the Hellenic tradition, the Le Mans windows follow the Syrian. An interesting characteristic of all these windows is that, although they are the earliest known examples, they reveal a highly developed technique with a knowledge of practically all the legitimate resources of the stained glass artist. Dom Norris writes:

> 'Germany had been receiving an infiltration of Byzantinesque elements from the time of Charlemagne, for was not his Palatine church at Aachen constructed in part from materials brought from Theodoric's palace at Ravenna? The revival of Art along the Rhine towards the year 1000 is accounted for by the influence of Byzantine artists following the marriage of Otto II with Theophano, daughter of Romanus II, Emperor of Constantinople. Speaking generally the Byzantine influence seems to have come to Germany via Rome, Venice and Ravenna. The Augsburg windows (Plate 1) bear a strong resemblance to the sixth, seventh and eighth-century mosaics at Ravenna. David at Augsburg and Justinian at Ravenna are obviously of the same tradition. Their garments are identical, while David's crown and jewelled borders are reminiscent of mosaic technique. The Augsburg windows appear therefore to belong

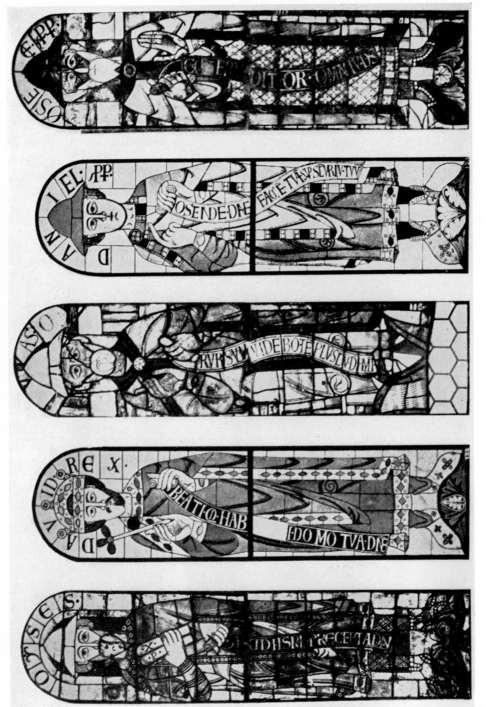

PLATE 1. Augsburg Cathedral. Attributed to the monks of Tergernsee, 1065.

York

Chartres

St. Denys

Plate 2.

to the Italo-Byzantine school, Hellenistic by tradition, static in expression, influences which came to Germany by the land route. On the other hand it is now known that France received much of its Byzantine influences directly by the Mediterranean sea route and from Spain. In the Le Mans Ascension the effects of a purer Oriental-Byzantine tradition, Syrian in origin and dynamic in style, is clearly traceable. It would seem likely therefore that the art of making stained glass windows arose in France and Germany independently and contemporaneously. Almost immediately, however, the French took the lead and all subsequent developments originated in France, and to a lesser degree in England.'

Unfortunately the black and white illustration (Plate 1) gives no indication of the real beauty of the actual windows with their pleasing colour pattern. Their position, high up in the south clerestory against a clear sky, gives the glass a luminosity in pleasant contrast to the mass of grey in the surrounding wall space. The lights are well worth studying on account of their quality and not because of any particular effect. The chief characteristic of their colour schemes is the successful use of green.

The colour scheme, beginning from the light nearest to the east might be tabulated thus:

1. *Green*, *Brown* and *Yellow* with smaller touches of red and blue.
2. *Green*, *Yellow* and *Red* with a touch of blue and one of quiet purple.
3. Quiet *Greyish-Purple* and *Yellow* with touches of green ruby and blue.
4. *Green* and *Ruby* with quiet yellowish-brown and biscuit.
5. *Green*, *Ruby* and *Yellow*.

It seems probable that the earliest example of twelfth-century glass in England is in York Minster. Part of the panel showing a seated King from the Jesse Tree window is so reminiscent of panels in St. Denys and at Chartres that it must be more or less contemporary (Plate 2). This would fix the date as somewhere between 1142 and 1151. On the other hand Eden says that four panels in the centre light of the East window of Rivenhall Church, Essex, were formerly in the apse of the church of Chénu-sur-Sarthe, France. These are of pronounced Byzantine character and may be the oldest glass in England.

An understanding of the historical development of technical processes is necessary for a balanced appreciation of the art of stained glass itself, since a stained glass window is the result of the technical, as well as the aesthetic and spiritual, development of the period in which it was created.

For example, the design of a medieval window was influenced by the fact that it was not possible to make large pieces of glass. The 'dim, religious light' so characteristic of the times—incidentally no disadvantage to a congregation that could not read —was therefore largely due to the limited skill of the glass makers.

Similarly, economic factors showed their influence. The small pieces of glass left over after the comparatively large pieces for heads, drapery, etc. had been cut, were far too valuable to throw away. They were therefore utilized in the borders which were common in this period. The artist thus made superb use of his limitations and refuted the idea that he was not a practical man.

CHAPTER 2

The Twelfth and Thirteenth Centuries

'The most beautiful experience we can appreciate is the sensation of the mystical. It is the source of all true science. He to whom the emotion is a stranger, who can no longer wonder and stand in awe, is as good as dead.' (Einstein.)

The great scientist says that the appreciation of the mystical is the source of all true science. It is equally true to say that it is the basis of the greatest art. Certainly it is those to whom the emotion is no stranger who will most readily appreciate the beauties of early medieval art. It is not so much that any mystical appreciation is necessary as the fact that those who are accustomed only to find enjoyment in purely materialistic and photographic representation may find it difficult to appreciate the impersonal qualities of the earlier work. The greatest visual art is akin to the finest music. Whall must have felt this when he wrote 'make your colour sing'.

The earliest stained glass is coeval with the development of heraldry and, as with every form of visual art of the period, fresco or tapestry, it is permeated with the same mental outlook. The treatment of the figures and the method of depicting them is precisely that of heraldic emblazonment. As in a coat of arms of the best periods, there is no attempt at realistic presentation; the figures, buildings or other objects are in no way natural but displayed after the manner of charges in heraldry. Nature is expressed rather than portrayed and with seldom more than three or four figures, the subject will be symbolically depicted so as to be understood by the most unsophisticated. Architecture depicted in the windows of this early period was purely decorative and symbolic and the colour of the building determined largely by the necessities of the general colour scheme. Any objects introduced are there for descriptive use, forming part of a pattern of beautiful decoration. The designs are two-dimensional in drawing and colour and the figures delineated with a flowing and sensitive line.

It is not easy in these days, when everyone can read and write, to appreciate the purpose and even the necessity of the early church windows. They were there for people to read just as in the Tsars' time in Russia, less than forty years ago, when the population was illiterate, the shop fronts were covered with colourful paintings of the merchandise and food-stuffs obtainable within. The medieval stained glass windows were designed under the direction of the clergy, and often by the

PLATE 3. Rivenhall Parish Church, Essex, east window.
Virgin and Child, late twelfth century.

PLATE 4. Rivenhall Parish Church, Essex.
East window, panel of knight, thirteenth century.

clergy themselves, to teach the gospel story to the populace and to impress it by pictorial means upon the popular memory.

Sir Herbert Read in his illuminating book *English Stained Glass* writes:

'The art that resulted from this subordination of the craftsman to the artist and of the artist to the authority of the church, had definite characteristics which are, in large measure, due to this process of control. It is, in the first place, a strictly impersonal art; it follows that it is an art devoid of sentimentality; and finally it is an universal art.

'An impersonal art implies a surrender of personality and the suppression of all those desires which, especially in the artist, seek the aggrandizement of self. In an impersonal art the artist is there not to express his ideas about the universe, or to record his wayward and trivial emotions, but rather to embody in universal images the ideas and emotions of the religious community of which he is a limb. He will naturally, in pursuance of this aim, seek the "type" rather than the individual, and the figures will be conditioned by intellectual concepts rather than by immediate observation. This does not exclude a generalized observation; indeed medieval art is marked by a heightened realism which does not, however, conflict with its abstract universality.'

The Frontispiece showing the well-known Ascension window in Le Mans Cathedral is a fine example of the earliest Byzantine influence. The figures of the Apostles are simply depicted on the mount, symbolizing the highest point of human understanding and the drawing states with direct simplicity the emotional reaction to a phenomenon beyond human understanding. The line work is simple, direct, decorative and sensitive, and the colour a bold and harmonious effect enhanced by the particularly beautiful quality of the glass, resulting from a fortunately imperfect knowledge of the chemical ingredients.

Ruskin's prolixity is understandably out of fashion these days but the following quotation from his appendix to *The Stones of Venice* is well worth studying.

'In the second place this modern barbarism destroys the true appreciation of the qualities of glass. It desires and endeavours as far as possible to conceal the transparency, which is not only its great virtue in a merely utilitarian point of view, but its great spiritual character, the character by which in Church architecture, it becomes most touchingly impressive, as typical of the entrance of the Holy Spirit into the heart of man, a typical expression rendered specific and intense by the purity of its sevenfold lines and thereby in endeavouring to turn the window into a picture we at once lose the sanctity and power of the noble material and employ it to an end which it is utterly impossible it should ever worthily attain. The true perfection of a painted window is to be serene, intense, brilliant like flaming jewellery; full of easily legible and quaint subjects and exquisitely subtle yet simple harmonies . . . this perfection has been consummated in the designs, never to be surpassed, if ever again to be approached by human art, of the French windows of the twelfth and thirteenth centuries.'

Ruskin speaks of the 'French' windows but it should be remembered that in Westlake's opinion there was no distinction between French and English glass in the twelfth and thirteenth centuries. He was convinced that the windows of Chartres and Sens were designed and executed by the same hand as the work at Canterbury. He further observed that the glass at Lincoln has borders which 'exhibit a different character from the work at Chartres, Canterbury, Sens and Rouen but are not unlike some at Bourges.'

Plate 2 shows a line drawing of panels from St. Denys, Chartres and from York Minster reproduced by kind permission of Mr. John A. Knowles, F.S.A. from his interesting book *A History of the York School of Glass Painters*. This clearly indicates some connexion between the schools of painting. Mr. Knowles writes:

'In the twelfth century, Archbishop Rogers' nave at York was filled with painted windows, one panel of which, and numerous sections of borders are still preserved, from which Professor Lethaby ("Archbishop Rogers' Cathedral at York and its Stained Glass", *Archaeological Journal*, March 1915, pp. 37–48) has reconstructed the original design. This panel, which is the earliest specimen of stained glass in England, represents Christ in Glory and originally formed part of a Jesse Tree. It is so exactly like similar panels in St. Denys and Chartres that it is extremely likely all three were derived from a common source. Whether that source was English or continental it would, however, be impossible to say. The York panel is supposed to have formed part of a window in Archbishop Rogers' choir, built between 1151 and 1181. But in view of the great similarity between the three, it might be argued, with some show of probability, that the York panel is earlier than the date usually attributed to it.

'The Jesse at Chartres dates about the year 1145, and the St. Denys glass between the years 1142 and 1151. It is quite possible that the York Jesse came, not from Rogers' choir, but from Thomas of Bayeux's church, pulled down in 1154. Although it is impossible to accept Le Vieil's suggestion that the source of the St. Denys glass was English, yet at the same time it is not impossible that there was a close connexion between English and French school's of glass-painting at that time.'

Plates 3 and 4 are taken from some of the earliest glass in England in the East window of Rivenhall Church in Essex. The window consists of four circular medallions of the late twelfth century, two fragmentary figures of bishops of the same period and a knight on horseback of early thirteenth-century date, besides several roundels and panels, some fragmentary, of the fifteenth and sixteenth centuries. They were originally in the parish church of Chénu-sur-Sarthe and were brought to England in 1840 by the Rev. B. D. Hawkins, the then parson of Rivenhall Church.

Mr. F. Sidney Eden gives a most interesting account of this transaction in the *Journal of the British Society of Master Glass-Painters* for October 1925, together with part of his report to the Royal Commission on Historical Monuments. The following are two extracts from his report relating respectively to the two illustrations:

'CHANCEL. East Window—central main light: A large circular panel, bordered ruby, with inner and outer narrow yellow margins ornamented with pellet pattern on brown enamel. The panel is set in white, ruby and blue geometrical-patterned glass, so as to form a square, the fillings in being green. The subject is Our Lady, with the Divine Child, enthroned. The Virgin's tunic is green, and her mantle ruby. Her crown is, merely, a plain yellow cap and her nimbus is green. She wears white pointed shoes which rest on a footstool, green-topped, diapered in squares, and with white round-arcaded sides.

PLATE 5. Twycross Church, Leicestershire. Crucifixion window, thirteenth century. (*By courtesy of Mr. H. T. Kirby.*)

PLATE 6. Canterbury Cathedral.
North clerestory window of the choir.
Adam Delving, *c.* 1178.

'The Child is on His Mother's right knee, clad in blue tunic with green sleeves. His right hand is raised in benediction over His Mother's left breast which she offers to Him with Her left hand. His nimbus is white, and shows one arm of a cross, the greater part of it being behind the Virgin's nimbus. A white dove, with neck outstretched towards the faces of the figures, hovers over the Virgin's left shoulder. The throne is green with yellow finials to its side posts, and the back is deep red and cross-hatched; the cushion is yellow and cross-hatched.

'On either side of the throne is a standing figure in a green mantle, yellow tunic and long green shoes, and nimbed green, holding a yellow sceptre with a finial of Fleur-de-Lys in his left hand and a yellow orb in his right.

'The background of the whole is blue. (Late twelfth century.) The above—iii, iv, v and vi are very Byzantine in type. They all show a few losses of original glass and consequent repairs, mostly with ancient glass, and there are some cracks.

'Sinister main light: (iv) A large panel representing a knight on horseback in white chain mail with deep yellow surcoat, trellised, and white pot helmet, holding a short sword (white) in his right hand. The horse is white and covered with yellow trappings, trellised like the knight's surcoat. The background is paly, yellow and blue, with a yellow bend and on either side is a border of oblong pieces of glass, yellow, ruby, blue and purple.

'Across the panel, behind the helmet, is a label shaded in brown enamel, bearing in Lombardic capitals, ROBERT/VS LEMAIRE (early thirteenth century).

'The tone of the ruby in these panels tends to scarlet, and it is very streaky; the blues are deep and rather violet on the whole, but some of the blue is very light. The greens are on the blue side and rich in tone, while the yellows are of the brownish tint characteristic of the early glass. The brown enamel is, for the most part, well preserved, and there is but little stick work, the line shading being done mostly with the brush.'

There can be no exact nomenclature for the various periods of art development. This is easily understandable because each period develops a new style whilst examples of traditional work are still being carried out, so that there is an overlapping and gradual merging which prevents any arbitrary classification by an exact date. The broad classification given by Sir Herbert Read is probably the most revealing, and in studying the various periods of glass it will be found useful to keep this broad outline in mind.

1. THE AGE OF REASON
   The rise and fall of the Classical period of Christian Art, generally
   known as *Early Gothic*.   1150–1350

2. THE AGE OF SENTIMENT
   The rise and establishment of humanistic standards. The Romantic or *Late Gothic*.   1350–1500
   The early beginnings can be traced long before the end of the classical Gothic period, but it may be said to have reached its fullest development about 1500.

3. THE AGE OF FANCY

The humanistic decadence. The age of 'fanciful' movements de-   1500
void of unanimity and religious sentiment.   onwards.

Perhaps the most beautiful twelfth-century work in England is to be found in Canterbury Cathedral. Plate 6 shows a panel in the choir clerestory representing Adam delving. This is surely a work of exquisite beauty. The line work is sensitive, decorative, direct and rhythmical. There is a fine sense of pattern in the arrangement of the glass. The earnestness of expression and simplicity of design is imbued with poetry, whilst the colour is restrained. The characteristic tawny pink flesh of this period, with white drapery is shown against a rich blue background; the figure is standing on a green foreground except for the oblong patch which has been dug; the yellow band near the base divides the green from the blue beneath. It is interesting that the tree and the leaves are white, and as green was available this is a definite example of choice of colour for design rather than for realism. The story or subject is clearly realized and the colour balance carefully maintained.

The colour in the Methusaleh panel (Plate 7) is much richer. There are varying shades of ruby, broken by bands of white, the deep Canterbury blue, a cool green and rich yellow, a brown madder scarf and the usual twelfth-century pink brown flesh. The whole design is indeed a magnificent conception and it has been suggested that this portrayal of 'The Thinker' is even finer than that by Michael Angelo. Certainly this is a dignified and impressive creation. The more one studies these two panels the more living they become.

It may be noted that in neither of these panels is there any predominant Byzantine influence, and that they are both definitely English in character.

The Crucifixion panel (Plate 5) from Twycross Church, Leicestershire (originally in La Sainte Chapelle, Paris), is an interesting piece of thirteenth-century work, but it has not the beauty or technical accomplishment of the Canterbury examples or the Ascension window in Le Mans. It is interesting to note the similar line technique. Unfortunately two or three of the original pieces are missing which to some extent destroys the rhythm of line, but the general design is bold and direct. A point of minor interest as regards design is the way in which Our Lady's halo on the left breaks the line of the cross, whereas St. John's halo on the right goes behind the arm and the cross.

Early medieval windows were designed with the emphasis on glazing. They are essentially mosaics of glass, and for that reason it may be said that the glaziers were more important than the painters. The white glass of this period is greenish and slightly horny in texture. The ruby varies considerably in tint, often streaky with brownish or orange patches. The blue also varies from deep indigo to a light blue, sometimes almost pale grey, and sometimes the deeper hues had a turquoise tint. Yellows were of course all pot metal, ranging from dark to light. Green varied from a dull colour to a bright emerald and from cool bluish tints to a warm pale green. The purple was rather brown and the lighter tones of this were used for the flesh.

PLATE 7. Canterbury Cathedral.
Methusaleh window in south transept.

PLATE 8. Hereford Cathedral.
Western window in south wall of Lady Chapel.

The very beauty of the glass must have been a deterrent to any sensitive craftsman who might have thought of painting it. To paint a diaper on the background glass of the Le Mans window would have destroyed much of its beauty. It must be remembered that glass was scarce and costly. To the craftsman it was precious, new and alive. He delighted in its qualities as a connoisseur might delight in the beauty of rubies and diamonds and all precious stones. It will be seen in later periods that these incentives to fine work had disappeared.

It may have been partly the desire to allow more light or possibly the influence of the Cistercian Order insisting upon the use of white glass, but a particularly beautiful and characteristic type of window was evolved which consisted of decorative subject panels introduced on to a grisaille background. A fine example of this type of design is to be seen in the Lady Chapel of Hereford Cathedral.

Plate 8 shows one of the two western windows in the south wall. At the top of the light is a vesica-shaped panel with a Majesty and four small panels with the symbols of the Evangelists and the remains of their names. Below this is a small round panel with the Agnus Dei, then a quatrefoil panel with the Marys at the sepulchre. The head of the angel is modern. Below this is a quatrefoil panel with the Crucifixion flanked by the Virgin and St. John, and in the base quatrefoil panel 'The Bearing of the Cross'. Three of the heads are modern.

In the thirteenth century the borders of stylized foliage of obvious classical derivation, so characteristic of the twelfth century, became more naturalistic with a suggestion of growth which foreshadows the developments of the fourteenth-century style. The figures, whilst still retaining their dignity and impressive impersonality, have more life and sense of movement. To understand this development in iconography it is necessary to know something of the history of the times and the gradual change in Christian thought of which it was the natural expression. For this purpose a study of Chapter 3 in Sir Herbert Read's *English Stained Glass* is immensely rewarding; from that chapter the following quotation is taken:

> 'The official Byzantine art, like the Gothic art to which it contributed a strain, was of the unearthly and rational type. It offered no harbour for the emotional longings of simple people, and with the building up of Scholasticism, the very humanity of the Christian doctrine tended to become lost in allegorical interpretation. Not only were the visual arts then devoid of sentiment, but the Christian story itself seemed to have become cold and inanimate. Against this paralysis of the emotions the Franciscan movement was an unconscious protest.'

No doubt a widespread longing for a more humanistic and intimate interpretation had developed and St. Francis and his followers gave it a welcome outlet for expression. From 1210, when Innocent III first gave his sanction to the order, the spirit of St. Francis spread throughout the land like an evangel. Read quotes from Henry Thode's work *Franz von Assissi*:

> 'A new Christian art was called into being by a conception of the Christian religion which was at once simple and natural, penetrated with love and intimate enthusiasm, and daily expressed in all its picturesqueness by Francis and his disciples in their preach-

ing and in their poetry. The Franciscan contemplation, unlike other mystic contemplations, provoked the study of nature, of that nature in which the Franciscans saw the faithful and the most exact image of God.'

Such observations as these are of profound significance to the student of stained glass and to the stained glass artist. The pleasures of aesthetic appreciation are sound and healthy and should add to the happiness of daily life. Nevertheless it must always be remembered that, in the production of a church window, they are but means to an end and in themselves quite incapable of producing the greatest art. Sentimentality is obviously no help or substitute. Nowadays every stained glass artist and every discerning connoisseur of the arts agrees that from the medieval period onwards something gradually evaporated from religious art. Alas, the recognition of this fact does not in itself bestow the ability to create any comparable work but perhaps it helps to keep standards from falling as low as those, for example, of the eighteenth century.

CHAPTER 3

The Fourteenth Century

It is generally considered that English stained glass reached its highest point of achievement in the fourteenth century though it is doubtful if any individual panels ever excelled examples like the 'Methusaleh' or the 'Adam Delving' of the twelfth-century Canterbury glass. The predominantly blue and red colour schemes, and the violet effects seen in France by the mixing of ruby and blue glass in the thirteenth century were superseded by designs with a greater proportion of yellow and white, and the use of a lighter and more luminous blue than the deep and rich blue so characteristic of Canterbury.

This change of colour scheme was considerably helped by the discovery, half-way through the century, of the use of silver nitrate to produce a yellow stain, but this accentuated or helped the tendency—it was not its prime cause. A study of the four-teenth-century windows in Wells Cathedral confirms that the use of pot metal yellow combined with white and green had produced a lighter and characteristic fourteenth-century effect as early as about 1327, which is the date ascribed to the two tracery lights of the first two windows from the west in the south quire aisle. Yellow stain had not then been discovered. Probably the finest example of four-teenth-century glass in England is the East window of the Quire of Wells, the well-known 'Golden Window'—c. 1328–1334, again earlier than the discovery of yellow stain. The subject is the Tree of Jesse, the motif of the twisting vine being combined with the canopy treatment so characteristic of this period. The masterly handling of the colour is well worth studying. The predominant effect is certainly that of gold but a careful analysis of the actual amount of the various colours used shows that there is in fact hardly more yellow glass than green or ruby, and to a large extent the effect is produced by the very sparse use of blue. This same rich yellow is found in earlier work but it is dominated by a full use of rich blue. In this golden window the blue is pale and in the five lights of the window it is confined to the borders of the two lights on either side of the centre, the pale blue alternating with yellow fleur-de-lys. The borders of the central and two outer lights show the golden leopards of England alternating with a ruby ground.

The yellow in the figure work is enhanced by the use of a cool green and supported by skilfully placed patches of ruby. The pale blue tint in the borders of two of the lights is delicately re-echoed in the traceries and thus prevented from overpowering the yellow. The twining vine and the shafts of the canopy are in silvery white and are so spaced, covering the whole design, that they give it unity and at the same time lighten the general effect and keep the whole conception two-dimensional.

The subject was very popular in this period. In his illuminating book *English Stained and Painted Glass* Dr. Woodforde writes:

> 'The "Tree of Jesse" occurs in fourteenth-century glass in at least seventeen places, and there are records of other examples now lost. Eight of those which survive, namely, in Bristol Cathedral, at Lowick (Northants), Ludlow (Shropshire), Madlow (Hereford), Mansetter and Merevale (Worcester), St. Mary's, Shrewsbury, and Tewkesbury Abbey, have so many points in common that it is difficult not to believe that some single and special influence was at work in the production of them. During this century the "Tree of Jesse" was sometimes, as in Wells Cathedral, at Winchester College, and at New College, Oxford, associated with the "General Resurrection", which was shown in the tracery lights. A panel of glass in Thaxted Church, Essex, shows a member of the Mortimer family, with shield and spear, encircled in a vine stem. It has been suggested that this is the only surviving example of a "secular" genealogical tree in medieval stained glass. Perhaps a more likely explanation is that at the bottom of a "Tree of Jesse" window one or more figures of donors were incorporated in the design.'

It has been noted that the lightening of colour had already begun before the actual discovery of silver stain and it will be readily appreciated that this knowledge further aided and accentuated the development. Before the discovery, yellow and white had to be leaded as separate pieces of glass, but the new process enabled both yellow and white to be combined in one piece. White pearls or diamonds could be shown on a golden crown, the crockets on a piece of canopy could be stained yellow leaving the main portions of the canopy white, on the heads of the figures the hair could be stained yellow, an ornament of yellow and white could be shown on drapery, and scrolls of lettering and patterns on quarries could be embellished with touches of gold. The quality and depth of the yellow could be varied according to the amount of silver nitrate applied. All this saved time and material by lessening the amount of leading required and in doing so lightened the general appearance of the windows. Coincident with this variation in the colour scheme came a development in the technique of painting. The traced lines were no longer entirely opaque. A more delicate and gradated line was used, strengthened as required to suggest the modelling. More shading was introduced and the smear of light tone slightly stippled. Towards the end of the century the smear painting was largely superseded by a stippled matt gradated to suggest the modelling, the stippled matt being more luminous than the smear painting. At this period the matt was not applied all over a piece of glass, as in later periods, and the parts of the glass where no paint was required were still left clear. The early decorative tradition still survived, and although the painting assumed

PLATE 9. Christ Church, City of Oxford.
Two left-hand lights in second north window of the Latin chapel.

a more realistic approach it had not gone far enough to destroy either the decorative line or the brilliance of the glass.

It should be remembered that the traditional development of the craft must have been considerably influenced by the national calamity of the Black Death, in which over a third of the population perished. The records of the Craft Guilds of this period indicate considerable replacements of master craftsmen which were almost certainly due to the decimations of the plague. This would seem to explain the lessening, towards the end of the century, of the traditional influence both in design and execution.

It is generally agreed that stained glass should subordinate itself to architectural requirements and should harmonize with the interior of the building. Architects were modifying and developing the traditional style to meet the prevailing demand for more light; windows were made larger. It would have been foolish to counteract these improvements by filling the larger windows with dark glass.

Although stained glass should be designed to suit the building, there are occasions and possibly periods when buildings have been designed to suit stained glass. For example, Sainte Chapelle in Paris, was deliberately conceived as a casket of coloured jewels. As far as stained glass is concerned the finest results are usually seen when the architect allows in his design for the colour emphasis to be placed on the windows. A propos of this view Sir Herbert Read quotes a passage from Fergusson in his *Handbook of Architecture*:

> 'The misfortune of the perpendicular was that it fell on evil days. Used as it was at first, or as it might in a better age have become, it may be considered nearly as the perfection of tracery. It possessed, however, within itself, a fatal facility which brought down the art to the meanest capacity and afforded no scope or exercise for the highest intellects. The tendency of the age was for the greatest possible effect at the least possible expense; hence the perpendicular tracery soon became prosaic to the last degree, and utterly unworthy either of its predecessors or of its own capabilities. Like all tracery, it was merely a framework, subordinate to the painted glass which filled the windows. In attempting to judge of its propriety or beauty, it is always necessary to bear this in mind. It may sometimes look cold and inartistic now, but when the stained glass was perfect the case must have been widely different.'

The difficulty of drawing any strict dividing line between various techniques is exemplified by the characteristics of the great East Window in Gloucester Cathedral. At first glance this would appear to be fifteenth century but on closer inspection the details reveal a quite definite fourteenth-century technique. It is generally agreed that it must be dated between 1350 and 1360. Not only is the glass a foreshadowing of the future development, but the architecture also shows how the two arts blended to express the requirements of their age.

Read, writing of this window, states:

> 'There can be no doubt that the glass must date the architecture; this being so, we have in this East Window the first example of the Perpendicular style; and from all appearances it seems that the glass design has determined the window design. For the

stained glass is within a regular development, and a development that, on its grand scale, required just such a sudden urge in architecture as this window reveals. Whatever the manner of its genesis the result is sublime.'

Plate 10 showing the canopy light of St. Peter in the East Window of Gloucester is a characteristic example of the fourteenth-century work at possibly its best period. The panel is boldly designed and realized as a mosaic of glass. The treatment shows significant and decorative line work, both in the figure and in the canopy, which is simple and not over-elaborate as it became in later periods. The two-dimensional character is still retained without any attempt at perspective.

More attention is, however, paid to minutiae than was the practice in the previous century. For example, a delicate pattern work covers the background behind the figure. To some extent this may have added to the glass a quality that was lacking, but on the other hand it tends to lessen its translucency and is a foreshadowing of interest in painting rather than in the qualities of the material itself. In contrast, the background blues and rubies of the twelfth-century Le Mans window are sufficiently interesting in themselves and could hardly have been improved by the addition of a diaper.

In Plate 11 showing the panel of the Virgin in the same window it will be seen that the background glass is not diapered, probably because the craftsman felt that the glass possessed the required quality without the addition of paint. Plate 12 shows the east window of Eaton Bishop Church, Herefordshire, one of the finest examples of glass painting of this period that has survived. Although incomplete it is notable for the excellence of design, colour and richness of decoration. Executed 1317–1321, approximately, it was reset between 1841 and 1854 and again in 1928.

The illustration shows the three centre lights of the five light window each with ornamental borders and the three middle lights with borders forming sub-heads above the figured panels. All the lights have two panels of figure subjects except the centre light which has three. The panels at the base show a series of kneeling figures of donors with Lombardic inscriptions. The window was probably given by Adam de Murimouth, Canon of Hereford, who later became Cantor of Exeter in 1328.

The left-hand light in the plate shows St. Michael weighing souls under a canopy and super canopy, and below a kneeling figure of a priest with inscription 'Magister Ade Ea'. In the centre light the Crucifix with the Virgin and St. John under a canopy and super canopy are to be seen, with, below, the figure of a Bishop in Mass vestments with fragments of inscription 'Joh Ca'. In the base panel appear the kneeling figure of a priest in white vestments with the inscription 'Magister A . . . mouth Cantor'. In the right-hand light St. Gabriel is shown with palm under a canopy and super canopy, and below a figure in pink gown with the inscription 'Dns Adam A ... oh Fra'.

Typical work of this period can be seen in the three northern windows of the Latin Chapel in Christ Church, Oxford, painted about 1365. Plate 9 shows the two left-hand lights of the second of three north-west windows. The borders alternate with a running vine motive and block patterning of leopard's heads between fleur-de-lys.

PLATE 10. Gloucester Cathedral.
East window, figure of St. Peter in first tier, *c*. 1350.

PLATE 11. Gloucester Cathedral, east window.
Panel of the Virgin, c. 1350.

PLATE 12. Eaton Bishop church, Herefordshire.
Three centre lights of five-light east window.

PLATE 13. Victoria and Albert Museum.
Window from Winchester College chapel.

The filling is composed of grisaille quarries of foliage and flowers. Across the middle of each light runs a band of elaborate spired and crocketted canopies containing figures, each with an inscription below. The illustration shows St. Margaret with dragon, cross and palm and St. Frideswide with book and sceptre.

The illustration (Plate 13) of the window depicting St. John the Evangelist, James the Less and the prophet Zephaniah from Winchester College Chapel, now at the Victoria and Albert Museum, shows clearly the development of style towards the end of the century. It is dated *c.* 1380 and makes an interesting comparison with the Gloucester Cathedral panels. The canopy is obviously much more elaborate, more delicate detail is introduced and there is a definite use of perspective. Large pieces of white glass are used, with a pale blue and sage green. The ruby glass is variegated and streaky and the stain varies from pale to deep tints. Use is made of counterchange in the colour pattern, the colour of the background of the two outer lights is ruby whilst that of the centre light is blue with the tunic of the central figure ruby. The tunic of the left-hand figure is blue and that of the right-hand figure a deep ruby.

The drawing of the heads is more delicate and realistic. Characters are approached as individuals rather than as stylized types. Winston writes:

> 'About 1360 or 1370 a remarkable change took place in the manufacture of the glass and this was simultaneous with a great change in the mode of painting. As late as 1350 there was little deviation from the earliest mode of painting, black lines represented the deep shadows and a very slight wash of enamel work indicated the shadow in half tint. But after this the lines diminished in thickness and intensity and were retained only as outlines; the deep as well as the light shadows being represented as a stippled coat of enamel brown.'

The craftsman was turning to nature for motivation; for example, the stylized borders of classical derivation were superseded by designs derived from natural foliage, particularly that of oak, vine, ivy, maple.

The influence of St. Francis and his followers had spread across Europe and was increasingly effective in England in the fourteenth century, awakening interest in the beauties of nature to which architects, artists and sculptors more and more were turning their attention. The place of the classical motif was taken by the portrayal of nature and contemporary life. The impersonal and universal was replaced by the humanistic outlook. Portraits of donors were introduced into the windows and for the first time heraldry made its appearance in glass.

The human personality became apparent in ecclesiastical iconography. The work was still primarily dedicated to God but the individualities of the dedicators were no longer concealed, and they indeed hoped for favourable consideration for the donations offered. The human personality was shown in its striving towards the divine. Christ crucified was no longer depicted as the sublime Godhead but rather as the Divine incorporated in the frailty of the flesh.

In this period all these influences striving for expression were still dominated by the Gothic tradition and from a technical point of view were kept subservient to the traditional design of a glass mosaic. So far the glazier had not been superseded.

c

CHAPTER 4

The Fifteenth Century

Whereas thirteenth-century windows were essentially patterns of coloured glass with a small proportion of white pieces introduced and fourteenth-century windows were similar except that the proportion of white glass had been increased, in the fifteenth century the proportion of white was such that the windows could be more accurately described as white glass with portions of coloured glass patterned upon it.

The traced line work of the heads and figures became entirely different, that is, delicate with little emphasis as to shading and making no allowance for halation. Shadow was no longer indicated by an opaque black line. Painting was subtle, to be seen close to the eye, and did not attempt to make the features or the expression readable from a distance.

The traced line of the previous centuries had a relationship to the lead. It had the same opaqueness and a similar weight. The leading delineated the main forms and the traced lines of the figures and drapery filled in the details. In the fifteenth century this unity between the leading and the painting disappeared, and the leading instead of being a helpful part of the craftsman's technique began to play a decidedly less important role in the construction of the design.

Haloes were no longer coloured but shown either as white or yellow stain so that the head and halo could be cut in one piece of glass. The chief interest of the window was in the painting, and although the quality and beauty of the glass was still appreciated, it gradually became subservient to the technical skill of the painting. In earlier periods the aim of the craftsman was more to interest the spectator in the general character of the figure portrayed and in the forceful realization of the subject as a whole. It had the vigour and forthrightness which characterizes the modern political cartoon, and the interest was rather in the message to be conveyed than in the minutiae of the detail. Westlake gives an interesting summary of the general characteristics of the period, but it should be noted that when he is speaking here of distinction in form, he is referring to the design as a whole and not the delineation of the figures:

'When we come to the glass of this period, the distinction in form is not so immediately marked as it is in colour; the shafting of the canopy work is, perhaps, generally

PLATE 14. Merton College, Oxford.
Figure of abbess in east window.

PLATE 15. Merton College, Oxford.
Virgin and Child in east window.

PLATE 16. Beauchamp Chapel, Warwick. St. Thomas and St. Alban, *c.* 1447.

PLATE 17. All Saints Church, North Street, York.
The 'Bede'—Pryke of Conscience window, *c.* 1430.

broader, and has more attempted perspective in its detail. The architectural details, however, gradually assume the same features as the stonework especially after the middle of the century. In the late perpendicular glass, the number of the pinnaclets, etc., which surmount the canopies, give the heads of the lights a pretty and animated appearance. An important characteristic is the increased use of white; in fact many windows are, in effect, little else than white or grisaille, with some dominating spots of colour, and this colour is often lower in tone and greyer than in the preceding styles, whilst the white glass is really whiter and more delicately covered.'

Westlake here stresses two points: the increased use of white glass, and the development of the canopy. Figure work in the twelfth or thirteenth centuries was framed by a border; in the fourteenth century these borders were broken by alternating symbols such as the fleur-de-lys and leopards. In the fifteenth century, however, the canopy usually framed the design and the conventional border disappeared. Although this lightening of the colour scheme was generally characteristic of the period, it must not be assumed that no richly coloured windows were produced. There were notable exceptions as for example the Beauchamp Chapel windows in Warwick (Plate 16). Dr. Woodforde writes:

'The Beauchamp Chapel glass is an example of the most costly window that a fifteenth-century English glass painter could produce. No trouble and no expense were spared to obtain the best available glass and every known method, such as inserting coloured glass "jewels" into the border of the robes was used to give the most splendid effect possible. When all the windows were still full of Prudde's glass and when the other decoration of the chapel was bright and newly painted, the splendid effigy of Richard Beauchamp, Earl of Warwick, on its equally splendid tomb must have seemed to lie in a casket of almost unbelievable richness.

'Another collection of glass which has a brilliance almost equal to that of the Beauchamp Chapel is in the Chapel and Audit Chamber of Brown's Hospital at Stamford . . . this glass must have been painted in about 1485.'

Nevertheless these windows should be regarded as a local or regional development rather than as characteristic of the period which was generally demanding a lighter type of glass.

The method of inserting coloured glass 'jewels' was occasionally used in the fourteenth century. Theophilus writing about the beginning of the thirteenth century, described the technique of grinding coloured glass, ruby, blue, green or purple into a powder and applying it as a paste to pieces of glass. When fired the paste fused on to the surface of the white glass to appear as jewellery on mitres, crowns or borders of robes. The practice was not a satisfactory one as in course of time the variation in expansion and contraction between the jewel and the white glass, due to temperature differences, caused them to come apart.

A sounder technique, though one that necessitated considerable labour in medieval days, was that of abrasion. The practice of abrading the flash from portions of ruby or flashed blue glass was common in the second half of the fifteenth century. By this means white, yellow and red or white, yellow, green and blue could all be shown in one piece of glass. The fine collection of fifteenth-century glass in York, despite some purely local characteristics, belongs more truly to the spirit of the age than the full coloured glass in the Beauchamp Chapel. The great East Window and other vast windows in York Minster and many fine examples in parish churches in the city are typical not only of the York school of painting but also of the general trend of development at this period. In his authoritative work *The York School of Glass Painting* Mr. J. A. Knowles writes:

> 'But in the fifteenth century this wide range of tints was abandoned and the number of colours was practically reduced to two—red and blue. A typical fifteenth-century York window can best be compared to a Union Jack, red, white and blue, the colours being separated by white. These three glasses were practically employed according to a mathematical formula, in the proportion of five of white, two of blue and one of ruby. We have in confirmation of this, not only the windows themselves, but documentary evidence also. We find Robert Preston making a bequest of tools and drawings and "ij sheff [i.e. sheets] of blew glass, i sheff of red, w^t v sheff of white glass", evidently enough glass and in the right proportions for carrying out one average-size window. In the fifteenth-century York work the white was very white and stain had ceased to be used as a colour but was merely employed to touch up details on the white glass. It was so pale and sparingly used as not to do more than very slightly modify the general tone of the white. Green is so seldom used, except occasionally in tapestry backgrounds, that for all practical purposes it can be eliminated. Purple is never seen and black, pot-metal yellow, pale blue, gold, pink and similar glasses so rarely appear that they can be disregarded.
>
> 'York artists had a passion for counterchanging the colour, thus a red bishop stood on a blue background with a red background to his canopy and so on. In the next light, this was merely turned round, whilst the whole of one window would be again counterchanged with the one next to it, as in the western clerestory of the choir. Colouring, therefore, was not a question of artistic feeling, but of mechanical procedure.'

Mr. Knowles does not, of course, condemn the use of counterchange in colour as a general principle. It is used in every period and its success depends upon the artistry with which it is handled. In windows such as the Golden Window of the quire at Wells, it is so skilfully employed that it is lost in the beauty of the design. It might be said to be successful when unnoticed. In some windows it is so obvious that the effect tends to appear mechanical.

The East Window of York Minster is reputed to be the finest and largest perpendicular window in the world, measuring 72 feet in height and 32 feet in width. It was designed and executed by John Thornton of Coventry from 1405–1408. Within a canopy framework it is divided into about 200 panels of approximately 3 square feet. The excellent state of preservation is due to the cultural influence of Fairfax who made death the penalty for anyone who fired a gun at the Minster. Unfortunately, his example has not always been followed in more recent and apparently less civilized times.

The upper panels of the main lights depict scenes from the Old Testament from

'The Creation of the World' to the 'Death of Absalom'. Below the upper transom are shown subjects from the later life of St. John, including his visions at Patmos and his martyrdom, and in the lower part figures of kings and ecclesiastics whose names are connected with church history in the neighbouring part of England.

The general colour scheme is simple with blue and ruby counterchanged as a background to the figures and canopy, which is characteristic of the treatment of most of the York glass. The colour scheme is comparatively high in tone but never approaching harshness.

Another notable window is that which occupies the whole of the north side of the Eastern choir transept. It is comprised of five lights and traceries being about 78 feet in height and 16 feet in width. It is divided into 165 panels depicting the life of St. William, patron of York, whose shrine was in the minster. In the traceries are figures of kings and bishops and at the apex 'The Coronation of Our Lady'. The colour scheme is again comparatively simple with ruby and blue backgrounds of rather lighter tone than in the east window, with pleasant variation of deep and lighter stain. Westlake considers it an interesting advance to a more conventional, perpendicular character compared with that shown in the east window. On the south side of the choir is the well-known window depicting the life of St. Cuthbert. The colour scheme is warmer due to the additional quantity of ruby glass in the background, appropriate to the south aspect. The Rev. J. Fowler in his monograph dates the work as towards the middle of the fifteenth century. It is definitely later than the St. William window, with greater brilliance and a liveliness due partly to the particularly pure green, and the use of intermediate tints so characteristic of later fifteenth-century glass. The 85 panels illustrate the life of St. Cuthbert, though unfortunately most of them are to some extent mutilated. In the panels under the lowest transom the donors of the window and their associates are depicted. Originally the traceries contained figures of saints and angels but these have now disappeared. In the centre is a figure of St. Cuthbert and figures of historical personages on each side of him under the lower transom give an idea as to the date and origin of the work. These are Archbishop Bowet (1407–1423), Cardinal Beaufort, Bishop of Winchester (1404–1447), Duke Humphrey (d. 1423), Cardinal Kemp (1426–1452), Cardinal Longley (1405), Henry V (reigned 1413–1421), Henry VI (reigned 1421–1461), John of Gaunt (1340–1399) and Henry IV (reigned 1399–1413).

Plate 17 shows the well-known 'Prykke of Conscience' window in All Saints Church, North Street, York, being the first from the east in the north aisle. It is based upon a poem written about 1325, and the window, illustrating that portion which deals with the pains and horrors of the last fifteen days of the history of the world, was erected about the middle of the fifteenth century.

It contains fifteen subject panels and characteristic donor panels at the base. The restoration, carried out in 1861, has faithfully preserved the medieval character of the glass. Apart from its interest as a typical example of fifteenth-century design, it illustrates the mentality prevalent at this period. It is, in fact, a Doom window as the following description by the Rev. F. Harrison denotes:

'The events of the fifteen days are terrible indeed. The sea first rises (first day), then falls (second day), and leaves the earth again dry (third day). On the fourth day fishes and fearful monsters of the sea rise up and invade the earth, and the sea is set on fire, burning with lurid red flames (fifth day). Trees are devoured (sixth day) an earthquake shakes the buildings (seventh day) and the rocks and trees are consumed (eighth day). In fear, men hide themselves in holes in the earth (ninth day) and only earth and sky are to be seen (tenth day). On the eleventh day, taking courage, men emerge from the holes in which they have taken shelter, and pray in their extremity. The bones of men in coffins come to life again (twelfth day), while death in the guise of a skeleton comes to claim all mortal flesh (fourteenth day). The stars fall from heaven with a blinding yellow light (thirteenth day) and finally the fire devours everything (fifteenth day) while St. Peter receives the souls of the blessed at the portals of heaven (tracery, left-hand compartment), and Satan, in the guise of a monster with a fork, helps the souls of the damned into Hell (right-hand tracery).'

Plate 18 shows the adjacent window to the west which is almost as remarkable and is particularly interesting in that it depicts the contemporary costume and the objects of everyday life. The subject is the Six Corporal Acts of Mercy, depicted in a canopy framework, with particularly rich background colouring of bright scarlet ruby alternating with a clear and definite blue in contrast to the more prevalent greyish hue. The canopies and crockets are the same as those used in the west window of St. Martin-le-Grand Church, Coney Street. Reading from the top and across, the Acts of Mercy are: feeding the hungry, giving drink to the thirsty, entertaining strangers, clothing the naked, visiting the sick, and ministering to the prisoners. In the left-hand base panel a priest, habited in a blue robe and almuce, is shown kneeling at an altar. In the right-hand base panel are the kneeling figures of a man and woman, both dressed in red with a scroll reading *Ora pro nobis*, whilst in the centre base panel the sun and the seven stars are represented in a blue sky shining over water.

With the exception of York the finest collection of fifteenth-century glass is to be seen at Great Malvern Priory. In this impressive building it is possible to judge the effect of a great church filled with glass of this period, although allowance must be made for the coloured mural decorations which no longer exist. These are typical perpendicular windows with single subjects or figures spaced between the canopy work. As a rule the whole of the light is carried out in white glass enriched with yellow stain except for the groining of the canopy, the background behind the figures and the robes of the figures themselves, the colours used being mostly blue, ruby and green. There are three windows of fine quality in the chapel south of the Choir depicting the story of the creation of the world and other subjects from Genesis.

Plate 19 shows a panel from the middle window illustrating God's Covenant with Jacob. On a blue background God is shown with a red mantle over blue, appearing in a glory edged with clouds with an adoration of angels in blue and the foreground figure of Abraham in red over blue with a green tree on the left. The inscription— 'D(omi)nus apparuit'—is perhaps Genesis 17.1.

On the north side of the clerestory of the choir there is an interesting window commemorating St. Werstan and the foundation of the Priory, and another showing

PLATE 18. All Saints Church, North Street, York.
'Acts of Mercy' window, c. 1475.

PLATE 19. Great Malvern Priory Church. Window in the south clerestory of the nave.

PLATE 20. Long Melford Church, Suffolk.
Donor panel in east window.

PLATE 21. Fifteenth century window, Margaretting Church, Essex.
(*By courtesy of the* Journal of Master Glass Painters.)

scenes from the life of the Virgin. The windows of this period on the south side of the clerestory of the choir are not in such a good state of preservation. All these windows, and the east window, date from about the middle of the century.

It is characteristic of this period to find small figures of the donors kneeling in the base, an indication of the gradual trend away from anonymity. It is also common practice for the artist's name to appear on the window.

Further examples of these figure and canopy windows are to be seen at Bardwell, East Harling and Long Melford in Suffolk, and at Stanford on Avon, Ludlow and South Mimms (Middlesex).

Plate 20 shows a donor panel in the east window of Long Melford Church (Suffolk). The figure is that of Anne Crane. It is interesting as showing the headdress and costume of the period and is typical of the growing attention paid to the individual rather than to a generalized type. The delicacy of the linework and the subtle shading of the face are in evident contrast to the treatment of the preceding centuries. It was painted in the second half of the fifteenth century and clearly indicates the general development of technique in painting though the design is still that of a glass mosaic.

The five-light east window in East Harling Church is a work of great beauty, one of the most beautiful of its kind in England. It has a border and canopy enclosing panels of scenes from the Life of Christ—The Annunciation, The Nativity, The Adoration of the Shepherds, The Adoration of the Magi, The Presentation in the Temple, The Boy Jesus Confounding the Doctors, The Miracle at Cana in Galilee, The Betrayal, The Crucifixion, The Taking Down of the Body of Christ from the Cross, The Resurrection, The Ascension and the Coming of the Holy Ghost.

The window is a mosaic of mellow colour of varying tints patterned upon a white ground delicately enriched with touches of yellow stain of modulating depth. The shaped heads of the lights above the springing line have been restored as is evidenced by the application of a dull and even stain of middle yellow. This could be brought into harmony with the rest of the window by unevenly removing some of the stain with acid and could be done without removing the window. As it is, the work below the springing line is that of an artist, whilst, in obvious contrast, that above is not.

Unfortunately the original traceries are no longer in position and, except for two lights, are filled with later glass mechanically repeating in each tracery a floral decoration out of scale with the rest of the window. The two angels, in the two central tracery lights, carried out in monochrome, are interesting but obviously not part of the original design. In a window on the south side of the church containing fragments of old glass, there is an angel which may have filled one of the traceries of the east window at one time. It is part of the same colour scheme.

The Jesse window was still a popular subject at this period. Plate 21 shows a fine example in the east window of Margaretting Church, Essex. It has been suggested that this work is Flemish but Westlake, who restored the window, has stated that it is Westminster work, probably by John Prudde, executed about 1460.

No doubt as the century progressed the style of the windows was affected by the rise of the middle classes. Whilst the feudal nobility were dissipating their energies and resources in wasteful strife, the wool and cloth merchants, amongst others, were increasing their wealth and consequently their power and influence. Through their munificence many fine churches were built and probably through their influence foreign craftsmen arrived, particularly from Flanders, to carry out commissions in this country; many of these foreigners eventually remained as naturalized citizens.

The merchants were men of widespread interests, infusing a new spirit into the country and welcoming any indication of emancipation from the feudal tradition. Whatever social benefits may have accrued from their influence, however, it is doubtful whether it was of advantage to the aesthetic development of stained glass. Up to this point in history the dominating influence had been that of the Church and the nobility; from now on the power of the commercial interests increased and the beauty of stained glass correspondingly diminished.

Merchant's marks of this period are to be seen in churches as far apart as St. Andrews, Norwich, Monk's Risborough (Bucks), and Newark (Notts). Heraldry and roundels showing secular subjects such as the twelve labours of the months, of which examples are to be seen in the Victoria and Albert Museum, became widely used to embellish the windows of the private houses of the affluent.

CHAPTER 5

The Sixteenth Century

As might be expected the transition from Gothic to the new Renaissance style was a gradual one, varying according to the district and probably dependent upon the age of the local craftsmen, but by degrees the tradition of the glazier and his appreciation of the material was lost in concentration upon pictorial representation. A similar misfortune befell the other crafts. Weaving suffered the same infliction as may be seen by comparing the tapestries at Hampton Court, designed by Raphael, with earlier Tudor tapestries in the next room. Referring to this period Lewis F. Day writes:

> '. . . by this time the donor had ceased to hide the light of his munificence under any show of modesty and his portraiture had become a feature in window design.'

This is far from an irrelevant consideration. Stained glass, probably more than other crafts, expresses the spirit of its age. It is significant that the artistry of the craftsman and the selflessness of the true religious motive both departed together. All the authorities in stained glass agree in deploring the deterioration which the craft suffered through the influence of the Renaissance; an opinion with which all the leading stained glass craftsmen in whatsoever country entirely agree. The interesting factor from the artist's point of view is that the overwhelming influence is one of national psychology, which, it would seem, is not to be overcome by the individual's appreciation of aesthetics. Sir Herbert Read comments:

> 'What characterizes the thought of this period, characterizes the Art. By the end of the fifteenth century (perhaps by 1455 when Fra Angelico died) Italian art had outlived the Franciscan impulse, and quite in keeping with the development of philosophy, had acquired the character of individuality. It was still capable of emotion, power and greatness—but only of the emotion, power and greatness of a personality. It had lost its universality, its humility, its subordination to a unity—all the qualities of classic art. The era of romanticism was born.'

Coming at the beginning of this transitional period is the great series of windows at Fairford Church, Gloucestershire, which are of particular interest not only because each light retains its original glass, thus giving an impression of its general aesthetic effect at the time of its installation, but also because the arrangement of the subject matter in its distribution throughout the church can be studied in its entirety. Whereas today the emphasis is perhaps on prayer and worship, in medieval days instruction had a very considerable part to play and the windows were obviously designed and arranged to reinforce by pictorial means the Church's teaching.

Most of these windows are of poor craftsmanship and are interesting rather for their subject matter depicting a medieval mentality rather than for any technical qualities.

The twenty-eight windows tell the story of the Redemption, beginning with the Fall and ending with the Doom or Judgement in the great west window (Plate 22). There have been several theories as to the origin of these windows but the Rev. T. G. Joyce analysing the evidence in his book, *The Fairford Windows*, comes to the following conclusion:

> 'There is but one view that will reconcile all the points in this evidence which appears to be conflicting; namely that the glass was made in England, under an English contract, but that both Flemings and Germans were employed in its execution.'

Eden in his *Ancient, Stained and Painted Glass* speaks of:

> '. . . the harmony which resulted from the unity of effort of mason, woodcarver, painter and worker in glass.
>
> 'In a sense, however, this decorative or artistic effect was but an accident, though one which invariably resulted from the medieval craftsman's work. Primarily, the idea underlying all this unified beauty in old buildings was usefulness—the notion of means to an end. Craftsmen of the Middle Ages knew nothing of art for art's sake; their object was to produce something useful and fitting to the end in view. If their work was beautiful it was so because it answered to that end according to the way in which it did so. Now, the end to be kept in view in all work connected with the church was, in the medieval mind, instruction—the driving home, through the senses, of the Church's message. As paintings on walls and pillars (such as we may see today in many churches, notably the thirteenth-century church of Our Lady and St. Lawrence at Trier, and St. Alban's Abbey church) shewed, to learned and unlearned alike, the story of the Church's life throughout the centuries, so painted windows did the same.'

The well-known sixteenth-century windows in King's College Chapel, Cambridge, are probably the finest examples of Renaissance glass in England. They are evidence of the new mental outlook in which the art of the glazier has been completely subordinated; that of the painter predominates. However much the technical skill in painting may be justly admired, it is impossible not to deplore the complete lack of architectural appreciation or understanding of the material they were using. They have lost the beauty of glass in a triumph of chiaroscuro and perspective, a gallant but misguided attempt to imitate oil painting.

The artist no longer strove to depict religious truths with piety and sincerity but rather revelled in an exhibition of materialistic effect which would have been appropriate to a town hall or other secular building but which, in a Christian church, was fundamentally an exhibition of bad taste. Mr. Kenneth Harrison in his instructive book *The Windows of King's College, Cambridge* writes:

'At the end of the fifteenth century an English glazier had scarcely more to offer than the fashions of his grandfather: every division of the subject was topped by a glittering frame or canopy; colour was mostly confined to the strong primaries; each figure or scene was bounded on both sides by a mullion; the drawing was sometimes delicate, as at York, but more commonly insensitive and crude. The foreigners brought freedom and imagination; they had a better sense of perspective; canopies were often dispensed with; the composition spread over the whole window, in defiance of the stonework; greens, pinks and purples were widely used to extend or harmonize the colour scheme; the development of stipple shading gave a roundness and softness to the drapery and human form. In other words glass began to be influenced by the painter in oils; it became pictorial.'

Mr. Harrison thus accurately describes the beginning of that degeneration in glass technique, the lack of architectural relationship and the introduction of perspective, the use of chiaroscuro, the attempt at picture painting which culminated in the disastrous enamel painting of the eighteenth century. In King's College Chapel we can see the development commencing and it is to be noted that it is at least partly due to Flemish influence.

Symonds in his *Renaissance in Italy* writes:

'As technical skill increased, and as beauty, the proper end of art, became more rightly understood, the painters found that their craft was worthy of being made an end in itself, and that the actualities of life observed around them had claims upon their genius no less weighty than dogmatic mysteries. The subjects they had striven at first to realize with all simplicity now became little better than vehicles for the display of sensuous beauty, science and mundane pageantry. The human body received separate and independent study as a thing in itself incomparably beautiful, commanding more powerful emotions by its magic than aught else that sways the soul. At the same time, the external world, with all its wealth of animal and vegetable life, together with the works of human ingenuity in costly clothing, and superb buildings, was seen to be in every detail worthy of the most patient imitation. Anatomy and perspective taxed the understanding of the artist whose whole force was no longer devoted to the task of bringing religious ideas within the limits of the representable. Next when the classical revival came into full play, the arts, in obedience to the age, left the sphere of sacred subjects and employed their full-grown faculties in the domain of myths and pagan fancies. In this way painting may truly be said to have opened the new era of culture and to have first manifested the freedom of the modern spirit.'

Nevertheless it is clear that however much this development of painting may have been of advantage to secular art it was undoubtedly detrimental to the creation of beauty in glass even for secular purposes; its influence upon Church windows was even more deplorable. It destroyed not only the beauty of the material but debased it still further by using it for secular and materialistic interests which were entirely out of place in a building of religious import.

The illustrations in this chapter are sufficient to show the decline in aesthetic achievement but it must be emphasized that they are even more to be criticized as expressions of mundane vulgarity in comparison with the more worthy and more truly religious creations of earlier centuries. It is a misapprehension to imagine that the technique of this period has more skill than that shown, for example, in the Canterbury 'Adam Delving' or 'Methusaleh' windows. The skill of the craftsman in both periods is superb but it is devoted to different purposes, and of the two the medieval objective is the more noble. It is the contrast between the simple but sensitive expression of sincerity and the accomplished exhibition of the commonplace. The glorification of the individual may be an excellent thing in a secular building for public assembly but it is not a characteristic of the worship of God.

The idea of a Universal Church had lost its power, and considering the behaviour of so many of the ecclesiastical authorities, including, of course, the Popes, this cannot altogether be deplored.

In Italy Savonarola had failed in his noble attempt to eradicate corruption but Calvin in Switzerland, Martin Luther in Germany and John Knox in Scotland had considerable success. The inauguration of the Church of England under Henry VIII was due to political and personal reasons rather than to any religious motives, nevertheless it had widespread national support and was in keeping with a growing mass of public opinion.

It may be said that the sixteenth century saw the beginning of the modern era. For the first time treaties were made chiefly on account of commercial and national interests. Increasing commerce assisted the spread of new ideas and the technique of stained glass was not immune from innovation. In 1550, Jean Cousin, the famous glass painter of Paris, invented a red enamel for use as a flesh tint which was another step in the direction of oil painting methods.

The five-light east window of St. Margaret's, Westminster (Plate 23), was carried out about 1525. In the three central lights the Crucifixion of Our Lord is depicted with the two thieves one on each side. Kneeling in the lower portion of the left-hand light is a figure of a monarch, with his patron St. George and the Tudor rose shown in the top half. In the lower portion of the right-hand light is a kneeling figure of a queen with her patroness St. Catherine, and the pomegranate of Granada shown in the panel above. The traceries are filled with angels carrying the instruments of the Passion.

This window was restored by William Price, the younger, in the eighteenth century, and Mr. Knowles has pointed out that flesh tints have been added and extra shading applied to the architectural details. Gothic canopy framing has been replaced by broad passages of typical Renaissance masonry such as might be found as part of the background in an Italian oil painting, but the use of pot metal is continued and the leading retained as part of the design. It has a fine rich colour effect, with a well varied blue ground, relieved with touches of deep and variegated ruby and secondary tints.

There has been considerable discussion and research as to the origin of this window, and the identities of the royal kneeling figures still remain in doubt. It seems very remarkable that the history of a window of this importance should be unknown especially as it involved the churchwardens in a law suit at the time of its installation.

Mr. F. Sidney Eden in his book *Ancient Stained and Painted Glass* after reviewing much of the evidence gives the following summing up:

> 'Clearly as the window stands, the kneeling figures cannot be meant for Henry VII and Elizabeth of York. The lady might be, and probably is, Catherine of Aragon with her patroness St. Catherine and her paternal badge. As to the male figure, the most likely supposition seems to be that it is intended for Henry VIII. Some have suggested Prince Arthur, his brother, Catherine's first husband, but it is hardly likely that Henry VIII would have set up the window in his chapel at New Hall—a favourite residence of his—had this been so. Perhaps the true tale may be that the window was, originally, intended to contain figures of Henry VII and Elizabeth, but that the plan was, after that king's death, altered by the substitution for them of Henry VIII and Catherine; or, again, even a more likely story seems to be that the window is not the one intended by the Dort folk for Henry VIII, but another window altogether, simply a gift to the canons at Waltham Abbey by Henry VIII, who, in his early days, was a constant visitor there. The probability of this last suggestion is increased by the fact that the window is distinctly late in style, highly developed as to its light and shade, and may well have been painted about 1525.'

Plate 25 shows an example, belonging to the early part of the century, of glass produced by English craftsmen in the traditional style before it had become submerged by the foreign renaissance. This window in St. Neot's Church, Cornwall, was given in 1523 by the wives of the western part of the parish and the placing of the kneeling figures of the donors in the base panels is characteristic of the period. The central figures are St. Mabena, Our Lady of Pity, the Risen Christ and St. Maberdus.

Earlier windows in the church are those showing 'The Creation' and the stories of Adam, Noah and St. George dating from 1480 to 1530. They are interesting examples of the glazing of windows in a country parish church of this period, though unfortunately they were rather drastically restored by J. P. Hedgeland soon after 1825.

Although the grace and decorative quality of the earlier canopy work has disappeared and become a rather ungainly mass of masonry, nevertheless the design is still based upon the technique of traditional glass mosaic and is not yet attempting the completely pictorial effects of oil painting. It is still in the Gothic tradition.

By the end of the century nearly all the colours were produced with enamel so that technically the use of pot metal became unnecessary, with disastrous results to the beauty of the glass.

The most successful use of enamel technique is in small domestic panels of genre painting which together with heraldic panels became very much the vogue at this period. This development undoubtedly owed a great deal to the growing wealth and importance of the middle classes, who were building more comfortable and refined houses and valued glass as an additional adornment.

Plate 24 shows a good example of late sixteenth-century heraldry, carried out at York, where craftwork still retained much of its traditional character. The panel has been to some extent repaired, as will be seen in the glass immediately below the shield which consists of a number of broken pieces leaded together. The leading is still a feature of the design though the light as a whole is a mixture of mosaic and enamel technique.

This new outlet for craft activity must have been at least a partial relief to the glass painters, since the ecclesiastical authorities were occupied with removing stained glass windows from their churches rather than in erecting new ones. This was of course due to the Reformation and break with Rome. Dr. Woodforde quotes part of Article 28 of the Royal Injunctions of 1547, which reads:

> 'Also, that they take away, utterly extinct and destroy all shrines, all tables, all candlesticks, trindles and rolls of wax, pictures, paintings and all other monuments of feigned miracles, pilgrimages, idolatry and superstition so that there remain no memory of the same in walls, glass-windows or elsewhere within their churches or houses. And that they shall exhort all their parishioners to do the like within their several houses.'

The extent to which this demolition took place can be judged by the comparatively few remains of medieval sculpture and paintings in our cathedrals and churches today. Queen Elizabeth's ordinance, roughly two decades later, that all superstitious painted windows in churches should be removed, undoubtedly resulted in some further destruction of existing glass, but fortunately the cost of extensive removal and replacement of windows with plain glass was an expensive business; indeed the cost was so prohibitive that the order was only partially obeyed. Nevertheless this ordinance must have proved a further deterrent to the commissioning of any new windows that might incur Her Majesty's displeasure or that of her advisers.

The Renaissance decadence in stained glass continued on the continent where indeed it had originated, though works of masterly technical skill and ability, retaining the use of pot metal glass combined with enamel, were still being produced, notably by the Crabeth brothers at Gouda and Linard Gonthier at Troyes.

The famous windows in the market town at Gouda have justly given it a more than continental renown. They are, in their style, a magnificent achievement and probably the draughtsmanship and technical skill is unsurpassed. It is certain that few modern artists could execute windows with such masterly handling. They were executed in the period from 1556 to 1601 and donated by such eminent personages as Philip II of Spain, Queen Mary of England, Margaret of Austria, William I, Prince of Orange and the Lord States of South and North Holland. The principal painters were the brothers Dirk and Wouter Pieterzz Crabeth.

To people unacquainted with the masterpieces of earlier periods, windows such as these, or for that matter those in King's College Chapel, Cambridge, must appear as the height of excellence, but this is only because they are momentarily impressed by pictorial realism on the grand scale, unconscious of the sublimity of a really fine window in an impressive cathedral setting or ignorant of the quality of, for example, the Le Mans 'Ascension' window which is set in an aisle window and owes little of its impressiveness to its surroundings.

Apart from its great technical excellence the scale of the Gouda glass is itself impressive. Thirty or more great windows, mostly of six lights, some twenty-five feet

PLATE 22. Fairford, Glos. Great West 'Doom' window.

PLATE 23. St. Margaret's Church, Westminster. East window, *c*. 1525.

PLATE 24. Heraldic glass by Bernard Dininckhoff, 1585,
formerly in Gilling Castle, Yorkshire.
(*By courtesy of the Abbot of Ampleforth.*)

PLATE 25. St. Neot's Church, Cornwall. Window in north aisle, 1523.

in height, are filled with scenes of Biblical events. However much the departure from two-dimensional technique and the lack of deep spiritual motive may be regretted, the craftsmanship is superb and recognition must be given to a great human achievement.

Examples of this transitional period where some of the beauty of the traditional technique is preserved may be seen at Auch, in St. Patrick and St. Vincent at Rouen, St. Gudule in Brussels, at Beauvais, St. Etienne in Paris, and other churches in France.

CHAPTER 6

The Seventeenth Century

The recognition of the further deterioration in the craft of stained glass during the seventeenth and eighteenth centuries is no modern twentieth-century revelation. As far back as 1848 Warrington writes:

> 'These periods introduce us to styles (if they may be so termed) differing so much in all respects from medieval work, that, with all the talent and ingenuity employed on them, they seem from first to last, to have been a misconception of this Art. As at this time, engraving and oil painting had become the ruling passion, so Church architecture to which these arts bore little analogy, became capricious and debased, assuming any form and style which the humour and fancy of the Architect or his employer might think fit, irrespective of order or precedent. Great artists in engraving and oil painting had now arisen, whom the practitioners on glass, misunderstanding its capabilities, vainly strove to rival. Now, as the latter art mainly depends for its beauties and effects on its association with appropriate architecture and upon principles opposite to those of oil and shadowy painting, it follows that the attempt to treat glass like canvas must prove a comparative failure.'

The activities of the Tudors, as we have seen, put a check not only upon the production of stained glass windows but also upon the form of religious observances. The infallibility and authority of the Church doctrines had been challenged and the numbers of the Nonconformists and Puritans greatly increased. It was not only that the traditional craft technique had been, to a great extent, lost, but the spirit in which the work was carried out lacked its earlier devoutness and simplicity. The invention and spread of printing to some degree weakened its purpose, the illustration of the Church's teachings. All these influences had their effect, together with that of the now wealthy middle classes, but none was so detrimental and far reaching as the failure to understand the proper use of the material.

Upon Westlake's statement in his *History of Design in Painted Glass* 'For works of this and later periods I have personally very little liking' Read makes the following interesting commentary:

> 'This instinctive aversion is quite free from any theoretical prejudice, and no doubt Westlake merely reacted to his sense of the orderly development of the art of glass painting. He did not, like Winston, appeal to the criterion of classical art, nor did he

PLATE 26. Merchant Tailors' Hall, York.
Window by Henry Gyles, 1679.

indict the course of art in general. In this he was wise, for the obvious truth is that once it has put itself under the domination of the false aesthetic the art of glass-painting fell into confusion and eventually perished.'

Plate 27 shows a section of a window in St. Mary's Church, Warwick. It is typical of the mentality of this period. Note the trivialities: the dog with the bone and the cast shadows of the dog's legs. It is well to remember that in the earlier periods of ecclesiastical iconography its aesthetics were in fact controlled by the Church authorities. The edict of the Council of Nicaea in the eighth century laid down a definite directive, no doubt to eradicate malpractices in design and execution. Far from this proving a deterrent to the artist, it is recognized that in the ensuing three centuries Byzantine art reached and maintained its highest state of perfection. Whether some edict in the seventeenth century could have brought the craft back to a higher level is problematical, but the ecclesiastical authorities in this period of political, religious and national ferment were no longer in the commanding position of the Nicaean Council.

Today Church authorities in England spread a benign influence through the functioning of the Diocesan Advisory Committees. Beneficial as this arrangement undoubtedly is to the general level of achievement, it is more of a safeguard than a source of enlightenment. An even more constructive policy, following the precedent of the eighth century, would be helpful alike to incumbent, parochial church councils and especially to stained glass artists.

At present the designer does not know what particular standards or criteria of subject matter the Diocesan Committees may have in mind. It is, however, true that in almost every case if he produces a design which has reasonable relationship to its architectural surroundings it will be accepted. Nevertheless if the designer had the benefit of a general directive issued, say, by a Council or Committee of Deans, and including some of our best architects, under the Chairmanship perhaps of the Dean of York not only would this be of advantage to him in solving his particular problem but also would be of help in guiding clients and parochial church councils in their appreciation of the true qualities of stained glass.

Such a directive is probably not so necessary in the case of the more important commissions for great east or west windows, where in most cases the control is exercised by people of knowledge and understanding, and probably under the guidance of an experienced architect. The difficulty is the constant addition of small windows to our churches, not in accordance with any co-ordinated plan, but as a haphazard selection according to the particular fancies of the client.

In no age has the name of freedom been more stridently invoked than at the present time. But it is always well to remember that freedom may all too easily develop into individual licence and if the course of stained glass is traced through the centuries it will be found that the best periods were those when the craft was controlled by the cultured authority of the church.

The ordinances of the Tudors had confined the use of stained glass almost entirely to domestic purposes, but the accession of James I enabled Archbishops Abbott and Laud, though disunited as regards theology, to encourage a revival of stained glass for

D

church windows, notably in Oxford where excellent examples of this period by Abraham and Bernard van Linge may be seen in the college chapels.

The windows by Bernard van Linge and contemporary craftsmen in Lincoln's Inn Chapel, London, were later saved from destruction by the iconoclasts through the protection of Archbishop Laud. They are mostly canopy and figure work with heraldic panels in the base. Painted 1623–1626, they are interesting examples of the prevailing false aesthetic, with flesh tints, rouged cheeks and reddened lips. The iris of the eye is tinted blue. Compared with much work of this date they are rich in colour. They were considerably damaged and some on the north side entirely destroyed by a bomb in the first world war. However the remaining windows have been repaired and restored and are sufficient evidence of great skill misapplied.

The van Linge windows in Oxford are larger and more important. The east window of Wadham College Chapel by Bernard van Linge is reputed to be the artist's finest work in this country. It was erected in 1613, when the chapel was built. Other examples by this painter are to be seen in the side windows of Lincoln College Chapel dated 1629 and 1630, and in Christ Church, showing the figure of Bishop Oliver King with the ruins of Oseney Abbey in the background, painted 1630–1640. Dr. Woodforde has pointed out that some of the prophets in Lincoln College Chapel, Oxford, are identical with those painted for the Chapel of Lincoln's Inn, London, and that the Oseney Abbey background is again used as the background for a window depicting St. Matthias (Plate 28). Winston writes:

> 'The side windows of Lincoln's Inn Chapel, which are dated 1623, 1624 and 1626, are generally supposed to have been painted by the Van Linges, but from their coarse and inartificial execution, I am inclined to attribute them rather to some inferior workmen employed as painters under the Van Linges. In their general style, however, they evidently belong to the Van Linge school. In the Lincoln's Inn windows, as in the works of the Van Linges at Oxford and elsewhere, enamel colours applied as an oil painting, are much used in the heads and naked parts of the figures, and in the backgrounds of the designs. Coloured glass is very generally employed in the draperies, and is occasionally diapered with an enamel colour of the same tint as itself. In some of the Oxford glass, the basis of the shading is stippled; in general, however, in the works of the Van Linges, it possesses no decided grain, but appears to have been suffered to dry without being stippled at all. The darkest shadows are universally formed by smear hatching and smear shading. The shadows are in general too opaque and heavy, and too much extended over the glass to the exclusion of clear light.'

Plate 29 shows a typical heraldic and medallion portrait window of this period in St. Mary's Church, Battersea. It was painted about 1634. The lack of feeling for design or pattern or relevance to the architectural setting is particularly apparent in the treatment of the traceries.

The windows in University College Chapel are by the younger van Linge and were painted in the reign of Charles I. They are signed and dated 1641. The subjects are 'The Temptation of Adam and Eve', 'Jacob's Vision', 'Elijah Translated', 'Jonah and the Whale' and 'Christ in the House of Martha and Mary'.

PLATE 28. Lincolns Inn Chapel. Third window in south wall. Attributed to Bernard van Linge.

PLATE 29. St. Mary's Church, Battersea, *c.* 1634.

PLATE 30. University College Chapel, Oxford. By Abraham van Linge, 1641.

PLATE 31. Magdalen College Hall, Oxford. King Charles I and his Queen, Henrietta Maria. By Richard Greenbury, 1633.

Plate 30 illustrates the 'Martha and Mary' window, the fourth on the south side of the Chapel. In the top centre tracery the Arms are those of Dudley and in the two smaller, rather rectangular, traceries are what appear to be extracts from some family photograph album. This three-light window is the apotheosis of vulgarity. If it were not for the halo round Christ's head it would be impossible to tell that this was a religious picture at all, and as it is, the right-hand light would look very appropriate in a wayside hostel.

If this window was painted to please the rising middle classes, as it undoubtedly was, it is not surprising that the bourgeoisie came to have the reputation of being lacking in good taste. The painter must take some of the blame for his failure to appreciate traditional technique but what sort of clients and incumbents must they have been to accept such trash, inferior even from an illustrative point of view—and this in Oxford, a seat of learning. It is somewhat surprising that the Dons did not show more discrimination than the Flemish merchants.

From the purely technical aspect the craft was deteriorating. The traditional canopy disappeared and a background of dull and meaningless Renaissance architecture took its place. Wherever possible the leading was divided into rectangular panes with no relationship to any observable design. The draughtsmanship, too, had little to commend it; for example, in the above-mentioned window the kneeling figure of Mary is an anatomical monstrosity.

A well-known earlier window of the younger van Linge, erected 1630–1640, in Christ Church, Oxford, depicts 'Jonah before Ninevah'. The whole surface of the two lights is leaded into rectangular pieces so that the impression is given of figure and landscape seen through a grille. It is as far from traditional decoration as is realistic oil painting, which no doubt was the criterion the artist had in mind at this period. So distrustful was the craftsman of his material that it became the common practice to matt over the outside of the glass to prevent any possible glitter.

Abraham van Linge also executed a window for Balliol College Chapel in 1637, showing 'The Sickness and Recovery of King Hezekiah', and carried out a considerable amount of work for Queen's College, which was much restored by Joshua Price in the eighteenth century.

Windows of this period are to be seen in the ante-chapel of Magdalen College. They depict a series of female saints carried out in sepia monochrome by Richard Greenbury, *c.* 1632. This craftsman was a goldsmith, portrait painter and copyist of pictures and one cannot escape the conclusion that his excellence in this latter capacity was a fatal deterrent to his success as a stained glass artist. He did, however, paint many highly accomplished portrait panels in glass, a number of which may be seen in the Oxford Colleges. Plate 31 shows an excellent example of his work in Magdalen College Hall. The portraits are of King Charles I and his Queen, Henrietta Maria.

With the exception of the van Linges, the best known stained glass artist of the period was an Englishman, Baptista Sutton. Two of his windows, dated 1634, are in the Chapel of Holy Trinity, Guildford. Unfortunately his east window in St.

Leonard's, Shoreditch, painted in 1634, was practically demolished by a bomb in the second world war.

An interesting work of this period by an unknown artist, is the east window in the Chapel of Trinity Hospital, Greenwich. It depicts the 'Crucifixion' with the 'Agony in the Garden' and the 'Ascension' on either side. Dr. Woodforde dates it as 1634.

Plate 32 shows an excellent example of early seventeenth-century work in the east window of Lydiard Tregoze, Wilts. The subject of the left-hand light is John the Baptist and an olive tree bearing six shields, showing the descent of the heiress of Beauchamp, wife of Oliver St. John. St. John the Evangelist is in the right-hand light. The window is characteristic of the period's almost predominant interest in heraldic emblazonment and it may be noted that this example still retains a traditional technique in that the leading forms a coherent part of the design.

In this century practically all the colours could be obtained in enamel which, as has been shown, together with the elimination of pot metal and (as far as possible) of the leading, side-tracked the craft into a simulation of oil painting. It is difficult to assess to what extent the development of stained glass technique was influenced by the sudden stoppage of the supply of pot metal glass in 1636. In that year King Louis XIII having invaded Lorraine and achieved complete victory, emphasized his success by razing to the ground its palaces and castles, and, no doubt, inadvertently, the glass works from which the glass painters of this epoch generally acquired their material. Pot metal became practically unobtainable and this must have constrained the stained glass artists, temporarily at least, to use an enamel technique.

But the century had further vicissitudes in store for stained glass. In 1646, Charles I fell a prisoner into the hand of the forces commanded by Cromwell and once again the power rested with the iconoclasts. The destruction and removal of stained glass windows ordered by the Tudors had not been extensively carried out. The 'purification', as it was felt to be, was mostly directed by men of culture and discernment, whereas the fanatical Puritans had less cultural background to act as a curb to their iconoclasm. Some of their leaders were, of course, men of culture, and in a few localities, notably at York, through the auspices of Fairfax, the fury of the mob was held in abeyance. But at best the production of stained glass windows for churches was at a standstill. Bernard and Abraham van Linge had already returned to Emdem at the outbreak of hostilities.

Painting on glass, however, had by no means ceased. Small subject panels for private houses were very popular in the latter part of the century, as were rondels depicting such subjects as the seasons and months with their various activities of sowing, reaping etc. Also much heraldic work was being done. Henry Gyles of York (1645–1709) was a well-known glass painter of this period. Examples of his work, a window in Staveley Parish Church, Derbyshire (1676) and one in the Church at Adel, Yorkshire, show that although coming from a family of glass painters and working in York where tradition died hard, he succumbed to the pictorial and enamel school of glass painting.

Plate 33 shows his window in Staveley Church, near Chesterfield. As was the

PLATE 32. Lydiard Tregoze Church, Wilts. Early seventeenth century.

PLATE 33. Heraldic window, Staveley near Chesterfield.
By Henry Gyles of York, 1676.

prevailing fashion, the leading shows no relation to the design. In fact there is little sense of design left. If the treatment of the mantling is compared with that of earlier work, it appears a shapeless mass of material with neither a feeling for line nor pattern. This applies equally to the wings and drapery. The coronets shown in perspective give an excellent idea of the artist's attempt at three-dimensional representation, an effect emphasized by the over-burdened cupids struggling with a lump of Renaissance architecture.

Before the end of the seventeenth century practically all the colours, blue, green, ruby, violet etc. could be produced with enamel paint, and thus an artistic poison was available which killed practically every aesthetic faculty the craftsmen of the period might have inherently possessed.

CHAPTER 7

The Eighteenth Century

This century is generally regarded as the period in which the craft degenerated to its lowest level of aesthetic production and, strange as it may seem, probably its greatest futility was achieved with a design by one of the finest portrait painters of his day and a President of the Royal Academy. This is the west window of New College Chapel, Oxford (Plate 34).

It was designed by Sir Joshua Reynolds and painted entirely in enamels by Thomas Jervais. The upper part depicts the Nativity and below are represented the three theological virtues, Faith, Hope and Charity together with the four cardinal virtues, Prudence, Justice, Fortitude and Temperance, all of which were received with general acclaim until Walpole, whose artistic taste must have been far above that of the majority of his contemporaries, dubbed them the 'washy virtues'. This caused a fashionable re-appraisement and finally their mythical aesthetic qualities disappeared in popular condemnation.

It would be difficult to find more convincing proof of the necessity for the craftsman to understand the elementary principles of his craft, or of the importance of his realization of an urgent and devout message to be conveyed. The artist must be vitally concerned with this subject. After the medieval period the interest becomes increasingly concerned with subsidiary details, and technical dexterity rather than on the message to be conveyed, a criticism perhaps not inappropriate to some of the windows produced today.

A work is sometimes condemned as being an illustration, ignoring the fact that the greatest masterpieces of the world have been illustrations. Christ's parables were illuminating illustrations of the highest order. If Reynolds had omitted the virtues and concentrated his heart and mind on the realization of the Nativity he might have produced a masterpiece. As it was he had his eye on Greek sculpture and classical representation. His work is a typical product of a purely academic mentality and has no relationship to or apparent understanding of the profundities or the humanities of the Gospel.

Dr. Woodforde in his excellent book *The Stained Glass of New College, Oxford* states that 'the work was a grievous disappointment to Reynolds' and amongst other

PLATE 34. 'Fortitude' and 'Faith'.
De signed by Sir Joshua Reynolds and painted by Thomas Jervais, 1778.

PLATE 35. Trinity College Library, Cambridge.
Alma Mater presenting Isaac Newton to King George III,
designed by Giovanni Battista Cipriani
and painted by William Peckitt, 1775.

interesting correspondence quotes a letter written by Horace Walpole to the Countess of Upper Ossory:

'I went to my passion Oxford and saw Sir Joshua Reynold's "Nativity". But, alas! it is just the reverse of the glorious masterpiece it made in the dark chamber in Pall Mall. It is too high, the ante-chapel where it is placed is too narrow to see it but foreshortened, and the washy virtues round it are so faint and light that the dark shepherds and chiaroscuro, that are meant to relieve the glory, Child and angels, obscure the whole. I foresaw, long ago, that Jarvis's colours being many of them not transparent, could not have the effect of old painted glass.'

Warrington writes:

'So far as regards the first half of this epoch but little can be said with reference to the Art which will not apply to the last. The same disposition to produce the effect of oil-painting on glass was continued and even further attempts were made towards this object by enamelling colours only. These last proved that the Art had exhausted itself in vain attempts to rival oil painting, which had in this sense entirely and long previously superseded it.'

This reliance of the glass painter upon the skill of the contemporary masters of oil painting was undoubtedly the cause of the low standard of stained glass design. The artist was thinking in terms of paint and chiaroscuro and not at all of glass. Unfortunately it was an all too common practice. Francis Eginton of Birmingham (1737–1805), one of the most popular glass-painters of his day, carried out the well-known window in St. Paul's Church, Birmingham, depicting 'The Conversion of St. Paul', and based upon a picture by Sir Benjamin West for the loan of which Eginton paid eighty guineas so that he could reproduce it in glass. His 'Resurrection of Christ' in Lichfield and Salisbury Cathedrals is 'after Reynolds'. Another window of his, 'Resurrection of Lady Letitia Dearden', may be seen in Aston Church, Birmingham.

A further example of the pictorial oil painter collaborating with the glass painter is the window in the Library of Trinity College, Cambridge (Plate 35). It was designed by Giovanni Battista Cipriani and painted by William Peckitt in 1775. As was the practice of the period the whole of the glass is divided into square panes so that the effect is given of a scene observed through a grille. There is very little pot metal used, but the wonder is that there is any at all. The subject is 'Alma Mater' presenting Isaac Newton to George III. Referring to this glass painter in his *York School of Glass Painting* Knowles makes the following interesting commentary:

'William Peckitt of York (1731–1795) was evidently a man of rare vision for unlike his contemporary Francis Eginton of Birmingham (1737–1805) who worked almost entirely in monochrome, Peckitt realized that colour is a sine qua non of Stained Glass. His windows, executed between 1764 and 1774 for New College, Oxford, display an array of colour not to be seen in glass with the exception of the work of the Prices, for a hundred years or more before his time.

'The query as to the source of Peckitt's coloured glass was finally solved by Mr. Harry J. Powell in his book *Glass Making in England* in which he quotes from Dr.

Pocock's *Travels through England*. "1751. 8. June, came to Stourbridge famous for its glass manufacture, which is here coloured in the liquid all the capital colours in their several shades, and if I mistake not, is a secret which they have here." '

Plate 36 is an illustration of what became possible at the end of this century. Incredible as it may seem it is a window in the south transept of York Minster painted in 1793 by William Peckitt. It is difficult to find any redeeming merit in a production of this sort either of design, draughtsmanship, colour or interest of subject. The artist was of course well past his prime when carrying out this work but in criticizing production in the next century it should be compared with this addition to one of our great cathedrals in the eighteenth century.

Of course throughout the history of stained glass the painters of windows have had recourse to the works of artists in other mediums. For example, illuminated manuscripts and later the *Biblia Pauperum* and the *Speculum Humanae Salvationis* were much used and indeed often illustrations were almost exactly copied. No doubt the artists who illustrated the early manuscripts working in the same brotherhood as the glass painters, often designed the subjects of stained glass windows. The earliest treatise on the craft is by the monk Theophilus.

Stained glass artists have naturally and necessarily always been influenced by the prevailing characteristics of the art of the day. So long as these were decorative and descriptive, relying upon line and pattern to create the effect, this influence was beneficial, but when the artist in oil and tempera painting developed a three-dimensional pictorial style introducing perspective and chiaroscuro, the situation changed completely. Succumbing to the general fashion of the day and neglectful of the true technique of glass, the stained glass painters destroyed their craft in an ape-like attempt to imitate the perfections of oil painting. They have a few survivors today.

The Price family of glass painters, consisting of the brothers William (d. 1722) and Joshua, and the latter's son William (d. 1765) were well known and did much work at this period. Authorities differ as to their history, training and the locality of their studios. It has been suggested that William Price, the elder, learnt his craft from Henry Gyles of York but Mr. Knowles states that:

'. . . there is nothing whatever to prove that Price had any connexion with York and much evidence against it. For Price was certainly a contemporary and, it would seem, even belonged to an earlier generation than Gyles. In 1683, when the York artist was but 38 years of age, Price was at the head of a flourishing business in London and was reported to have already amassed wealth.'

No one who has read Mr. Knowles' book *The York School of Glass Painting* will feel inclined to dispute his conclusions in this matter.

It is generally agreed that Joshua Price, working after the manner of the van Linges, was the most worthy representative of the family and his work may perhaps best be studied in Queen's College Chapel, Oxford, and also in a series of ten windows in Great Whitley Church (Worcestershire) (Plate 37). The Rose window in the north transept of Westminster Abbey was also painted by him from designs by Sir

PLATE 36. York Minster, window in south transept. By William Peckitt, 1793.

PLATE 37. Whitley Church, Worcs.
Window in north aisle by Joshua Price, 1719.

James Thornhill. William Price the younger, is best represented by five windows on the south side of New College Chapel, Oxford. In these windows he has incorporated some of the original fourteenth-century glass, more especially in the canopies. Dr. Woodforde records that he painted glass for the west window of Westminster Abbey in 1735.

James Pearson (1750–1805) another well-known stained glass craftsman of this period, painted numerous windows for various London churches, also for Brasenose College, Oxford, and for Salisbury Cathedral. He was born in Dublin but came over and established himself in London. Plate 38 shows a small panel painted by him in 1783, now in the Victoria and Albert Museum. The subject is that of a female figure representing Comedy and the work shows a very high degree of technical painting ability and draughtsmanship. Painted with enamels, it is more in the nature of genre painting than stained glass.

Eglington Margaret Pearson (d. 1823) also painted windows in this period and one of her works, based upon Guido's 'Aurora' was carried out for Arundel Castle.

It is of course natural that all the arts should be similarly affected by the prevailing spirit of their time and it is interesting to note that a fine and sensitive intellect such as that of Coleridge (1772–1834) was well aware of the contemporary general decline in cultural and aesthetic appreciation. In his *Biographia Literaria* in commenting upon the differences between poetry of the fifteenth and sixteenth centuries and that of his own age, he states that these differences may also be seen in the sister art of painting.

'The poet seems to propose to himself as his main object, and as that which is most characteristic of his art, new and striking images; with incidents that interest the affections or excite the curiosity. Both his characters and his descriptions, he renders, as much as possible, specific and individual, even to a degree of portraiture. In his diction and metre, on the other hand, he is comparatively careless. The measure is either constructed on no previous system and acknowledges no justifying principle but that of the writer's convenience; or else some mechanical movement is adopted, of which one couplet or stanza is so far an adequate specimen, so that the occasional differences appear evidently to arise from accident, or the qualities of the language, not from meditation and an intelligent purpose.

'Something analagous to the materials and structure of modern society I seem to have noticed in our common landscape painters. Their foregrounds and their intermediate distances are comparatively unattractive; while the main interest of the landscape is thrown into the background, where mountains and torrents and castles forbid the eye to proceed and nothing tempts it to trace its way back again. But in the works of the great Italian and Flemish masters, the front and middle objects of the landscape are the most obvious and determinate, the interest gradually dies away in the background, and the charm and peculiar worth of the picture consists not so much in the specific objects which it conveys but to the understanding in a visual language formed by the substitution of figures for words, as in the beauty and harmony of the colour, lines and expression, with which the objects are represented. Hence novelty of subject was rather avoided than sought for. Superior excellence in the manner of treating the same subjects was the trial and test of the artist's mind.'

It is now very evident from the aesthetic point of view that the decline in the quality of stained glass was due to contemporary indifference to traditional glass technique. The draughtsmanship and the painting skill were adequate but they were used for mistaken purposes. It should perhaps be emphasized that an appreciation of tradition or better still, an understanding of tradition, in no way prevents an expression of the prevalent modernity. Indeed it is almost certain that no great work of art can be created unless it truly represents the spirit of its time. This is beautifully expressed by Coleridge:

> 'A lasting and enviable reputation awaits that man of genius, who shall attempt and realize a union: who shall recall the high finish, the appropriateness, the facility, the delicate proportion and above all the persuasive and omnipresent grace, which have preserved, as in a shrine of amber, the Sparrow of Catullus, the Swallow, the Grasshopper and all the other loves of Anacreon; and which, with bright though diminished glories, revisited the youth and early manhood of Christian Europe, in the Vales of Arno, and the groves of Isis and Cam—and who with these should combine the keener interest, deeper pathos, manlier reflection and the fresher and more various imagery, which give a value and a name that will not pass away to the poets who have done honour to our own time and to those of our immediate predecessors.'

PLATE 38. Panel representing Comedy. By James Pearson, 1783.

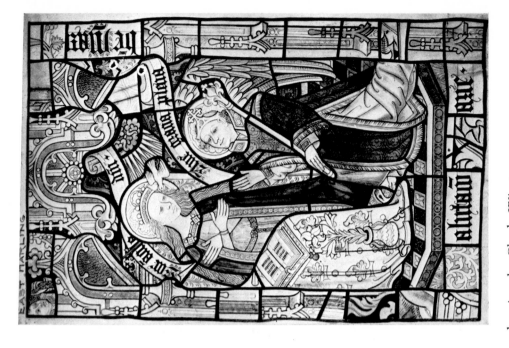

PLATE 39. East Harling, Norfolk. Full size drawings by Charles Winston.

CHAPTER 8

The Nineteenth Century

It has long been the custom to condemn the period of Victorian art but it was in fact a time of reassessment and revival, especially as regards stained glass. Pugin and Ruskin created a renewed interest in native Gothic tradition in contrast to the somewhat insipid and often meaningless repetition of classical forms. The maligned industrial era did at any rate release vast amounts of money for creative artistic effort.

Many new churches were built and many existing ones restored or rebuilt in the Gothic tradition. Innumerable church windows were commissioned. The general level of work was admittedly poor but craftsmen were slowly regaining an understanding of the value and merit of the earlier traditions and most windows, although heavily overpainted in a realistic manner, were nevertheless carried out in pot metal and with due regard to leading. Moreover, it was increasingly recognized that this modern pot metal glass could not compare in colour or texture with early medieval glass.

Probably no single individual has had such far-reaching effect upon the craft of glass as Charles Winston (1814–1864), barrister, archaeologist and connoisseur of glass. Being deeply interested in the craft of stained glass and, after collaborating without any satisfactory result with several smaller firms, he finally approached the Whitefriars Glass Works and samples of medieval glass which he had collected were analysed. With the information gathered, glass was produced the quality of which equalled, and in some respects surpassed, that of medieval times. These results greatly interested many of the best artists of the day, not only stained glass craftsmen, but men like Burne-Jones, Rossetti and Morris. Rossetti and Burne-Jones (1833–1898) both designed windows for the Whitefriars Studios. Charles Winston, as well as being a connoisseur of the arts had himself considerable talent as a draughtsman. Plate 39 shows two copies of fifteenth-century glass in East Harling Church, Norfolk, executed by him. It is true that these are copies and not originals; nevertheless, the technical execution and appreciation of the subtleties of form and delineation are those of a sound draughtsman.

Burne-Jones' earlier cartoons, some of which are still to be seen at the Whitefriars studios, are in some ways better than his later work. They are simpler, less mannered and less imbued with the romanticism which rather weakened his later style. Plate 40 shows two of his cartoons for the St. Frideswide window in Christ Church, Oxford, drawn in 1857, when he was twenty-three years of age.

From 1861 onwards he worked exclusively, as regards stained glass, for his former undergraduate friend at Oxford, William Morris (1834–1896). It was Morris's practice, as a rule, to get those of his colleagues who were professional painters to design the figure subjects whilst he mostly confined himself to choosing the glass and supervising the interpretation of the design. It was mostly due to Morris that the importance of the glazier in the creation of a stained glass window was once more recognized, and under his influence leading became once more part of the design.

This improvement in the colour and quality of the glass naturally attracted widespread interest amongst the leading architects. Dr. Woodforde writes:

> 'Thereafter J. R. Clayton, at the instance of Gilbert Scott, made a careful study of ancient and modern stained glass at home and abroad, with a view to improving the art as a whole. He met William Edward Chance, who had a wide experience of English and foreign methods of making glass. Chance, after years of experiments in his stained glass works at Oldbury, produced results, especially in the making of red glass, far superior to anything that had been produced since medieval times.
>
> 'He was first successful in producing "antique glass" in 1863. The first window in which it was used was by Hardman. Other "antique glass" was soon made by Lloyd and Summerfield of Birmingham and Hartley's (later Hartley, Wood & Co.) of Sunderland, both of whom were closely connected with Chance in 1870–2, when many obstacles connected with the construction of furnaces were overcome.'

The popular idea that the secrets of medieval glass had been lost and that equally good contemporary glass could not be produced might have been true of the beginning, but it was certainly not so by the end of the nineteenth century, and in fact today the range of colour and quality of glass far exceeds anything that the medieval craftsman was able to produce. It must in fairness by emphasized that the greatest advance was achieved in the despised Victorian era. The obloquy should be confined to the eighteenth century.

At the beginning of the century, Eginton at Birmingham and Betton and Evans at Shrewsbury, were discarding the false enamel technique and gradually returning to the true glass tradition. William Raphael Eginton (1778–1834) the son of Francis Eginton carried out windows for George IV, and was appointed glass painter to Princess Charlotte, when he received numerous commissions for windows in the mansions of the aristocracy. In co-operation with Samuel Lowe, his brother-in-law, he executed a great library window at Stourhead (Wiltshire) based upon Raphael's 'School of Athens'. Other examples of his work may be seen in Barr Chapel, near Chester, and in the churches of Brockley (Somerset), Colley (Yorkshire), Digswell (Herts) and Hatton (Warwickshire).

The firm of Betton and Evans renewed in the Gothic technique with excellent results the old fourteenth-century glass of Winchester College Chapel, sent to them

PLATE 40. St. Frideswide window. Cartoons by Burne-Jones, Whitefriars Studios.

PLATE 41. Panel of St. Lawrence. By Charles Eamer Kempe.

for repairs in 1820. Most of their work was for churches in Shropshire, particularly for those in Shrewsbury. Two more of their windows painted in 1838, can be seen in Wadham College Chapel, Oxford. Both partners, Sir John Betton and David Evans, were admitted to the Glazier's Company in the years 1775 and 1819 respectively.

One of the most prolific craftsmen of this period, Thomas Willement (1786–1871), Heraldic Artist to King George IV and Artist in Stained Glass to Queen Victoria, is best known for his memorial window in the great hall at Hamptom Court. He carried out numerous heraldic windows, a type of glass that he helped to revive and popularize, and was influential in restoring a pot metal treatment as opposed to the debased enamel painting of the eighteenth century.

W. Wailes of Newcastle was another pioneer of this period and excellent examples of his work are to be seen in the Church of St. John the Baptist, Newcastle. Hedgeland of London is also note-worthy for his west window in Norwich Cathedral. Like so much work of this period, it has few qualities that would arouse enthusiasm in the modern craftsman or connoisseur of stained glass, but it should, in fairness, be judged in comparison with the work of the previous century. Only then can it be realized that this craftsman was indeed a pioneer struggling to restore to his craft a true appreciation of the medium, although it must be conceded that work such as this must be regarded as an example of historic or archaeological interest rather than of great beauty. It has the effect of an enormous illuminated oil painting placed behind the masonry of the west window with little if any relationship to the architecture. Full use is made of flesh tints and Renaissance realism. The colour scheme, predominantly blue and purple, is not in itself unpleasant but the work as a whole fails because of its irrelevance. Nevertheless Winston described it as 'the best window of modern times'.

Hedgeland is perhaps best known for restoration work in the Chapel of King's College, Cambridge. Amongst the many windows he executed are those in the south aisle of the nave and also in the south-east transept of Lincoln Cathedral, and windows in St. Matthew's Church, Ipswich; Jesus College, Oxford; Holy Trinity Church, Upper Tooting, London; and St. Neot's Church, Cornwall.

Plate 41 shows a small panel, 24″ high by 13½″ wide, of St. Lawrence designed and painted by Charles Eamer Kempe (1837–1907). He was a well-known representative of this period, but like most of his contemporaries very much criticized by the next generation. The illustration shows the merits and weaknesses of this transitional period. The treatment of the head is competent, sincere and sensitive, but the design as a whole is a rather futile conglomeration of meaningless ornament, and the ugly and mannered folds of the drapery are entirely lacking in any sense of design, suggestion of form or appreciation of the beautiful flow of line in draped material which is so characteristic of the earlier periods. Nevertheless in spite of all its defects the figure does retain a semblance of dignity. An excellent example of his work is the 'Milton' window in Horton Church, Bucks. His four windows in the Choir of Bury St. Edmunds Cathedral, based upon fifteenth-century tradition, have a rich and varied colour and the figure work an obvious sincerity. With the exception of the

Flemish late fifteenth-century glass in the westernmost window of the south aisle, these are the best windows in the church.

Gibbs of London is represented by windows (1849) in the south aisle of All Saints Church, Margaret Street, London.

A firm of repute, known for the high standard of their work, was that of Clayton and Bell; James Richard Clayton (1827–1913) and Alfred Bell (1832–1895). The Bell family has carried on the craft to the fourth generation. The best-known windows by Clayton and Bell are in the Cathedrals of Bury St. Edmunds and Truro, and the west window of King's College Chapel, Cambridge. Their windows in Bury St. Edmunds Cathedral, on each side of the Nave, show competent craftsmanship but the general effect is dull, monotonous and uninspired. Nevertheless they should be judged by the prevailing standards of the period and it should be remembered that they are a great improvement on the work of the previous century.

Another outstanding artist of this period was Henry Holiday (1839–1927), painter of the famous picture 'Beatrice and Dante', who began his stained glass career by working for the Whitefriars Studios. His work is now dated, but it was vastly superior to that of most of his contemporaries in quality of glass and in fine draughtsmanship. His designs were extremely competent and devoid of the meaningless embellishments of, for instance, the Kempe panel.

Although Holiday carried out innumerable windows in England among which those in St. Peter's Church, Bushey Heath, Herts (Plate 42), or in Worcester College Chapel, Oxford, show his characteristic style, his finest work is to be seen in America. A visit to the Rhinelander Memorial Church of the Holy Trinity in New York is convincing evidence that he was a fine artist and a master of his craft. The whole church is filled with his windows, which are a perfect enrichment of a fine architectural setting. He eliminated all meaningless ornamental padding and designed his windows as mosaics of glass expressive of their subject. His treatment of figures, although beautifully designed, was still too pictorial, nevertheless his international reputation was founded upon undoubtedly outstanding capabilities.

Nathaniel Hubert Westlake (1833–1921) is best known as the author of the excellent *History of Design in Painted Glass* (1894). Amongst his numerous windows are those in Worcester Cathedral, and the Churches of St. John the Baptist, Brighton, St. John the Divine, Richmond, the Sacred Heart, Hove and St. Philip Neri, Arundel.

John Hardman and Co. (now Hardman's Studios) produced some good work in this period of Gothic revival. Two examples are the 'Te Deum' window in the south transept of Sherbourne Abbey, carried out after a design by A. W. Pugin, and the five-light east window of Bury St. Edmunds Cathedral, depicting the Transfiguraation (Plate 43). The treatment of the latter is that of pot metal glass mosaic based upon sound traditional technique, boldly designed with the main subject covering the three central lights and with subsidiary subjects in the two decorative panels in each of the two outer lights. The colour has not the quality of medieval glass but it was an immense improvement upon the enamel technique of the previous century, and,

PLATE 42. St. Peter's Church, Bushey Heath, Herts.
Window by Henry Holiday, 1918.

PLATE 43. John Hardman & Co., 1868.

PLATE 44. All Saints Church, Middleton Cheney, Northants.
East window designed by William Morris, Burne Jones,
Madox Brown, S. J. Solomon and Philip Webb.

Lo! the joyful Princess was borne home again

PLATE 11. Scene from 'St. George and the Dragon.' Designed by D. G. Rossetti

considering the limitations of the period it should be recognized as a fine pioneering achievement.

William Morris (1839–1896) had, as on all crafts, an important influence on stained glass. The greatly improved quality of the glass was used to produce rich and striking colour effects, and in collaboration with Burne-Jones outstanding windows of characteristic pre-Raphaelite style were evolved.

It was Morris's practice to have his figures drawn by well-known artists while he filled in the background and ornament (Plate 44). It is understandable that he felt the general level of work produced by other firms to be too much of a mechanical copying of traditional designs and that a more modern and contemporary note was desirable. The weakness of this period was that the pictorial figure painter inevitably realized his work from the point of view of picture rather than glass painting. To prevent the artist from carrying out the design as a whole in glass is to deprive him of the very discipline and understanding of his craft that he needs. In the very early centuries this practice had not the same defects because the artist drew his subjects in line work which was easily adaptable in the event of its not being suitable to a glass technique.

The Morris-Burne-Jones windows in Birmingham Cathedral are generally regarded as their most successful. Other windows to be noted are two in Salisbury Cathedral (1879) and St. Cecilia (1874–5) and St. Catherine (1878) in Christ Church, Oxford.

Plate 45 is an example of domestic glass which Morris to some extent popularized. It is a pleasing pattern of colour in glass mosaic combining the traditional technique with modern interest. The panel, $22\frac{1}{4}''$ high by $25\frac{3}{4}''$ wide, depicts a scene from 'St. George and the Dragon'. It was designed by D. G. Rossetti and executed by William Morris about 1860.

It is very obvious to the modern critic that all the work of this period was still marred by the attempt to realize the qualities of pictorial oil painting. The window was regarded too much as an easel picture and not sufficiently as decoration in an architectural setting. This was well understood by many art critics of the period not only in this country but also on the continent. Weale in his quarterly paper on Architecture, Midsummer 1845, prints a translation from the German of an article by Emmanuel Otto Frumberg part of which reads as follows:

> 'In the sixteenth and seventeenth centuries, correct delineation completely gained the ascendancy in painted windows and we find in these neither the effects of symmetry nor of the mosaic. It underwent a change in every particular, to an historical kind of painting . . . but which was no longer so rich or so brilliant; in the eighteenth century the art of painting on glass seemed to be completely lost.'

After developing the argument that the craft must be carried out with proper understanding of the legitimate resources of the art he emphasizes the fact that 'the painter on glass must refrain from attempting to imitate oil-painting'. It is unfortunate that the artists of the period, no doubt influenced by the prevailing popularity of oil painting paid too little attention to the discerning critics of their day.

Mr. Knowles has pointed out that even in the earlier periods craftsmen would resort to practices which savoured of commercialism and artistic insincerity. For example the figure of St. Paul with a sword would be used in another light to represent St. Peter, by turning it round to face the other way, two keys being substituted for the sword and the colouring of the robes altered.

However, the amount of journeyman work of this sort was never such that it seriously affected the general aesthetic standard of the period, but by the Victorian era the increase of commercialization did have a very serious effect indeed. It is hardly an exaggeration to say that eventually the discerning public turned away from church windows in boredom, if not in disgust.

The larger firms developed a streamlined process of production that might have served as a prototype for a twentieth-century car factory. The designer prepared a sketch, probably from a previous design, adapting it to the size of the new window with little regard either for adjacent windows or the general architectural environment. Not infrequently it would be a copy of a design chosen by the client from an illustrated catalogue.

The sketch was then handed to the cartoonist who was not given the slightest information as to the setting in which the window was to be placed. Having completed his full-size cartoon, as if it were an easel picture in monochrome for the next exhibition of the Royal Academy, he handed it over to the man whose sole job in life was to make cutlines, no doubt in the shortest possible space of time, and again with no idea of the general conception of the window. The cutline and coloured design were then taken to the glazing shop and handed to the cutter, an expert at his work, possibly possessing an excellent colour sense, the only trouble being that he had never seen the position of the window in the church and had never been given any information as to what was needed. It is of course very doubtful whether anyone really knew.

The glass, when cut, would be taken to the painting shop where it would be parcelled out to various painters according to their degree of skill. The heads, hands and feet would be handed to the flesh painter, who in those days always arrived in a top hat, to preserve respect for his craft. The draperies were handed to a less skilful painter and such parts as canopies were reserved for even less qualified painters, probably boys in their teens.

The mere description of this procedure is enough to horrify any sensitive artist or lover of the arts, whether practising or not, and it exemplifies one of the tragic aspects of modern civilization, that too often mankind's creative activities are controlled by semi-educated men of business with little or no appreciation of culture.

The modern architect is too often compelled to design, not a piece of architecture but a structure with the maximum numbers of offices for rental purposes. Regent Street used to be a cultural asset in the heart of the Commonwealth but the authorities insisted on proving that the English were indeed a nation of shopkeepers. It was pulled down to make way for the existing conglomeration, the sole merit of which is its increased letting space. This is all the more to be deplored because it is Crown property.

The above description of a successful stained glass firm of the nineteenth century is in no way exaggerated and it truly portrays circumstances which explain the opportunity and indeed the reason for the success of men like William Morris and Burne-Jones. Unhappily the process of commercialization is accelerating until it is practically impossible in the present age of automation for the craftsman to carry out his true work and earn a reasonable livelihood.

In the stained glass world today there are roughly two categories of producers, the Individuals and the Firms, though it is not easy to draw an exact dividing line because some individual artists organize their production as effectively as any firm and some firms are far less commercial in practice than individual craftsmen are sometimes known to be.

The danger with the artist is that he or she may not go through a sufficiently long or arduous training with a master craftsman and when this is not the case the work is apt to be amateurish—limited in capacity and lacking in knowledge and strength.

The great value of a firm is that it has a tradition and continuity. This will probably have varied with good and bad periods, the good periods when an artist had been in control and the bad periods when a business mentality has predominated, but nevertheless a valuable amount of knowledge and experience is gathered and when placed in the hands of an artist, enables him to accomplish better work than as an individual working on his own. The great masterpieces of the past impress, not by their individuality, but by their beauty.

On the other hand if the artist does not exist and the control passes to the hands of the business man a reversion to the worst type of Victorian procedure is only too likely to take place.

It is precisely from such a possible calamity that the Diocesan Advisory Committees are there, to safeguard an unsuspecting and uninformed public.

E

CHAPTER 9

The Twentieth Century

The interest in and appreciation of stained glass, renewed in the nineteenth century, continued in the twentieth century which has in fact experienced two boom periods occasioned by the catastrophes of two world wars. After the first world war the Church authorities, aware of the demand created by the commissioning of memorial windows to the fallen and fearing a flood of poor quality work which would accentuate or possibly depreciate the none too high standards of the nineteenth century, very wisely instituted the Diocesan Advisory Committees in an attempt to eliminate the worst types of design. This was a development for which all true artists and connoisseurs of the arts must be very sincerely thankful.

One of the pioneer craftsmen of the beginning of the century, Christopher Whall (1850–1924), is perhaps best known for his excellent book on stained glass, written very evidently by a man who loved his craft. His axiom 'let the colour sing' stamps him at once as a true craftsman and glazier.

His windows, however, though well composed and full of colour, suffer from his too realistic and pictorial conception of his subjects and therefore lack the profundities of religious iconography, substituting a sentimental prettiness.

Examples of his work are to be seen in the Lady Chapel of Gloucester Cathedral (Plate 47), the south transept of Canterbury Cathedral, Ashbourne Church, Derbyshire, and Tonbridge School Chapel.

Undoubtedly one of the finest artists of this period was Louis Davis (1861–1941). He was one of the last of the pre-Raphaelite group dedicating his exquisite sensibility to the service of the Church. His windows show a complete appreciation of the craft of the glazier which he uses to serve the aesthetic purpose of illustrative decoration to complete the architectural environment. The artistry of his windows is characterized by culture and distinction, with perhaps more of a humanistic approach rather than universality and mysticism. He was held in high regard by his fellow artists and had, in his lifetime a continental reputation.

Examples of his work may be seen in Dunblane Cathedral; St. Anselm's Church, Hatch End, Middlesex; Paisley Abbey (Plate 48); Cheltenham College Chapel; Holyrood Palace; the English Church of Stockholm; St. Peter's Church, St. Albans;

PLATE 46. 'Conversion of England', by A. K. Nicholson Studios.

Christ Church, Derby; St. Peter's Church, Broadstairs; Ludlow Parish Church; St. Matthew's Church, Surbiton and many other churches throughout the country.

Another notable stained glass artist of the beginning of the century was Archibald K. Nicholson (1871–1937), brother of the well-known ecclesiastical architect, Sir Charles Nicholson. During his lifetime he carried out 700 windows. His first big work (1906) was the large south transept window of the Irvingite Church, Gordon Square, London, which he carried out with the assistance of Gerald E. R. Smith, thus originating a collaboration which continued for the rest of Nicholson's lifetime.

It is pleasant to record that he was a pioneer amongst model employers. All his staff were paid for Bank holidays, getting two weeks' holiday a year on full pay, and were paid when they were ill, a privilege almost unknown at the beginning of the century.

In the nineteen-twenties Nicholson was commissioned to carry out all the windows in three important churches, the Church of the Ascension, Bitterne Park, Southampton, St. Thomas', Bedford Leigh, Lancs, and Holy Trinity, Jesmond Dene, Northumberland. Plate 46 shows the central window in the north aisle of the Church of the Ascension. The subject is 'The Conversion of England' with the central figure of the beardless Christ in blue overmantel bordered with gold. In the two side lights and the base of the central light are scenes of missionary ships, four of them bordered by coasts of pictorial maps, showing the vessels on the high seas, and in the three scenes in the bases the ships are shown making land. The treatment of the sea is excellent glass mosaic and the colour scheme of the whole window is a well-controlled harmony.

The series of windows in this church is representative of the best work of the period and is particularly interesting on account of the fact that the Very Rev. Eric Milner-White, Dean of York, collaborated in the designs, and that the windows were commissioned by his mother in memory of his father, Sir Henry Milner-White, a prominent citizen of Southampton.

Other important works of Nicholson's can be seen in Newcastle Cathedral, the cloisters of Chester Cathedral, the Cathedrals of Norwich, Southwell, Bradford, and at Harrow School Chapel, Christ Church, Northampton, and the west window in Crewkerne Church, Somerset. Later came his Elgar memorial window in Worcester Cathedral and then perhaps his most remarkable work, the great centre light of the west window of Wells Cathedral, where he had to fill a gigantic space to harmonize with the existing eighteenth-century glass to the right and left of the centre light.

He was a pioneer in the removal of the crude blue and red backgrounds of so many Victorian windows for which he substituted creamy antique white, an example which has been followed by many present-day artists when repairing blitzed churches with dark interiors.

A memorial window to him at St. Sepulchre's Church, Holborn, was composed by Gerald Smith, from some of Nicholson's own cartoons, including his favourite St. Joan of Arc. This church also contains the Stephen Harding window which he gave as a votive offering for his recovery from a serious illness.

Karl Parsons (1884–1934), like his friend Edward Woore, graduated in his craft at Whall's studios and although he later developed his own individuality he never entirely broke away from the Whall tradition. He was an extremely competent designer, an excellent draughtsman and a fine colourist but his work suffers from a too realistic and sentimental approach. For some time he was a teacher of Stained Glass at the Royal College of Art and also at the Central School of Arts and Crafts.

Plate 49 shows one of his early windows in All Saints Church, Eastchurch, Isle of Sheppey, carried out as a memorial to Charles Stewart Rolls, and Cecil Stanley Grace, the first window ever designed to commemorate airmen. The two central figures depict Fortitude and Hope, with wording on the scroll 'Turn you to the stronghold ye prisoners of hope' (Zechariah 9.12).

The east window in Pangbourne Church (Berks) is an excellent example of his work, well designed and rich in colour. He also carried out the west window in Christ Church, Fulham, as well as numerous windows throughout the country.

Robert Anning Bell, R.A., R.W.S., R.B.C., LL.D. (1863–1933) added distinction to the stained glass craft with his excellent sense of design and fine draughtsmanship. For a time he was professor of design at the Royal College of Art, Kensington, and also in the Glasgow School of Art.

A delightful window of his may be seen in the Parish Church of Amberley, Sussex, designed in memory of Edward Stott, R.A. Unfortunately an important window of his, the east window in St. Jude's Church, Hampstead, was destroyed by enemy action. Plate 50 shows one of his windows in the Rochester Alms Houses. Interesting examples of his work are the Sir Walter Raleigh window in Merton College, Oxford, and the Shakespeare window in the Central Library, Manchester. Amongst the many windows he carried out are those in Copegrove Church (Yorks), Wytham Church (Oxford), Old Parish Church, Renfrew, near Glasgow, and Hornsley Church (Derbyshire).

Probably the two most important stained glass artists of the first half of the century are James Hogan (1883–1948) and Martin Travers (1886–1948) each a master in his own style of work. Hogan carried out the whole of his life's work at the Whitefriars Studios. He was a remarkably gifted designer, an excellent draughtsman and a particularly fine colourist as may be seen from his series of windows in the great central space of Liverpool Cathedral, designed in collaboration with Sir Giles Gilbert Scott, and particularly from the last window carried out just before his death, the east window in the Church of St. Francis at Petts Wood (Kent). This is a beautifully designed Te Deum window in pure glass mosaic, the figures delineated almost entirely in line, with a minimum of shading, giving the beauty of the translucent glass its full value in brilliant but harmonious colour.

Although Hogan's full-coloured windows are superb he was equally successful in light windows with quarry backgrounds. Lack of space prevents a list of his works, but a fine example of lighter design is the east window of St. Bartholomew's Church, Herne Bay (Kent). This is a fine example of heraldic treatment of colour on a white ground.

Hogan also carried out innumerable windows for the U.S.A. Perhaps the best known are those in St. Thomas' Church, New York (Plate 55), where he executed a series of large five-light windows of outstanding beauty and remarkably fine colour. His mastery of design, draughtsmanship and colour is also evident in the superb windows of the Church of the Heavenly Rest, New York, and at Beverly Hills.

Martin Travers was trained as an architect and built several churches in collaboration with T. F. W. Grant, F.R.I.B.A., including the Church of The Good Shepherd, Carshalton, the Holy Redeemer, Streatham Vale and Emmanuel at Leyton. Also, apart from stained glass work he designed and executed many beautiful altars, reredoses, rood screens, font covers etc. and, in Romsey Abbey, Hants, an image of the Blessed Virgin Mary over the High Altar. His impeccable taste made all his works in whatever craft, objects of beauty. He executed the altar, crucifix and candlesticks for St. Helier's Church, Jersey, which were commissioned by the Queen as a commemoration of the liberation of the island.

In 1925 he obtained the Grand Prix de Paris for stained glass and in the same year was appointed instructor in stained glass at the Royal College of Art, South Kensington, where he continued until his death. Several of the best-known stained glass artists began their careers as assistants in his private studios. It is significant that every one of them, after years of wider experience and development, retains an admiration for the work and talents of their old master, regarding him as the finest artist of his day in his own particular sphere. His commissions were usually not of such magnitude as those of Hogan but any work of his was always of especial interest to the craftsmen and cognoscenti of the stained glass world, and whenever a new window of his was placed in position, if within reasonable distance, Hogan would always take his staff to study it.

A one-time pupil of Sir Ninian Comper, the famous church architect, his early work showed definite Byzantine influence but travels in Spain and France developed in him a strong leaning towards the Baroque, until finally his own characteristic style emerged.

Dr. Woodforde records that his favourite window was that of St. Nicholas (1928) in St. Sampson's Church, Cricklade (Wilts) (Plate 51), but Travers also considered his east window in Tyneham Church (Dorset) (Plate 52) to be one of his most successful. He has a fine series of windows in St. Martin's Garrison Church, Liss (Hants) and also in the same county, windows in Cheriton Church, near Alresford, and Beauclare Church, near Newbury.

An excellent east window of his may be seen in Woodbridge Church, near Ipswich (Suffolk), and a fine 'Te Deum' in the east window of St. George's Church, Headstone, near Harrow (Middlesex). His series of windows in St. Andrew's Church, Catford, South London are particularly interesting as they date from 1921 to 1937 and show the development of his style.

Some of his major works were for St. Stephen's Church, Portsmouth, St. Andrew's Church, Plumstead, Barham Church, near Canterbury, and Swanick Church (Derbyshire). Unfortunately many of Travers' windows were destroyed in the blitz.

Sometime in the late twenties he carried out a large war memorial for New Zealand, showing great men climbing the Hill of Life and New Zealand soldiers killing a dragon at the base.

Douglas Strachan, LL.D., F.R.S.A. (1875–1950), was another well-known artist of this period, carrying out his windows in an individual mosaic technique with flowing line and arresting colour. His early windows such as those in St. Machar's Cathedral, and King's College Chapel, Aberdeen, have a quality not unlike that of Whall and Davis. In 1912 his group of windows made for the Palace of Peace at the Hague brought Douglas Strachan's name before a wider public and his reputation was later still further enhanced by his windows for the Scottish National War Memorial in Edinburgh Castle. His finest work in England is in the Church of Winchelsea although here the total effect of colour is rather overpowering for so small a building. Another excellent example of his work is in the Church of Hotham (Yorks).

Reginald Bell (1886–1950) produced excellent work of more traditional type, consequently more in harmony with its architectural setting. Although showing strong fifteenth-century influence his style was completely his own (Plate 54). His 'Victory' window (1920) in Salisbury Cathedral is much admired, as also his series of historic medieval personages in St. Mary's Hall, Coventry, which fortunately survived the bombing of the city. In both Exeter Cathedral and Exford Church (Somerset) he has well-designed windows depicting 'St. George and the Dragon'.

F. C. Eden (1864–1944) designed in quiet, sincere, if rather sentimental mood. He carried out the east window in Abergavenny Priory, Wales, and windows for other churches including those in Clare (Suffolk), Duxford (Cambridgeshire), Eastingham (Gloucestershire) and Thorpe (Derbyshire).

Evie Hone (1894–1955) contributed a distinctive note to the craft of stained glass. Her windows are undoubtedly the work of a fine and sensitive artist with a masterly sense of colour. Unfortunately she allowed the influence of the Parisian ateliers to outweigh her responsibilities to the architectural surroundings. Whilst her sincerity and her colour schemes compel admiration, it is difficult not to regret her lack of any sense of scale and want of appreciation of architectural requirements. As easel pictures her windows may be great achievements, but as embellishments to architecture they are not without defects.

This is especially evident in her east window in Eton College Chapel (1952) which is so overpowering that the beautiful lines of the architecture can no longer be appreciated. Another window of hers in St. Michael's Church, Highgate, has the same merits and defects. Her work should be studied and admired for its strength, sincerity and colour values, but its lack of architectural fitness cannot be passed over.

One of her windows is in Washington Cathedral, U.S.A., and some of her finest are to be seen in Ireland, at Clongowes Wood College Chapel, St. Stanislaus College, Tullabeg, and St. Mary's Church, Kingscourt.

Wilhelmina M. Geddes (d. 1956) was one of the best stained glass artists of her period. Her first important commission was in 1919 from the Duke of Connaught, for a three-light window for the War Memorial of Ottawa. Another fine three-light window of hers is 'The Crucifixion' in St. Luke's Church, Wallsend, carried out with the minimum of painting and relying largely on the design of the leading.

Her work is full of character, strong yet sensitive. It is pleasant to record that her great memorial window in Ypres was not destroyed in the last war. Plate 56 shows one of her finest works, the figure of Moses, which, very unfortunately, was destroyed by fire in the bombing of Belfast in 1941. Other windows of hers are in the Presbyterian Hall, Belfast, The Museum and St. John's Church, Belfast, St. Anne's Church, Dublin, Laleham Church, Middlesex, and many others.

Harry Clarke (1889–1931) was one of the best artists of his day. In 1913 he won a gold medal in London for a Judas window and in 1916 he was commissioned to carry out a series of windows for the Honan Collegiate Chapel in Cork, which, as Mr. James White has recorded, almost alarmed the critics by their daring originality and pure glowing colour. However, the beauty of the work assured his instant success. Working in his studio in Dublin, he achieved an international reputation, sending his work all over the world. Plate 57 shows his Annunciation window in St. Joseph's Terenure, Dublin, in which Church he also has a three-light Crucifixion window and a Coronation of the Virgin. Among his more important works are a three-light window of St. Paul, St. George and St. Hubert in the Protestant Church, Castleknock, Dublin; windows in the University College Chapel, Cork; three windows in the Catholic Church, Tully Cross, Connemara; a three-light window in Notre Dame Convent, Dowanhill, Glasgow, and a series of windows in the Notre Dame Convent Chapel, Ashdown Park, Sussex.

His work always has a beautiful decorative quality, emphasized by glowing colour, and is imbued with religious sensibility. His comparatively early death was a sad loss to the stained glass brotherhood but his fine tradition is still carried on and worthily upheld in the Harry Clarke Studios, Dublin, by William Dowling, David Clarke, son of Harry Clarke, Terence Clarke, his nephew, and assistants, some of whom were trained by Harry Clarke.

PLATE 47. Gloucester Cathedral. Window in Lady Chapel by Christopher Whall.

PLATE 48. Abbey Church of Paisley. Portion of window in north transept, 'St. Margaret, Queen of Scotland', designed by Louis Davis.

Within the illustration, the following text appears on the windows:

having done all, to stand.

turn ye to the Stronghold ye prisoners of hope

To the Glory of God & in memory of Charles Stewart Rolls & Cecil Stanley Grace

Aviators July December 1910

This window is given by friends AD 1912

PLATE 49. All Saints Church, Eastchurch, Isle of Sheppey.
Window by Karl Parsons.
(*By kind permission of V. J. D.*)

PLATE 50. Rochester alms houses, window by Robert Anning Bell, R.A.

PLATE 51. St. Nicholas. Aisle window, St. Sampson's Church, Cricklade, Wilts.
Martin Travers.

PLATE 52. Tyneham Church, Dorset. East window and altar piece by Martin Travers.

PLATE 53. Corfe Church, Dorset. North-east window in Lady Chapel by Martin Travers.

PLATE 54. All Saints Church, Worcester.
Cartoon by Reginald Bell.

PLATE 55. St. Thomas' Church, New York City, U.S.A. Clerestory window, designed by James Hogan, Whitefriars Studios.

PLATE 56. Moses, by Wilhelmina Margaret Geddes.

PLATE 57. St. Joseph's Church, Terenure, Dublin.
The Annunciation, by Harry Clarke.

PART 2

Technology

CHAPTER 10

Glass Making

━━━◦◦◦◦◦◦◦◦◦◦◦◦◦◦◦◦◦━━━

Glass is melted sand. It is more accurately described by Angus-Butterworth in his book *The Manufacture of Glass* as a congealed solution.

> 'Glass may be termed a congealed or supercooled liquid. In a crystalline body there is a definite temperature at which the substance freezes or passes from the liquid to the solid state. The change is accompanied by considerable evolution of heat, with the curious phenomenon that the cooling of the mass is temporarily arrested. In contrast to this, glass passes from one state to another by a perfectly continuous and gradual process, so that there is no evolution of heat or temporary retardation of cooling. Thus in vitreous bodies there is a gradual stiffening of the liquid until the viscosity or stickiness becomes so great that the behaviour is that of a solid.'

Pure sand can be melted to make glass but this result can be achieved with much less heat if a flux is used; so the ingredients from which glass can be made include the following:

(1) *Silica* (Sand).
(2) *Soda* and *Lime* (most often used as a flux).
(3) *Potash, Lead Oxide* (used as a flux).
(4) *Colouring Agents*.
(5) *Decolouring Agents*.

Originally flint stones were crushed and powdered to make the finest flint glass but nowadays silver sand is in common use. The sources of supply include Norfolk in England, Loch Aline in Scotland, Fontainebleau in France, Campine in Belgium and Limburg in Holland. In the United States silica is obtained mostly from the Oriskany Quartzite of Pennsylvania and West Virginia, and the St. Peter sandstone of Illinois and Missouri. The quality depends on the size and shape of the grains and its freedom from impurities. It is usually calcined after arrival at the works to burn off organic matter and to remove any moisture.

Vitreous silica or melted sand or quartz is the simplest form of glass chemically and physically but the melting temperature—1,710° C.—is far too high for ordinary commercial furnaces. The addition of 25 per cent of sodium lowers the melting point to 793° C. To overcome the water solubility of such an alkaline silicate

75

other materials must be used. C. J. Phillips in his book *Glass: the Miracle Maker* states:

> 'One of the most satisfactory—the very one used by the ancients—is lime. These soda-lime silica glasses, usually called simply "lime glasses" comprise about 90 per cent of the total tonnage melted today.'

He also quotes A. L. Day as saying:

> 'As the addition of the akali reduced the silica melting point, so the addition of the lime produces a further reduction, until finally the lowest temperature of the triple entente is reached at about 725° C. A diagram published by George W. Morey of the Geophysical Laboratory, showing the measured freezing temperatures of mixtures of soda, lime and silica . . . (confirms) the stubborn facts which have guided or driven the ancients and moderns, from somewhat different viewpoints to be sure, toward this composition because it is the lowest-melting, stable glass which is available to us. It is within the reach of such fires as may have been available to the ancients; it is also easier for us to work at a lower temperature than a higher one; furthermore, the viscosity of such glass is appropriate for convenient working, and there is little tendency to devitrify at any temperature—above melting point none at all.'

This mixture is itself not chemically very endurable. This defect is corrected by adding other oxides, often alumina, boric oxide or magnesia. Further to correct any chemical impurities which may affect the colour, other oxides known as decolorizers may be added. Tableware of the cheaper kind usually made automatically had this composition but the better grades, those made by hand, are usually lead glasses. On these C. J. Phillips says:

> 'The lead glasses, made by melting lead oxide or lead silicate with alkalis, silica and minor ingredients, are very interesting. They are used for special purposes where high electrical resistance, ease of manipulation or extraordinary optical properties are necessary. Glasses having a lead oxide content as high as 92 per cent have been made, and such glass, having a density of approximately 8·00, is as heavy as cast iron. The lead glasses have a range in refractive index from 1·507 to 2·179 and the mean dispersion varies from 0·0092 to 0·0988, a range of 10 to 1. These glasses are very important in the optical field, for obvious reasons. The very finest tableware and art objects are also made from lead glass because of these characteristic properties.'

The colour of the glass is produced not only by the chemical ingredients as such but also by the temperature to which they are subjected and the length of time this process may take. Generally speaking blue glass is coloured by cobalt, green by uranium, copper and chromium, pink by selenium, yellow by cerium and titanium. Amber is made on light lead base and coloured by carbon. Red glass is coloured by cadmium, selenium, copper and gold.

The process is an extremely complicated one and for a fuller explanation *Glass: the Miracle Maker* by C. J. Phillips should be consulted. In his chapter on coloured glasses he says:

> 'The manufacture of coloured glass involves many problems of glass chemistry, some of them complicated and perplexing. Therefore the story of coloured glass cannot

be made wholly simple and straightforward. Briefly the colouring agent may be one of three types: (1) The colour is produced by absorption of certain characteristic frequencies of the incident of light by substances in solution in the glass; or (2) the colour is produced by particles of submicroscopic size precipitated within an originally colourless glass by appropriate heat treatment; or (3) the colour may be produced by larger particles, which may be either coloured themselves as in aventurine glasses, or colourless as in opals. Weyl has further divided the colourants into two groups: (*a*) those in which the colour is due to differences in the ionic environment; and (*b*) those in which it is due to differences in the state of oxidation. The composition of the parent glass has a profound effect on both groups of colouring agents and when more than one agent is present the interaction of these various factors makes it almost impossible to predict the final result.'

Perhaps it would help towards an appreciation of these technical difficulties if an example is given of the seemingly eccentric manner in which glass is liable to behave during process of manufacture. Again the quotation is from Phillips:

'A classical example of the second type of colour—that produced by colloidal suspension—is Gold Ruby. First described by Neri, it is produced by adding a relatively small amount of gold or gold salt—perhaps one part in 50,000—to the glass batch. When melted and cooled, the glass is first colourless or, at most, a light straw colour. But when properly reheated, the colour "strikes" and an intense red develops—the red of ruby. The best colour appears with potash–lead base glass. The cost is high and only luxury products can be made from gold-ruby. The colour is so intense, however, that a thin gold ruby layer can be "flashed" as a casing over crystal glass with effective results. Copper ruby is made in much the same way.'

There is an additional difficulty in making coloured glass to be used in stained glass windows. When glass is made for tableware, it is taken molten from the pot, blown and fashioned into shape, and annealed. Except with certain types of cooking utensils the glass is never again subjected to intense heat. In contrast, after glass for a stained glass window has been made, it has, after being painted, to be subjected to a considerable amount of heat in the firing kiln. It has therefore to be so constituted that it will not again alter colour, during the second application of heat. Occasionally some window glass does prove unstable during firing. Neutral tints particularly are apt to be unreliable but generally speaking the colour is definitely fixed and does not alter again in the process of firing in the kiln, which may have to be repeated two or three times.

The pots in which the raw material of the glass is melted are made of fire clay, roughly 3' 6" in height, domed and with a small aperture at the front through which the melted glass is finally extracted by means of the blow-pipe.

The fireclay of which the pots are built up is first kneaded to work it into the right consistency and particularly to extract every particle of air, which otherwise would cause the pot to crack when subjected to the great heat of the furnace.

These pots when made have the date marked on them and are placed in a room with a moderate but carefully regulated temperature to allow them to dry out thoroughly; a process which takes at least twelve months.

Before a new pot can be set in the furnace it must be brought up to the same temperature as that which it will meet therein; this is done in an adjoining kiln called a 'Pot Arch', and it needs no very vivid imagination to realize what a hot and tricky job it is to transfer the cumbersome and heavy pot, glowing with yellow heat, from the arch to the furnace, with the mouth at just the correct height from the floor or 'siege'. The necessary adjustments are made with firebricks placed under the pot and when this has been done the whole of the front is bricked up, all the crevices and cracks being filled in with wet fireclay. This process is a particularly arduous one as it has to be done literally by hand with a furnace heat of 1,400° C. The number of pots in a furnace varies. At Whitefriars Glass Works there are ten in two of the furnaces and only eight in another.

When the pot, which holds about 15 cwt., is ready for use, the 'batch' of prepared ingredients is gradually fed in at intervals for easier melting and because, as the contents melt, they contract. The process may take up to two days, especially if the glass contains a high percentage of lead. When the mixture is thoroughly melted, the scum of impurities is cleaned off the surface of the molten glass.

There are roughly three categories of glass that are used for Church work, ordinary sheet glass being obviously omitted. These are Cathedral, Antique and Slab or Bottle glass. As regards the first category its nomenclature tends to the practice of getting money under false pretences. To anyone, except the expert, Cathedral glass suggests the highest grade of material reserved more especially for our finest Cathedrals, whereas it is in fact the lowest type of glass which should never adorn anything higher than, let us say, a domestic bathroom. This type of glass is produced in large sheets obscured by a mechanical surface and guaranteed to take the light and lustre out of any window of whatsoever aspect.

The second category—Antique—has a justification because it possesses the qualities to be found in medieval glass. It is first blown into a cylinder, for obvious reasons called a 'muff'. This is then cut down its length and placed in a spreading kiln when it opens out and forms a rectangular uneven sheet of glass roughly $\frac{1}{8}''$ in thickness. The particular quality of this type of glass is that it is not uniform in thickness and the colour varies accordingly in its shading and colour value. Our Antique glasses give us all the qualities that can be found in ancient glass. The third category of Slab or Bottle glass surpasses in quality and texture anything to be found in medieval glass. Moreover, with this type of glass as with Antique there is a far wider range of colour than the earlier craftsmen ever possessed. The glass is blown into a square-shaped mould forming a rectangular bottle or jar. The process of blowing it into the mould causes the sides of the jar to be very much thinner at the edges and corners.

The blow-pipe seems to have been invented by the Egyptians about 300 B.C. and it is remarkable that this implement is still used in making the best type of glass today. It is a hollow tube about 4 feet in length with a 'gathering' knob at one end and a mouthpiece at the other. Today it is made of steel.

The glass blower puts the gathering end through the opening in the furnace wall coincident with the opening in the pot containing the molten glass and draws out his gather. He gives this a gentle blow through the tube expanding the gather adhering to the other end of the blow-pipe by a few inches at a time.

When making slab glass he will have a rectangular-sided mould on the floor and as soon as the width of the ball of glass approximates to the width of the mould, though a little less, he will carefully lower the ball of glass into the mould keeping the blow-pipe vertical above it. Then by further gentle blowing he will enlarge the size of the glass until it fits into the rectangular mould, thus forming a square jar with a slightly domed top. The blower then removes the jar still on the end of the blow-pipe, places it gently on to his steel table, and gives the blow-pipe a sharp tap near the glass. This causes the jar to crack off from the end of the blow-pipe. It is then placed in the lehr and annealed.

After annealing the jar is cut down each side of the corners, thus producing four slabs of glass from the sides of the jar and one small one from the base. The particular advantage of this type of glass is that it has much greater variety of thickness, so that when held up to the light it catches and refracts the light, as with a prism, to an extent that neither antique nor medieval glass can do.

The final process in the production of glass is the annealing. This is important because if not properly carried out the glass will sooner or later fly or crack and break into more or less small pieces. This process is one of gradual and controlled cooling. The usual type of annealer consists of a heated tunnel about seventy-five feet long, with a moving track upon which the glass object is placed. This moves slowly down the tunnel, at the rate of about one foot per minute, which controls the gradual cooling until after a few hours it emerges properly annealed.

I am indebted to Mr. Hugh Salmond for the following interesting account of the medieval method of making glass, written by his father the late Mr. Frederick Salmond:

'In all probability the earliest glass used in church window making was made in circles, such as large roundels, roughly from 12″ to 18″ in diameter. This accounts for the great variation in thickness, as when getting near the knob or centre, and it also accounts for much of the brilliancy. Later the glass was made in small "muffs" which turned out sheets when flattened about 12″ by 10″ and smaller. This process continued until the present day excepting the fact that the muffs are much larger and when "spread" or flattened leave sheets about 24″ by 14″.

'A man, or in those early days a monk, took a blow-pipe, i.e. an iron pipe about three feet long by three-quarters of an inch in diameter and dipped it into the pot of molten metal, twisting it on to the pipe as we would stiff treacle. When this formed as a solid ball he commenced to blow, twisting it round and round to prevent it falling off the iron. When he had blown it to the required size another monk would come along with just a small knob of glass on his pipe, hot out of the pot and stick it in the middle of the ball thus:

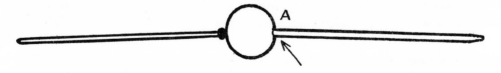

Then by simply putting a cold piece of iron or even a wet finger at the place marked A the ball comes away from the original blowing iron, leaving the hollow ball of glass on the knob or as it is technically called, the punty.

'By this time the glass is getting cold and has to be warmed before a hole in the furnace known as the "glory hole". The monk would then take the plastic glass ball, twisting all the time, to a chair with two bars attached and running the blow-pipe up and down these with the left hand, he would use a tool with the other, not unlike a large pair of calipers to open the ball until it assumed a flat form precisely the same as a large roundel.

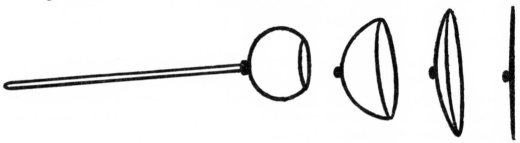

'When flat this would be put in a kiln and slowly cooled or annealed, in those days probably for about twenty-four hours. Flashed glasses were made by putting the original ball of glass into another pot of the required colour, taking on this extra layer and then blowing it out just as described.

'Later on it was found that they were able to get larger pieces of glass by making cylinder or muff glass. This system continues to the present day excepting that the old muffs did not exceed 9″ long by 4″ diameter, whereas those today go up to 16″ long by 8″ in diameter or even larger without difficulty.

'The medieval furnace was quite a small affair, not more than four feet round or square, built of fireclay brick and heated with charcoal. The pots were of elongated shape, most probably about 18″ long by about 8″ diameter.

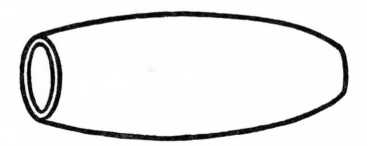

These were laid flat on the furnace, the mouth coming almost to the face, probably only two in a furnace, or two one side and two the other in the larger furnaces. These little furnaces made excellent church window glass. It has never been beaten for this purpose, but as one can readily imagine it must have been a lengthy process for the amount of footage turned out. However, the early fathers gave of their labour in love for their church and religion. The present furnaces are of two kinds round and square, 20′ diameter or square (very roughly). About eight pots would be in a furnace of this size various in shape but each holding about six or eight cwt. of metal. These furnaces run at a fair heat say 1,200 degrees Centigrade and are built of Welsh bricks, or silicate bricks and Stourbridge bricks much the same as the old furnaces.

'The pots are made of a certain kind of fire clay, exactly the same as the medieval pots, ground down, wetted up, and built by hand. These stand for twelve months to dry. In the furnace they may last only three days or thirteen weeks according to luck, this item being the most uncertain from the glassmaker's point of view. Pots, like babies, must be tenderly treated. Even a slight draught will cause them to crack and go to pieces within twenty-four hours after being put in the furnace. The writer has known a whole furnace of pots break within two days, the pots alone involving a loss of £300, let alone the cost of getting the furnace ready again, also a costly matter. [Written in 1920. Author.]

'ANTIQUE GLASS. Rough description of the present method of manufacture.

'The molten glass is gathered from the pot in the furnace upon a pipe about five feet long and three-quarters of an inch in diameter. The metal is gathered or collected upon the end of the pipe by a twisting motion, in much the same way as one gathers treacle on a spoon. When a sufficient amount has been collected, the blower begins to blow down the pipe always keeping the pipe on the twist and swinging backwards and for-wards. This takes some little time and as the metal cools it becomes necessary to reheat it in the glory hole, sometimes once, sometimes twice. Owing to the constant swing-ing backwards and forwards of the metal which is in a plastic state, the circular ball (the blower gently blowing all the time) begins to assume a cylindrical form thus:

When it has reached sufficient length, the blower takes it to his chair and rolling the cylinder round and round, he proceeds with his caliper-like tool to open out the end A, until the cylinder has an open mouth. Some workmen open this end out by a large pair of scissors. By the time this bottom end A is open, the cylinder is getting quite set and hard and a boy then brings a thread of hot glass and puts it round the end B next the pipe.

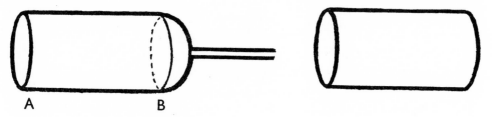

The action of the hot thread of glass on the colder glass causes it to crack, leaving a cylinder which is now placed in the kiln for about twelve hours. When taken from the kiln it is of course quite cold. It is then cut along its length with a diamond and cracked through.

F

The cylinder then goes to the spreading kiln which is an open-mouthed furnace like a brick oven, inside of which, on the ground is a flattening stone almost red-hot. Above the stone and gently stealing round the furnace is a glowing flame keeping the furnace at a nice steady heat. The cylinder is placed on the flattening stone with the split side uppermost. When the heat begins to tell the opening in the cylinder widens and the worker or flattener as he is called takes a stick with a wooden block on the end, usually pear wood, and gently presses the glass down, first one side and then the other. When flat this sheet is removed and annealed, a process of gradual cooling taking three to four days. This method of flattening is much the same as that used in the early days.'

CHAPTER 11

Designing

The designer of a stained glass window has one great advantage. He is, or should be, working for a definite purpose. A very small minority of artists in glass regard their work as an easel picture, but this is a hangover from Victorian days when the public collected pictures very much as a schoolboy collects postage stamps and with about as much aesthetic appreciation.

Churches and Cathedrals were not built as art galleries. Their architecture, throughout their development, has been functional, and the object of a stained glass window is to preserve and accentuate the general architectural style.

For the artist this is a saving grace. So much modern art, predominantly the result of an artificial education in a so-called Art School, seems to have no purpose. The painter, having no definite objective, falls back on the excuse of self-expression. A more fatuous or debilitating theory of Art has never been invented. It is fatuous because you cannot walk down the road without expressing yourself, possibly to your own detriment, and it must surely be fatuous to strive after the inevitable. One can hardly believe that personalities like Florence Nightingale, Livingstone, Leonardo, Schweitzer, Bach, St. Francis or Fra Angelico could occupy their minds with any self-centred concern about self-expression. On the other hand it is quite conceivable that such a preoccupation is characteristic of an accomplished courtesan.

Some artists, having nothing to say, invent a new language to say it in, and both amongst artists and art critics are to be found those artistic perverts who are so blasé of the whole business that they need aesthetic pin-pricks to stimulate their jaded emotions.

From all this confusion the designer is saved as soon as he enters the building of which his work is to form a part. He at once acquires the supreme sanity of a purpose in life. The general architectural effect will give him an intuitive feeling for what is desirable and it is upon this reaction that his conception should be based.

Of course such a visit is not always practicable. It may be that the church is in New Zealand, South Africa or America, when only a work of major importance would justify the expense. But it is always possible to obtain elevations and descriptions from which a general idea can be formed.

83

A design for a stained glass window may be divided into two parts, its architectural fitness and its subject. The latter, usually, though not always, emanates from the client. It may be by letter but a personal interview is always far the more satisfactory. If the commission comes from an architect many of the difficulties are automatically overcome. Other clients, not unnaturally, do not always realize what a stained glass window ought to be. When visiting Canterbury Cathedral or York Minster or Chartres their appreciation of glass may be very sound but when it comes to commissioning a window themselves they are apt to have a family photograph album or some religious illustration in mind as a suitable criterion.

In such cases a general discussion of the subject and an explanation of the technique of making a window will remove misunderstanding and promote confidence. Without a sympathetic understanding of the sentiments of the client and an appreciative respect for the subject, a successful window is not likely to be evolved.

The designer is now aware that the style must be Gothic, classical or modernistic as the case may be, and he knows the theme of the window, but it has still to be decided whether the window should be full coloured or of a lighter type with figures on a quarry background.

For an east window the full coloured treatment, emphasizing the focal point of the church, is often the most appropriate. Not only does the harmony of colour in a fine east window complete the architectural effect but a further consideration is that the congregation, as a rule, do not want to sit facing a glaring light, and this modification is likely to be gratifying. The lighter type of window is most suitable for the aisle windows where nowadays a maximum of light is required. In earlier days stained glass windows provided splendid opportunities for the pictorial representation of Christian beliefs to an illiterate congregation. In the west window full colour can again be effectively used though perhaps not to the same extent as in the east window.

Although the subject for the window is often given to the designer by the client with the approval of the Vicar, on other occasions he is asked to suggest a suitable one and even, at times, to plan the subjects for all the windows in the church. It is therefore useful to have a knowledge of traditional practice. It must be remembered that in the early period there was a decided emphasis on eschatology. Men's minds were particularly concerned with the Last Judgement and the world to come. Our present humanistic outlook suggests a revision in the choice of subjects. For example, it is doubtful if one can find a better subject than the Te Deum for a large east window. The Risen Christ or Our Lord in glory surrounded by the Prophets, the Apostles, the Saints and the Holy Catholic Church, typifies the highest aspirations of mankind. This seems to be a more obviously inspiring theme than that of a Jesse Tree window which was frequently used in the medieval period. The Tree of Jesse was a popular subject throughout the Middle Ages. It represented Christ's paternal descent from Jesse, the father of David. Isaiah 11.1 reads: 'And there shall come forth a rod out of the stem of Jesse, and a branch shall grow out of the roots. . . .' At the base of such a window there is a recumbent figure of Jesse and from his body rises a vine which spreads across the various lights. The inner branches enclose the kingly an-

PLATE 58. 'Mother and Child' by Ervin Bossanyi.
Oval window in house at Winchcombe.

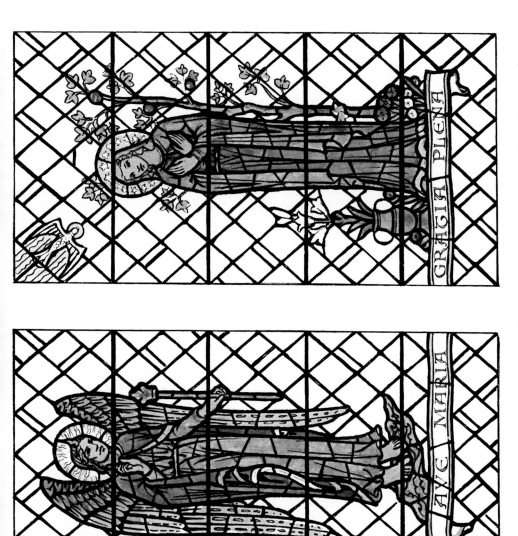

PLATE 59. St. James' Church, Jersey. Window by E. Liddall Armitage, Whitefriars Studios.

PLATE 60. Queen Mary Road United Church, Hampstead, Montreal.
East window by E. Liddall Armitage, Whitefriars Studios.

cestors of Christ and the outer branches enclose the prophets who foretold His coming. The Tree culminates in St. John the Baptist and the Blessed Virgin Mary with the Christ Child.

As a rule the eastern end of the church was used to give the story of the Gospel: the Birth, Life, Death and Resurrection of Christ. The nave was used to show representations of the Apostles, Saints and Prophets and the west window to remind the departing congregation of the Last Judgement.

Subjects for the Lady Chapel at the east end of the church were frequently the Annunciation, the Nativity, and the Adoration of the Wise Men and the Shepherds. If other windows were available to lead up to this, the Temptation of Eve or perhaps Moses and the Burning Bush were used, and for subjects connected with Our Lord's Childhood, the Flight into Egypt, the Presentation in the Temple and the Child Christ teaching the Doctors. The Crucifixion was commonly used for the subject of the main east window, and in the panels in the lower part of this, or perhaps in other windows in the chancel, were shown the Triumphal Entry into Jerusalem, the Agony in the Garden, the Judgement of Pontius Pilate, the Scourging at the Pillar, the Taking down from the Cross and the Entombment.

In the chapel on the south side we might find the Transfiguration in the east window, and in the other windows the Resurrection and events in Our Lord's subsequent life such as the Visit to Emmaus, the Ascension and the Descent of the Holy Ghost upon the Apostles.

The Twleve Apostles were often depicted in the windows of the south aisle, beginning from the east end, and, as at Fairford (Glos), to these were sometimes added the four great Doctors of the Church, SS. Jerome, Gregory the Great, Ambrose and Augustine of Hippo, leaving the north side for representations of the Prophets beginning with Jeremiah and ending with the Four Evangelists.

Again taking Fairford as an example, in the windows of the clerestory on the south side are the figures of the saints and martyrs: Dorothy, Sebastian, Agnes, Margaret; a bishop, an emperor, two kings, a pope and two cardinals, whilst in the opposite windows of the clerestory on the north side are twelve figures of persecutors of the Church including Annas and Caiphas, Judas, Herod and Diocletian.

Finally in the great west window, Our Lord sits in Judgement, enthroned and surrounded by the Heavenly Hosts, Angels, Cherubin and Seraphim and by the Twelve Apostles. On His Right Hand is depicted the Lily of Mercy and a scroll inscribed 'misericordia', and on His Left Hand the Sword of Justice and a scroll with the word 'Justitia'. The Blessed Virgin Mary and St. John the Baptist kneel before Him in intercession for humanity, with the world on fire crumbling beneath His feet.

Although this note of doom is singularly appropriate to modern conditions and was never more needed as a warning to mankind, it is not in accordance with modern mentality and people prefer to leave the Church with a more consolatory message. Certainly a pleasanter and very beautiful alternative is a Benedicite Window.

The designer's consideration of a suitable subject must, to some extent, be influenced by the construction of the window. For example, it is never satisfying to put an Annunciation into a three-light window. The figure of Gabriel will appear in the left-hand light and the figure of the Blessed Virgin Mary in the right-hand light, leaving a hiatus in the central light where normally the principle character is found. James Hogan has attempted this, no doubt unwillingly, but for all his skill the result is unsatisfactory. The centre light is lacking in interest and meaning however well drawn or patterned.

Unless stained glass windows introducing figures are to be completely excluded from the church, a four-light east window is an architectural faux-pas. It seems evident that the central figure of the east window should be Christ and for this a window with an uneven number of lights is essential.

The first concern of any creative craftsman is to suit his conception to his medium. Basically there are two types of design. A pattern of colour on a white ground as in a heraldic window, where coats of arms are emblazoned on a white quarry background, or a full coloured treatment which consists of placing lighter or contrasting colours on a dark ground. The designer may be in a position to make this decision himself or it may be stipulated in the commission. At times he will be asked to emulate the glories of Chartres; this can only be attempted if the architectural setting is appropriate and provides the necessary brilliance of light.

A visit to the church is obviously desirable. The general architectural setting and possibly existing windows will dictate the type of window that is appropriate. If the subject has already been decided upon together with any additional detail, the artist may come away with the design almost completed in his mind.

Without a deep appreciation of his subject an impressive window is not likely to be created. The subject can of course be pondered upon equally well in the studio, but, as has been pointed out, a visit to the church is of great advantage because a stained glass window is not an easel picture to be considered apart from its potential surrounding; it is part of an architectural effect supplementing and emphasizing the quality of the building. It may well be that architectural style is practically nonexistent but nevertheless in such cases there remains the question of scale. That distinguished architect, the Duke of Wellington, stressed the importance of scale in his speech at the Master Glass Painters' Annual Dinner on 14th October, 1952. Scale in architecture means the relative proportion of the main features of the building and its various ornamentations and details, i.e. the cornices, mouldings, window sills, pediments etc. In a stained glass window a suitable relationship should be felt between the figures and ornamentations in the glass and the main proportions and details of the building. Even the work of such a fine artist as Evie Hone suffers from lack of this consideration. However beautiful both in colour and general religious feeling her east window in Eton College Chapel may be, it shatters the architectural beauty of a fine medieval interior. In contrast a delicate appreciation of scale, coupled with excellent colour, may be seen in the east window of the Temple Church designed by Carl Edwards. Here the beauty of the glass in no way disturbs but rather reinforces the beauty of the Gothic architecture.

Another completely successful treatment is seen in the east window by Christopher

PLATE 61. Ely Cathedral. Bomber Command Memorial Window, illustrating the mosaic effect. E. Liddall Armitage, Whitefriars Studios.

Webb in St. James's, Piccadilly. Here again scale and colour are most satisfactorily treated: the yellow of the silver stain in the window is delicately re-echoed in the gilded capitals of the adjacent columns producing a most satisfying harmony of effect.

As a further example the windows for Coventry Cathedral by Lawrence Lee, Geoffrey Clarke and Keith New are excellent in scale and appropriate to their modernistic setting, which shows that the consideration of scale is equally important in any type of architecture.

It is of course impossible to lay down any definite rules for designing, but it seems obvious that the more one can visualize the completed window before commencing the sketch the more successful the result will be. Sir Albert Richardson used to advise his students to design with the rubber. This may seem a contradiction, but as usual the truth can best be explained by paradox. It is one thing to have a conception in mind and quite another to delineate it on paper. For example, one may have visualized a central figure of Our Lord in glory, but the exact position of this figure in the light and the exact size may not be at once determined. This is partly what Sir Albert meant; pencil in the central figure and do not hesitate to use the rubber to try the position a little higher or a little lower, to increase or decrease the stature. The figure must not be so dominant in silhouette that it seems to interfere with or detract from the shape of the window, nor must it be too small so that it loses in dignity and significance. This also applies of course to subsidiary figures and it should be remembered that subtlety in these matters will contribute considerably to the success of the window. As Browning says, 'The little more, the little less and oh, what world's away.'

The silhouettes must be impressive and show rhythm of line. They have therefore to be gradually developed and refined though not to the detriment of the whole, for it is only too easy to be sidetracked by detail and to lose sight of one's first conception, or to produce a design which seems completely satisfactory in line and then to find when finishing it in colour that the unity has been destroyed.

The reason for this is simply that the original conception has been lost and instead of designing in terms of a pattern of coloured glass, one has been led away into considerations of line and rhythm or some details, quite felicitous in themselves, but detrimental to the whole. Here again the rubber might have saved the day.

A friend of the writer caused surprise by saying 'Of course the window looks quite different to the design.' In contrast it is always a little surprising to find how closely the finished window resembles the original sketch, when one has knowledge of the many vicissitudes of its creation. Every stained glass craftsman sees, or should see, his completed sketch as GLASS, for, as Aldous Huxley has pointed out, and experience verifies, we see with our minds and not with the physical apparatus of vision.

When a church is first built and the windows filled with plain quarry work, there is a pleasing unity about the whole interior, in which the shapes of the lights and traceries form a pleasant pattern. The designer should be careful not to destroy this harmony but to add to its beauty by rectifying its possible lack of warmth and significance. Unfortunately too many of our churches would look better if the stained glass windows were removed.

It is difficult to over-emphasize this architectural aspect because the merit of a window cannot be judged until it is seen in position. The illustrations in this or any other book cannot give either the full beauty of the glass or convey the effect that the windows have in their position in the church.

That is why exhibitions of glass are never very satisfactory. It is to be hoped that they do some good by calling attention to the existence of stained glass artists, but it is doubtful if any member of the public can visualize the effect of a fine east window from a water colour sketch. Nor can small panels of glass give any adequate idea of an artist's work in its appropriate surroundings. Stained glass can only be properly studied and appreciated by viewing good work in position, which, however interesting, requires both time and money.

The question of money has a considerable bearing upon the type of window that can be made. A full-coloured window is more expensive than a window which has a large proportion of quarry work. However the amount of money to be spent on a window does not necessarily affect its aesthetic qualities. Economy can be made not only in the quality of the work but in the type of design. A quarry window with a well-designed coat of arms is just as artistic as a window with considerable figure work. In fact, if the figure work is of poor quality the coat of arms may be preferable. There are, nevertheless, limits within which no worthy work of any sort can be produced, and it is obviously wise not to be involved in such a case. It would be a mistake to put in a quarry type window where the architectural requirements called for rich colour.

In by far the majority of cases a simple type of window will be completely satisfactory. The quarry window which lets most light into the building is justly popular nowadays.

If the design is for a church of the Anglican establishment, after it has received the approval of the Vicar and the Parochial Church Council, it must be forwarded to the Diocesan Registrar with an application for the granting of a faculty from the Chancellor. Special application forms can be obtained from the Registrar. A coloured tracing or photograph should also be enclosed so that this may be retained and filed in the archives. Before a faculty is granted, the design must be submitted to the Diocesan Advisory Committee, a body of experts whose approval must be secured before the Chancellor will grant a faculty. This may mean a delay of a month or so, but whatever inconvenience this may cause it should be remembered that since the institution of these advisory committees the standard of work has improved, and that they are a safeguard for the client and the artist, preventing the future erection of any window or other feature which might be detrimental to the general aesthetic effect.

CHAPTER 12

Grisaille

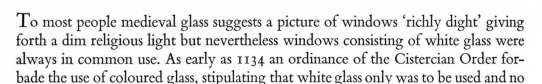

To most people medieval glass suggests a picture of windows 'richly dight' giving forth a dim religious light but nevertheless windows consisting of white glass were always in common use. As early as 1134 an ordinance of the Cistercian Order forbade the use of coloured glass, stipulating that white glass only was to be used and no figures or crosses.

Coloured glass was costly and difficult to obtain as is known from surviving correspondence of that period. It would have been almost impossible to fill a newly built church with full-coloured windows. Plain quarry work was used but the urge for additional beauty undoubtedly instigated the creation of the grisaille window. This could be removed and probably placed in another position when an opportunity occured for a full-coloured window.

The word Grisaille (French *grisailler,* to paint grey) shows it to have been of Norman origin, and it is reasonably sure that this type of window was in common use in England early in the twelfth century and no doubt much earlier on the continent. There was in fact more white glass in use in the twelfth century than in the thirteenth when more coloured glass was available.

As has been mentioned, this term does not denote a coloured decorative window but it is so associated with pattern work that the writer has been asked on more than one occasion to design a full-coloured grisaille window. Of course a grisaille window can be developed and decorated until it has become practically a full-coloured window. This approach has the advantage of keeping the design architectural. Pieces of jewel-like colour may be added, perhaps in a border, and then simple panels which may become enlarged to take important subject matter until the result is a rich pattern of colour held together by an underlying grisaille ornamentation.

The 'Five Sisters' window in York Minster, erected in 1282, was once considered to be not only the finest grisaille window in England but the finest in the world. Today its glory is a little diminished. Dr. Christopher Woodforde observes, 'The glass of the well-known "Five Sisters" window is still impressive although it is but a shadow of its former self.' This apparent deterioration is at least partly caused by the face light coming from the clear glass of the adjacent window now in position on the west wall of the north transept.

Dr. Woodforde further expresses the opinion that the best examples of grisaille glass in England today are those in Lincoln and Salisbury. The Salisbury grisaille is far more comprehensive both in quantity and variety of pattern and treatment. In Lincoln the five lancet lights below the large rose window in the north transept are interesting as showing various treatments of early grisaille. The two outer lights are composed of quarry work with small rondels of blue and ruby introduced at intervals down the centre of the light. In the two lights on each side of the centre one, circles and crosses are placed centrally on a quarry ground with a yellow fillet running down the inside edge of the outside border. The centre light is glazed with portions of two different grisaille windows both showing ornamental treatment without any quarry ground and with a larger amount of colour. In this light three colours are used, ruby, blue and yellow, so that we have three different colour schemes in the five lights. In the two outer windows small amounts of ruby and blue, in the next two yellow only, and in both portions of the centre light, ruby, blue and yellow are introduced.

The great west window of Salisbury Cathedral consists entirely of fragments of thirteenth-century grisaille with six shields dating from 1270 to 1280 taken from the Chapter House and assembled with the window in 1894. The west windows of the north and south aisles are also beautiful examples of the same period, giving a silvery effect with glints of jewel-like colour.

The clerestory window in the south-west transept is particularly interesting not only because it is a fine example of thirteenth-century grisaille, but because it is thought to be the only glass of this type which is in its original position in the cathedral. It also gives one an opportunity of contrasting it with the glass in the great window immediately below it, which was executed in 1880 with the object of reproducing the thirteenth-century grisaille in the two central lights immediately above it. The modern replica has certainly not the quality of the original. This is partly on account of the weathering which has mellowed the 700-year-old medieval glass, but very largely because of the uninteresting quality of the nineteenth-century glass. This replica was carried out at an unfortunate period when there was a dearth of good quality glass, and the craft itself was largely commercialized. The work was not executed or supervised by artists, but carried out by poorly paid technicians with no appreciation of the aesthetic side of the job they were doing.

There can be little doubt that the glass of today has at least as good a quality as the old glass and that there are half-a-dozen or more modern artists who could produce a facsimile with all the qualities of the old glass. There is, however, quite rightly, a strong prejudice against anything suggesting faking. When a similar occasion arises it would seem best to execute modern grisaille, similar in scale and general weight of line and colour to the old glass but not copying it.

Some such attempt was made in 1900 in the great window in the north transept of Salisbury, but it fails through being neither medieval nor modern in style. It has not

Plate 62. Salisbury Cathedral, Grisaille.

the clarity of design that characterizes the early work, which was designed to give a silvery and pearly overall effect with contrasting passages of glinting colour, whereas this modern window is a little too mellifluous in appearance. Its lack of contrast in breadth of design and colour gives it a tendency towards monotony. It is merely pleasantly innocuous.

In the great window of the south-east transept there are fragments and sections from seventeen windows. Not only do they make a particularly beautiful ensemble but they are extremely interesting to study for the variety and ingenuity displayed in their various designs. Although Salisbury has not so much fine old glass as other ancient cathedrals on account of the misplaced zeal of that notorious architect James Wyatt, of the eighteenth century, who removed so much of the original glass in the process of restoring the cathedral, this great window is a superb artistic treasure and probably the finest of its kind in the country.

Dr. Woodforde makes the following observation:

'Grisaille went through interesting stages of development. At the end of the thirteenth century or the beginning of the fourteenth century the trend towards naturalistic representation was exemplified by the glass painters in a new way. The lights were frequently filled with twining stems springing from a central and thicker stem, the twining stems bearing leaves, flowers and fruit. Vine, oak, holly, ivy, maple, sycamore and suchlike are often seen. Sometimes the leading followed the main stems and an irregular or flowing trellis pattern to emphasize and strengthen the whole design. [Plate 62.] In other examples the glass is cut into diamond-shape quarries to make a regular or formal trellis pattern, and the foliage was drawn as if to grow against it. In the chapter-house at York which was glazed about 1300 to 1307 the flowing design was combined with the older geometric pattern. In the interesting series of grisaille windows at Chartham, Kent, which were painted about the same time as the chapter-house windows at York, the transition from the earlier to the later style is also apparent. In Exeter cathedral the formal patterns were retained and formed a background for heraldic glass, as may be seen in the chapel of St. Mary Magdelene and the Archangel Gabriel.'

It is not surprising that Professor Sir Albert Richardson, P.P.R.A., F.R.I.B.A., is such a keen advocate of grisaille and has done so much to further its revival. Most of the leading architects realize its advantages. Sir Giles Gilbert Scott, R.A., F.R.I.B.A., used it extensively in a very large church he has recently built in Canada, and again in the Guildhall windows (Plate 63).

Another of our leading architects, Mr. S. E. Dykes Bower, M.A., F.R.I.B.A., F.S.A., architect in charge of Westminster Abbey and joint architect with Mr. Godfrey Allen, for the new work at the east end of St. Paul's Cathedral, has recently shown his appreciation of grisaille windows by installing eight really beautiful windows in Westminster Abbey. These windows give just the note of colourful enrichment which their position required. At that height any subject matter would be incomprehensible but the colour value gives additional impressiveness to the soaring architecture. Mr. Dykes Bower stresses the usefulness of grisaille windows where subject matter is not of primary importance and the main consideration is one of architectural enrichment.

Perhaps the particular difficulty in designing a grisaille window is the lack of a given subject. As in all other cases the design will be influenced by the architectural setting. Possibly the shape or part of the shape of one of the traceries can be re-echoed in the design for the window and used as the silhouette of the panels, or as an inter-lacing line, to produce a pleasant pattern.

It is essential to have a general conception of the design before the beginning. It must be decided whether a plain design is desirable or whether the setting calls for more elaborate treatment. For a large five-light window it will be necessary to make more variation in the details, the silhouettes and weights of the panels than if the window were a small one. The panels or points of additional interest need just as careful placing as the main subjects of a window with figures. They will lose or gain dignity in just the same way by their position. Once these silhouettes and the main lines of the design have been determined, the rest of the design can be gradually evolved by complementary and contrasting additions as fancy dictates. The general scale of the design must be determined by that of the architecture, and from the commencement of the design the thickness of the lead is an important consideration, especially if the window is a large one, or if it is to be placed at a great height from the floor, or again if it will be receiving a strong light as in South Africa, when the consequent halation must be allowed for. In such a case an inch lead, or even more, round the main silhouettes will not appear excessive when in position. Without this strengthening the window might easily appear to be weak, thin, or lacking in quality.

The white background glass must be varied in tint and again this variation must depend to some extent upon position and light; the further the window will be from the eye and the stronger the light, the greater the variation needed in the tints of the glass. These variations of tint are too subtle to be shown satisfactorily on the small scale drawing; they tend to dull the effect of the sketch rather than to suggest sparkle, but the thickness of the leading must be definitely indicated, otherwise the propor-tions of spacing in the cartooning and cutlining will be seriously impaired.

PLATE 63. Part of windows in the Guildhall, London. Designed by E. Liddall Armitage, Whitefriars Studios, in collaboration with Sir Giles Gilbert Scott, O.M., R.A.

CHAPTER 13

Heraldry

The study of heraldry is an important part of the training of a stained glass artist, not only because he is constantly required to incorporate emblazonments into his designs, but also because it teaches him the soundest method of design and applications of significant colour patterns for glass. The success of a window with figures in the main lights and heraldry in the tracery can always be judged by the way the figure work stand up to the clarity and pattern of the heraldry above it.

Good heraldry tells its story in the simplest possible terms of line and colour effect. It was originally designed for that purpose so that it could be read at a glance rather as a newspaper cartoon is designed today. A good political cartoon has a clarity and forcefulness which enables its meaning to be understood at once. That is also the test of good heraldry. It is regrettable that the College of Heralds seems unaware of this fact. A twelfth-century heraldic eagle depicted in a few significant lines is a creature of fierceness and power, whereas an eagle as depicted nowadays in some official emblazonments shows the details of every feather so minutely drawn that one feels they must have been studied in a poulterer's shop. The result is equally lifeless.

It is well to remember that heraldry originated far back in history as a product of the living conditions of the times. It was not co-ordinated into a science until this was necessitated by the complications of the first Crusade at the end of the eleventh century, a date which roughly coincides with early stained glass. This Crusade, as Warrington explains,

> 'brought together numbers of princes and nobles from many countries, a circumstance which created a necessity, for the sake of distinction, discrimination, order and arrangement of heraldic blazonry and the more especially so as the surnames were not then generally adopted, the chiefs being designated by their general characteristics such as strength, conquest, colour, learning, place of birth, courage etc., as is the case with all our earlier monarchs. Yet a certain portion of blazon had long previously prevailed in their banners, and in their professional accompaniments, such being attributed to the tribes of Israel (they were indeed commands given to Moses by God himself—"And the children of Israel shall pitch their tents, every man by his own camp, and every man by his own *standard*"—Numbers 1.52) and certainly to both the Greek and Roman warriors. Thus in the play by Aeschylus, called the *Seven Chiefs against*

93

Thebes, a full account is given, almost in modern terms, of the devices, mottoes and coloured emblems by which the shield of each warrior was distinguished.'

The aeroplane markings in the last war denoting England, France, Germany, Russia etc. were heraldic emblazonments conditioned to the necessities of modern war.

It is interesting to note that the colours chosen for blazonry in medieval times were the ones which modern science proves to be the primary ones, namely: *Gules,* red or ruby; *Or,* yellow or gold; *Vert,* green or emerald; *Azure,* blue or sapphire; *Purpure,* purple or amethyst; *Argent,* white or silver; *Sable,* black. Or and Argent were treated as metals and it is a rule of English heraldry that one metal must not be super-imposed upon another. To these colours various furs were added.

Diagrammatically the tinctures are expressed thus:

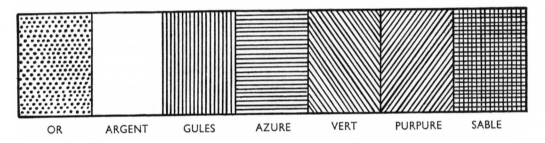

| OR | ARGENT | GULES | AZURE | VERT | PURPURE | SABLE |

THE PRINCIPAL FURS ARE

ERMINE   VAIR   POTENT

There are several variations on these devices such as counter-vair or counter-potent and other furs which may be studied in textbooks on heraldry such as G. W. Eve's *Heraldry as Art,* Boutell's *English Heraldry,* and for further general information on the subject Webber's *Church Symbolism.*

Nearly all early heraldry is displayed upon shields, and the main divisions of the shield are shown below and described heraldically.

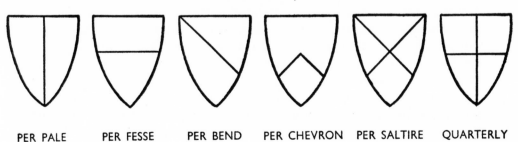

PER PALE   PER FESSE   PER BEND   PER CHEVRON   PER SALTIRE   QUARTERLY

Originally these would be described as party per pale, party per fesse etc. but later the word party was omitted. Many variations of these ordinaries and additional ones are to be found and the previously mentioned textbooks and others should be consulted for information about these.

Multiples of the ordinaries produced further divisions, and here are some of the principal ones. Again, many variations are to be found.

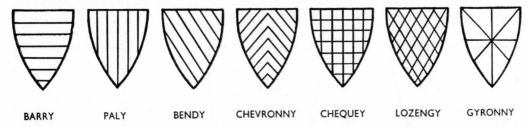

BARRY   PALY   BENDY   CHEVRONNY   CHEQUEY   LOZENGY   GYRONNY

The blank spaces about the ordinaries, and sometimes the ordinaries themselves were often filled by devices of every possible kind, known as charges. It is quite impossible to list more than a few of these, and the reader is once again advised to consult the appropriate textbooks. Almost any object, animate or inanimate has been used, and the list includes animals of all kinds, real and fabulous, flowers, birds, trees, and, amongst hundreds of inanimate objects, articles such as cushions, combs, battle axes, shells, cinquefoils, and so on. An example of one such charge, the crescent, will be seen below.

Quite obviously some method of describing a coat of arms was necessary, and the method evolved (called technically 'to blazon') was at once an accurate and a precise one. It aimed at describing unambiguously what was on the coat of arms so that there could be no possibility of a mistake being made in the drawing and emblazoning of it. It was an heraldic abbreviation, evolved to facilitate the compiling of records and registers. Below is shown a coat of arms with its blazon underneath.

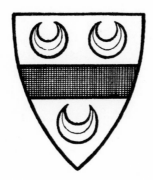

ARG. a fesse SA. between 3 crescents GU.

This description indicates that on a silver field there is a black fesse between three red crescents.

Heraldry was not confined to tournaments and martial pursuits. Ladies of the realm, Councillors of State and the higher Clergy made use of armorial bearings. Heraldry was, like Latin, part of the international culture and language of the period. It arose from the pattern of medieval life, but through the centuries, as its usefulness diminished, it degenerated into the rococo absurdities of the sixteenth century onwards, from which state it has been to some extent rescued today. This degeneration can clearly be seen merely by studying the actual form of the shield as depicted in the various centuries.

The earlier type of shield as exemplified by the arms of France (ancient) in the east window of Selling Church, Kent, is composed of two curved lines running from the ends of the top horizontal to the centre line at the base. In the fourteenth century the shield slightly changed in shape: the sides were parallel for a quarter of the length then curved to the lower point. It also became narrower, whereas the earlier shields were almost as wide as they were long. The length of the fourteenth-century shields was definitely greater than the width by a proportion of roughly five to four. By the middle of the fifteenth century the shape of the shield had developed further fullness approximately to the shape of a capital U. Towards the end of the century the shape began to assume every possible sort of variety, until in the middle of the sixteenth century the influence of the Renaissance had produced this sort of heraldic monstrosity.

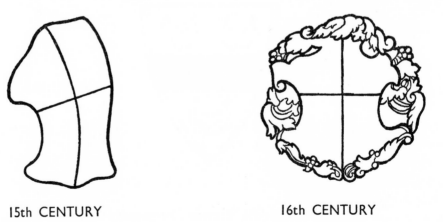

15th CENTURY   16th CENTURY

In England the first complete achievement appeared about the middle of the fifteenth century although it came into use a little sooner on the continent. For the first time there were helmets with mantling and crests, supporters and mottoes on the label. There are no examples of this before 1450. Heraldic crests came into general use about the beginning of the fourteenth century, as devices for surmounting helms, putting on seals and for general armorial purposes. When used in the tournament they were made of some light material such as leather or canvas, or even paper fashioned on a wicker frame, and boldly designed with surface details modelled in plaster, and finished with paint and gilt. Up to the sixteenth century the crests showed purpose and virility, but later, when tournaments were no longer held, the clerical pedants took charge and rules were made with no regard to their practical or artistic application. Flowing water, for example, would be designated as part of a crest. Rules were now made that the helm must face this way or that, with the vizor open or shut, according to rank, so that from this period onwards a helm might be facing one way and the crest the other. Moreover the ratio of shield, helm and crest became disproportionate, showing a deterioration of aesthetic appreciation, as illustrated in the following diagram.

15th CENTURY

16th CENTURY

An Esquire or gentleman has a helm of steel, with gold ornaments in profile with vizor closed, though it may be shown three-quarter view.

A Knight's helmet is the same except that it is full-faced and the vizor is open.

The helmet of a Peer is of steel or silver and gold, but bars or grilles replace the vizor. It is shown in profile.

The Sovereign and Princes of the Blood Royal have barred helmets of gold full-faced.

The torse or wreath is a silken decoration and should not be treated as a support for

G

the crest. Originally the colours of the torse had no especial relationship to the colours of the shield, but custom has gradually decreed that they should be the principal metal and colour as shown in the blazon. They are usually shown with alternating twists beginning with the metal, but this is not essential.

The mantling or lambrequin hanging from the helmet was, like the surcoat, designed as a protection from the rays of the sun. It is usually shown with shaped edges and forms a valuable addition to the decorative treatment. The colour of the mantling followed the same development as that of the torse and is now confined to the first metal and colour of the blazon.

The origin of the supporters is not exactly known. They may first have been used decoratively to fill in the side spaces which arise when placing a shield in a circular crest. Examination of early crests certainly suggests this is probable, but it remains only a surmise. The shield is the essential part of an heraldic achievement, with the crest next in importance. The supporters are hardly more than fanciful ornamentation sanctioned by custom, and they are sometimes employed without shield or crest to support monograms or badges.

Of other insignia the Imperial Crown is the most important. It originated as a circlet; fleur-de-lys and cross pattees were then added and later a number of arches to support the central orb, the emblem of sovereignty.

16th CENTURY

18th CENTURY

The most satisfactory design, as in the sixteenth century, shows the orb strongly upheld and predominant in dignity. In the seventeenth century the arches sag and the weight of the orb appears to be a little too much for them, giving an unpleasant appearance of weakness. This weakness was further emphasized in the Georgian period. Design implies meaning so that the royal crowns of this period can hardly be said to be well designed. Their heraldic significance implies that the weight of sovereignty was causing its supports to sag, but it is doubtful if this was intentional. It was almost certainly a matter of ignorance. The drawing or emblem was created without any understanding of its significance.

The cap which is enclosed in the crown is made of purple velvet, though shown heraldically as crimson with the ermine fur along the lower rim.

Where necessary, clients supply the details of heraldic achievements but if the information is not complete, Burke's *General Armoury*, Burke's *Peerage, Baronetcy and Knightage* and also Debrett can be consulted. Should there still be any doubt as to the accuracy of the blazonry, the College of Heralds should be approached as they are the final judges.

CHAPTER 14

Colour

The best designers do not seem to have much faith in theories of colour though they always seem interested in discussing the subject in general terms. Anyone can be taught to draw just as anyone can be taught to produce an engineering design, which is a product of applied knowledge. This is not to suggest that anyone can be taught to produce a drawing that has artistic merit; that is quite another matter and there is only too much evidence of this particular difficulty. It is equally difficult if not impossible to teach anyone to produce a good colour scheme, for this especial sensitiveness is either innate or it is not.

With regard to stained glass perhaps more than to any other form of colour work, it is important to realize the theory or indeed the actuality of light vibration. The beauty and brilliance in the colour of a flower is due to the fact that it is made up of a number of varying shades. It is not one flat tint such as on a door which has been painted one even colour. The colour of the flower consists of a variety of minute specks of different shades that can be seen through a microscope.

White light can be broken up into varying vibrations by passing it through a prism and the resulting band of colour or spectrum is the stained glass artist's palette. The quality of a colour scheme, however, depends not only on the blending or combining of various distinguishable colours but also in the variations in the tints themselves. This was fully realized by the early masters. Careful study, for example, of a portion of green surface in a Ravenna mosaic will show that the apparently even passage of green colour is in fact made up of at least a dozen different shades of green in the small tesserae. It is this variation of tint that gives it its quality of freshness. The same quality can be seen in medieval glass and it is well understood and utilized by the best colourists today.

The treatment of colour varies of course to some extent with the individual and also the school or locality in which he is painting, but it is also very much affected by the particular supply of raw material that is available. In his *History of the York School of Glass Painting* Mr. Knowles makes the following interesting comments:

'York artists seem to have preferred to use colour to obtain contrast rather than an all-over effect of harmonious tones and tints, as was the case in the south-west of

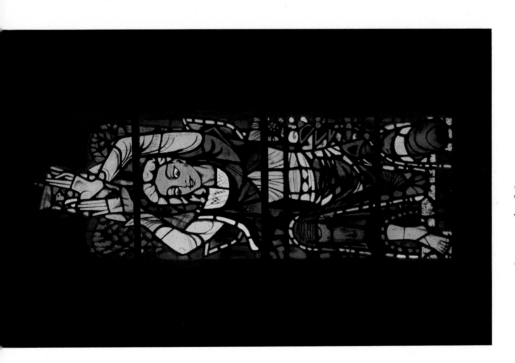

The Angel of the Resurrection.   The Angel of the Annunciation. Gabriel.
Windows in Michaelhouse School Chapel, Balgowan, Natal, South Africa. By Ervin Bossanyi.
PLATE 64.

England, where the artists employed a rich range of deep colours such as dark rubies, indigo blues, olive greens, rich browns, and pot-metal yellows, which, when contrasted with deep stain and again with pale yellow, harmonize with each other so wonderfully. To see this at its best one should study it in ornament founded on plant forms such as was used in tracery pieces, where the colours can interlace and the designer has the opportunity of bringing one close up against another. Practically the only example of this at York is the easternmost window of the north aisle of St. Denys Church, which, as will be shown later, probably owes much to Wells influence. But the whole of the credit for this successful result does not, however, belong to the glass-painters for deliberately selecting and arranging the colours with an eye to obtaining colour harmonies; though in the fourteenth-century examples such as the one above mentioned, there cannot be the slightest doubt that they did so. For in Decorated glass the colours were more secondary and less primary than those of a later date, there was less pure colour and more mixed tints, the red-browns, brown-purples, brown-yellows, olive-greens, green-yellows, yellow-whites and so forth being due to the impure materials used by the glass makers, each chemical containing impurities in the way of other oxides which gave broken tints, so that each colour contained a trace of some other colours. All this aided the colour harmony, for being all more or less secondaries they could be placed right up against each other without clashing. We are therefore frequently liable to give credit to the artist, which rightly belongs to the glass maker, for with such a palette it was not easy to go far wrong.'

To some extent these are technical considerations and the subject has far wider connotations than mere technique. That fine modern colourist, Ervin Bossanyi recommends the study of the earlier chapters of *Form and Colour* by March Phillips. In the later chapters the author loses his way in a fog of chiaroscuro, but the opening chapters are well worth reading. His main thesis is that form appeals to the intellect and colour to the emotions. The matter is not quite as simple as that, but there is little doubt that colour appeals to the emotions, though Phillips himself implies a qualification:

'So long he says, as forms are presented to the eye in salient relief their colour is bound to remain primarily descriptive and accordingly the mitigation of their clearness of outline is an indispensable preliminary to the display of substantive colour. The rough test is whether or not an object strikes the attention by form or colour. If the former—then the possibilities of colour are in subjection to the intellectual control of form. If the latter—if colour asserts its influence direct on the feelings without the mind having a chance of raising the question of form—then colour is asserting its own inherent emotional power. In order that it may be able to do this, however, it is essential that the self-assertion of form and natural tendency to thrust itself forward should be checked and toned down.'

That this is essentially true, at least, of stained glass windows, is borne out by the fact that anyone describing the beauties, say, of Chartres or Bourges, will inevitably dilate upon the brilliance of the colour. It seems to be generally agreed that the first thing that should appeal on seeing a full-coloured window in position is its colour rather than its significance.

It has often been remarked that art is the elimination of the unnecessary. In many examples of abstract art the elimination of form has been carried to such an extent that colour alone remains. Since it is mostly the intellectuals who are grateful for this release, it must be that they are thankful for the temporary relaxation.

If these considerations are useful in designing a full-coloured window, do they apply to heraldic windows or windows in which the figures are silhouetted against a white quarry ground? It is evident that they do. To be successful any type of window must first please by the quality of its colour. The visitor, entering a large hall, with a series of windows displaying heraldic devices on a white quarry ground, will first receive a pleasing sense of colour pattern, long before he has formed any idea of the significance of the armorial bearings. Possibly some useful suggestions can be gained from the heraldic stipulations of colour. It is practically impossible to produce a bad colour scheme when following the rules of heraldry, and it should be emphasized that early medieval glass was essentially heraldic in treatment. Figures and objects were displayed not as realistic representations (realistic in the sense of photographic) but rather as statements of historic fact, and even the statement of fact was subordinated to the general colour scheme. For example, a brick wall would be green or red or blue or indeed any heraldic colour that gave the most pleasing sense of pattern.

The heraldic palette is a limited one, and it has been noted in the history of oil painting that the greatest of the old masters restricted their palette as they advanced in age and experience. As has been said there is today a far wider range of colour in glass than was ever available in earlier times, but this, like atomic energy, has its dangers as well as its possible advantages. It is beneficial only when a variety of range is used to give quality to a simple colour scheme rather than to produce a complicated one. But these are matters upon which no one can dogmatize. Beautiful windows have been produced with a marked predominance of one colour; on the other hand the masterpiece, showing the Ascension, at Le Mans, delights with its vivid contrast of ruby and azure. Colours largely depend upon the particular mood of the window; those near to one another in the spectrum giving the softer effect and those farther away giving contrast and emphasis.

In selecting the colour for a stained glass window the additional factor of halation has to be taken into consideration and controlled. This spreading of light causes one colour to overlap and affect the adjacent colour. For example, in the transept windows in Notre Dame and, of course, in some of the windows at Chartres, Bourges and Le Mans, some blue, placed adjacent to ruby causes a definite violet or purple hue. Some artists do not like this effect but it can easily be avoided by placing a narrow band of white glass between the ruby and the blue. The spreading of the white light keeps the ruby and blue colours distinct. There is no doubt, however, that in these medieval windows the violet hue was deliberately planned, and that the early craftsmen could have avoided it had they so wished.

In stressing the importance of colour it must always be remembered that it is possible to have too much of a good thing. Emotion may degenerate into hysteria. In all these considerations there is the overriding proviso of architectural fitness. Phillips eulogizes the emotional aspects of colour but he may perhaps not have visited Winchelsea and seen the Strachan windows there. Individually they are excellent, but as they completely fill a small edifice without receiving from their architectural setting a corresponding and balancing amount of quiet grey contrast as at Chartres, the effect of the colour is overwhelming, particularly on account of the preponderance of purple. The strength of colour in this case is a distraction rather than an attraction, and the main purpose of the church seems hardly to have been kept in mind. It cannot easily be imagined that anyone would wish to pray there, except for a speedy release. The brilliance of the windows in the great cathedrals is offset by the surrounding wall space and the distance from the eye. The dignity and solemnity of the interior is in no way interfered with but rather enhanced by the jewel-like colouring of the windows.

The lessons of heraldry, of the old masters, and of the best of medieval art suggest that the aim must be simplicity and strength, but strength does not imply lack of sensitivity and refinement, nor does simplicity imply emptiness. In a really successful design the subject produces an emotional reaction that surges to an expression in colour. It was not only skill in combination of colour that produced the early masterpieces. They were the natural emotional statements of an age of faith. This emotion was not analogous to the superficial enthusiasm of modern aesthetic appreciation. It was not an emotion that was concentrated upon the glories of ART with a capital A, but something that really strived for the glory of God. This is not an irrelevant consideration but the crux of the whole matter. It is not enough to evolve in the mind the design for a great window; its conception must also be the result of a spiritual experience.

Phillips stresses the point that oriental life, with its essentially emotional and intuitive impulses, is soaked with colour. It is part of their daily life. He writes:

> 'The gypsies who bivouac on English commons impart a whiff of their living sense of colour among us and emphasize thereby our consciousness of their foreign origin. Colour as they use it is a matter of life and assumes accordingly that note of depth and richness which no amount of studio-culture seems able to bestow upon it.'

As a generalization it may be said that Greek art is characteristic of western thought, being essentially intellectual and producing perfection of form, whereas Byzantine and Gothic art have assimilated the ideas of the east which receive an emotional expression in colour. Phillips writes:

> 'the mystical or spiritual element which belongs to medieval life and in the sphere of life expresses itself as monasticism, expresses itself in art in depth and richness of colour. While that spirit lives in life it lives in art; when it dies out of life and makes way for the renaissance the deep colour ebbs out of art, making way for the exactitude of form.'

No doubt there is deep truth in Phillips' assessment, but it should be remembered that other influences besides mysticism are involved. There is no doubt that the Elizabethan period was far more colourful than present-day England. The Englishman of today has become acclimatized to drabness, partly through the negations of Puritanism but largely as a result of the sordid beginnings of the industrial era. The human counterpart of the peacock no longer exists, and today only women keep alive any sense of colour.

Some years ago the writer carried out an east window for Burma which was naturally compared with the local colour of the Burmese countryside and it was the particular choice of vivid blues that by good luck made the work a success. Recently with reference to a window designed for Jamaica, that distinguished architect, Mr. Alik Low, insisted upon the use of particularly rich colour. He emphasized the fact that what might be considered as an effective but subtle colour scheme in this country would not be appreciated out there.

This raises the question as to whether it is not so much a question of subtlety but of lack of robustness. Have we got the physique to stand rich colour nowadays? Probably the Elizabethans would have had similar tastes to those of the Jamaicans. Strong colour is always characteristic of less sophisticated societies. The first reaction of the healthy infant is towards colour, the other senses develop later. It is also evident that grandmother cannot becomingly bedeck herself with the same brilliance that might appear charming on her grand-daughter. It would seem that the question of vitality is involved. No one would contend that the absence of colour is a healthy sign in our national life. Whatever other advantages the West Indians may have brought with them they have certainly added a pleasing note of colour to the drabness of our streets. It is a pity that our young bloods do not emulate them, but the height of their sartorial achievements appears to be a particular shape in a black bowler hat. But how interesting it would be to see a pair of scarlet trousers, a canary waistcoat and an emerald green jacket coming down the street. The choice and pattern of a tie would then be of minor importance. Such a fashion would help to cultivate a robustness and a breadth of vision that might even be a help to modern statesmen.

It is generally accepted that the three primary colours are red, yellow and blue, but this is only true or useful as regards pigments. If red and blue are mixed, the result is a purple colour, a combination of blue and yellow produces green, red and yellow produces orange. These results are termed secondaries. When all three primaries are mixed together to form other tints these are termed tertiaries. If red, yellow and blue are mixed in correct proportions a grey is obtained, and it was formerly thought that if the pigments were sufficiently pure, the correct mixture would produce white.

Science has shown that this theory is fallacious. It is now known that white light can be broken up, for example, by passing it through a prism, into all colours of the rainbow. This colour band is known as the spectrum, categorized as red, orange, yellow, green, blue and purple. Any of these colours are in fact white light with all the other tints of the spectrum deleted, so that it is more true to call each one of these primaries.

It is a scientific fact that colour has no objective reality, but only exists as a sensation in the mind. Light is in fact a vibration which reacts upon the retina of the eye and causes a sensation of colour in the brain. The different colours are different vibrations which individually excite in the brain the sensation of each particular colour. The effect of the total vibrations of all the colours reacting simultaneously gives the sensation of white.

Each primary colour has what is termed its complementary colour, which in combination with it will also produce the sensation of white. The complementary colour of red is green; the complementary colour of purple is yellow. The accompanying diagram shows the colours of the spectrum arranged so that their opposite complementary colour can be read at a glance.

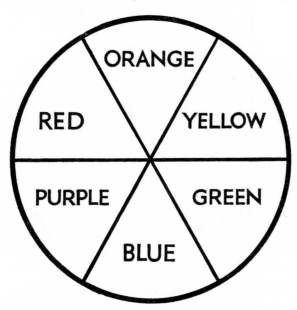

If anyone is at all sceptical about these facts they can easily be verified by experiment. The simplest method is to place a spot of bright red colour on a piece of white paper and stare at it concentratedly until the eyes are fatigued. Then look at another piece of completely white paper, i.e. red plus green vibrations, or even just shut the eyes, and an image of the complementary colour will appear. The scientific explanation of this is that when one has been looking concentratedly at a bright spot of red, the red nerves of the retina become temporarily atrophied, and for the moment one is blind to the sensation of red, so that when the eye is focused on the white paper the red vibrations for the time being have no effect, and can only react to the complementary green sensations.

This knowledge has a certain practical use for it is a warning not to look too long at a coloured sketch when working or the colour nerves may become tired and one's judgement thereby affected. Most designers will agree that after a lengthy period of work without a break, there comes a time when almost any change or alteration in the design appears to be an improvement.

There are other ways of proving these facts about colour but they require a little apparatus. The following quotation from *The Tricks of Light and Colour* by Herbert McKay gives an example:

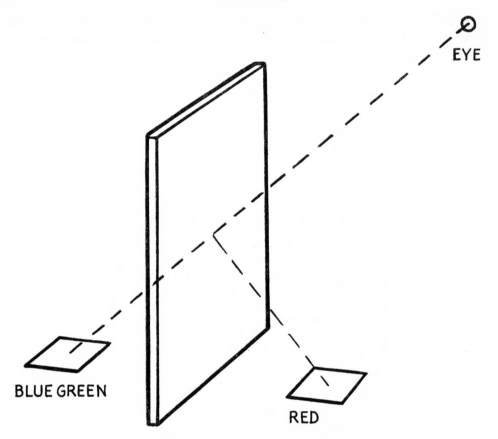

'There is another simple way of combining two colours. We paint squares of white paper, one with each colour, and we place them on a table. We hold a sheet of plain glass half-way between the two colours. If we are seeing red and another colour, it is usually better to have the red in front of the glass because red is probably the brighter colour. We stand at the side of the glass from which the light comes and we look down through the glass at the colour behind it. We should see at the same spot the reflection of the colour in front of the glass, but a little adjustment may be necessary. When we combine red, blue-green in this way we get a near approach to white.'

It must not be imagined for one moment that scientific knowledge of this sort will enable anyone to produce a beautiful colour scheme. The creators of the windows at Chartres were quite unconscious of the scientific facts of the spectrum and the theory of light vibrations. Such beauty is created instinctively or by trial and error, through the emotions rather than through the intellect. Nevertheless this knowledge need not be detrimental and can even be useful. It can be completely ignored but it can also be helpful as a guide. If a colour scheme proves unsatisfactory, knowledge of primary and complementary colour may be of help in detecting the cause of failure. For example, it is useful to know that a combination such as red and green, primary and complementary, add up to the effect of white, and therefore of brightness or luminosity. In contrast, to combine red with blue or violet is to lower the general tone of the colour scheme and thus to deaden it.

It is quite true that normally anyone with a good colour sense will feel these things instinctively, but even the finest composer with the keenest sense of tone values may on occasion check up with a tuning fork. No one has ever supposed that a good musical composition was derived from a tuning fork and similarly no colour chart based on scientific knowledge of colour vibration will create a beautiful colour scheme.

If one is seeking inspiration the illimitable examples of nature are far more likely to be of help. Indeed the mind unconsciously absorbs the lessons she puts before us. It is customary to view her expanses of blue and green, her usually limited and concentrated use of red, purple and yellow, and mankind in general seems to prefer the things to which it is accustomed. To most people the old thatched cottage has a more pleasing appearance than a modernist dwelling of severe, rectangular line. Future generations, industrially conditioned, may come to regard the cube as the perfection of form, but for present-day considerations of colour, colour in nature undoubtedly makes a more beneficial study than, say, a scientific treatise on colour. A walk in the garden can be more educative than a talk in the studio.

CHAPTER 15

Imagination

The craft work of the best periods is imbued with the quality of imagination. It is not confined to the conception of transcendental subjects, imaginings such as the classical phantasies of Blake or the germanic horrifics of Hieronymous Bosch, but pervades in quiet fancifulness and delicate charm all the craft work of the medieval period. It is a sign and proof that the craftsman loves his work and is living with it. The quality is not obtrusive, but subtle though it may be, it is easily apparent when craft work is compared with the commercialized and standardized products churned out mechanically by a streamlined process. It is the difference between the creative work of a human being and the production of a human automaton who has been trained in time and labour actions by an expert in rhythmic motion. What does it matter if he loses the joy of creation provided he saves his employer's time? What does it matter if his work no longer gives a sense of aesthetic appreciation to the beholder provided the ephemeral figures in a profit and loss account give an entirely different satisfaction.

The craftsman is the surviving trace of salt in a world that has lost so much of its savour in the unhealthy conditions of industrialization. So much of the charm of medieval work lies in the happy imaginings of the details. The capitals, the poppy heads and all the minutiae of the craft work are evidence of the happy phantasy of the craftsman adding warmth and enjoyment and aesthetic charm to buildings that have inspired and given pleasure to mankind throughout the centuries.

The Very Rev. E. Milner-White, Dean of York, once complained of the lack of imagination shown by the continual repetition of diamond quarries as patterned background, and invited study of the variety of design in the windows of his Cathedral. It was a salutory lesson, showing how one can unconsciously lose a quality not only from lack of care but also from lack of imagination. It is quite true that most artists will give variety to their quarry backgrounds but this is to avoid mechanical harshness rather than to employ a pleasing phantasy.

The earlier workers had the inestimable advantage of time. Today few people have time to think. One cannot live at more than four miles an hour; beyond this speed touch is lost with life. It is no doubt exhilarating to have a trip on the Gigantic

Switchback, but one does not want to live on it. Nor is it the ideal place for the creative imagination.

Unfortunately the work of the finest artist is no more than the most perfect expression of the age in which he is born. Today the craftsman has not only to contend with the prevailing mentality but to endeavour to maintain suitable conditions for work. The time factor becomes increasingly despotic. Possibly the artist has always demanded too much in this respect. Tradition tells of the portrait that was begun by depicting the subject as a youth and completed with the necessary addition of a beard.

Nevertheless it is true that human beings really only live when unconscious of time. A symphony concert cannot be appreciated with one eye on a wrist watch, nor will good literature be enjoyed with the ear waiting for the clock to strike the hour. It is only possible to live, just as it is only possible to evoke the creative imagination, in timelessness. It is necessary to specify creative imagination because statistics show that it is in those countries where time consciousness is most prevalent that one finds the largest proportion of the population in mental hospitals.

It has been stated that the finest examples of art and literature have always been created when the chief town of a nation has grown big enough to attract the best intellects but has not become so large that it has lost touch with the country. This seems a reasonable theory. Shakespeare could leave the artificialities of the theatre and with a short walk find himself amongst the realities of the countryside. There was then no distinction between the language of the town and that of the country. This was still a common heritage in which he could blend the sanity of the village with the wit of the town. His art was no studio product of esoteric appreciation, which had to be explained to the less educated who otherwise could not understand what he was talking about. His appeal was to the nation and not to the coteries.

Imagination is the especial characteristic of the creative artist whether he be a bricklayer, master craftsman, architect, composer of opera or literary genius. The following personal experiences illustrate two widely different aspects of the imaginative faculty. I once put a problem to a Mr. Steggles who was building a cowshed for me in Suffolk. It concerned some brickwork that he was working on. He scratched his head and said thoughtfully, 'That will require some pillow work', and I realized in a flash why he had such a fine reputation as a craftsman. He used his imagination. I felt humbled, for I realized that he was not an automaton but in fact carried out his creations and solved his problems in his imagination before materializing them in the light of day.

Of course imagination like most human faculties has its dangers. It can lead one astray. This truth was made painfully obvious to me years ago by an incident which temporarily shattered my faith in my fellow craftsmen. A society of artists to which I belonged had arranged a competition amongst its members for the production of a poster announcing the annual exhibition. I had spent some time carefully preparing my attempt but at the last moment I forgot all about it. On the appointed evening I was working in my studio when I suddenly remembered the meeting. Hurriedly snatching up a sheet of discarded cartoon paper from the floor, I wrapped it round my design and quickly made my way to the studio in Chelsea. Just in time I handed my roll to the secretary who unrolled it and to my consternation pinned up both pieces of paper on the wall amongst the exhibits. Fortunately the exhibits were un-signed and anonymous, merely being given a number for voting purposes, so that I felt thankful that the meaningless scrawls on one piece of paper could not be gener-ally attributed to myself.

When the result of the voting was announced my serious effort secured third place, another competitor secured second place, and my meaningless scrawls were acclaimed first by a large majority. I like to think that it was due to my innate honesty that I got up and rather shamefacedly and apologetically explained what had hap-pened. My memory of a painful situation is not very clear but I do remember that the design accorded second place was eventually adopted for the poster.

The incident disturbed me very much at the time. Most of the members were well known to me and I am still convinced that they were a sincere and hard-working group of genuine craftsmen. We were all comparatively young and therefore our ideals were fresh and vigorous, but nevertheless not at all immune from self-decep-tion. Confronted with the incomprehensible, possibly ashamed to expose their ignorance or delighted at the novelty the majority acclaimed the work because they were impressed by the fact that they could not understand it. Our sophistication is only skin deep. The supposed merit of the work was due entirely to their unbalanced imagination. I have sometimes wondered whether I did the right thing. 'There is a tide in the affairs of men, which if taken at the flood etc.' Ought I to have kept quiet and accepted the position as leader of a new art movement? No doubt the more ad-vanced critics would have accepted me. No doubt I had quantities of discarded and meaningless oddments littered on the floor of my studio, with which to uphold my reputation. Unlike diamonds they did not even require cutting and polishing. It would possibly not have lasted very long but one wonders.

Coleridge's own skit (published in *The Times*), on *The Ancient Mariner* perhaps contains the truth:

> *'Your poem must eternal be*
> *Dear Sir, it cannot fail*
> *For 'tis incomprehensible*
> *And without head or tail.'*

That fine artist and delightful wit Fougasse, when giving a talk at the Art Worker's Guild, of which he was then the distinguished master, maintained that the public can draw better than the designer. Each individual will, as it were, fill in the omissions of the drawing to suit his own imaginative taste. A novel seen subsequently on the films is often unsatisfactory because the impersonations do not reflect the images that the reader has subconsciously created. In other words there is much to be said for leaving something to the imagination. Prolixity is just as much to be avoided in designing as in writing.

This is the obvious defect of realistic art. The fine draughtsmanship of Raphael's cartoons for tapestries on view at the Victoria and Albert Museum, South Kensington, seems commonplace in comparison with the Ravenna mosaics. The tapestries themselves can be seen in one of the rooms of Hampton Court and comparison made with the Tudor tapestries in the next room. The medieval work conveys a sense of music and poetry that is lacking in Raphael's superb photography. A visit to the authentic realism of Madame Tussauds is no doubt very interesting, but there is more aesthetic enjoyment to be had in inspecting the equally truthful statements in an Assyrian bas-relief at the British Museum. Apart from its aesthetic value, mere realism can but reflect the obvious; otherworldiness is beyond its capabilities, hence perhaps, its appropriateness for renaissance architecture.

Great truths whether in mathematics or religion seem to be best expressed by symbols, and medieval windows in their use of symbolism convey greater profundity of religious truth than those of more recent times. At least as far as religious art is concerned the great tradition of spiritual significance was lost in the upsurge of renaissance materialism.

The pre-Raphaelite Brotherhood realized this and attempted to regain it, a noble project which failed in the bogs of romanticism. Perhaps it is not too fanciful to suggest that modern abstract art may succeed where the pre-Raphaelites did not. The aesthetic shackles of realism and humanism have been unloosed but whether abstract art exists only as an artistic reaction or whether it will be generally accepted as a significant form of religious art will depend upon the motives of the designers who create it. Until the impetus of novelty and intellectual snobbery has been exhausted it will not be reasonable to judge, but it seems possible that this is a foreshadowing of the form in which the future religious masterpieces of the world will be created.

Probably the most inspired writing on the subject of imagination is in Coleridge's *Biographia Literaria,* admirably annotated by Professor Basil Willey in his illuminating book *Nineteenth Century Studies.* Coleridge does, however, make a categorical distinction between Fancy and Imagination which has been described as 'celebrated but useless', since sharp divisions may be useful, but they are seldom accurate. There are, in fact, varying degrees of imagination. Like most human faculties it can be used for lower or for higher purposes. When used as a playful fancy it can be charming enough and a relief to the humdrum and prosaic, but obviously such a practice makes no worthy comparison with the deep insight of the true poet, artist or mystic.

Nevertheless his description of a poem by Wordsworth could serve as a balanced summary of the qualities one would wish to find in a successful stained glass window:

> 'The union of deep feeling, with profound thought; the fine balance of truth in observing, with the imaginative faculty in modifying the objects observed; and above all the original gift of spreading the tone, the atmosphere and with it the depth and height of the ideal world around forms, incidents and situations, of which, for the common view, custom had bedimmed the lustre, had dried up the sparkle and the dewdrops.'

The primary imagination, he declares:

'I hold to be the living power and prime agent of all human perception and as a repetition in the finite mind of the eternal act of creation in the infinite I AM,'

Willey comments:

'This is not to be dismissed as metaphysical babble; a weight of thought, indeed a whole philosophy, lies beneath each phrase. Coleridge is here summarizing the great struggle and victory of his life—his triumph over the old tradition of Locke and Hartley, which had assumed that the mind in perception was wholly passive "a lazy looker-on on an external world".'

That is beautifully expressed, but when Coleridge discusses reason and understanding, he seems to use the words with inverse meaning and weight. He implies that reason denotes a wider comprehension than understanding. Surely the truth is just the reverse. Reason, with experiment, has enabled us to make practical use of electricity but we do not understand it. If we did we should probably not have to reason about it. A philosopher will reason about his fellow men but Christ understood them and there is no doubt as to the relative depth of wisdom. Study of the lives of great poets or mystics reveals that imagination gave them glimpses of a higher truth and profounder reality than reason can ever vouchsafe. The writing of a great scientist like Einstein confirms this in his own experience. Reason at best is but a half-truth because it parallels but does not pervade life. Understanding can never be achieved without participation in life. Understanding is essentially emotional. The work of art comes first and theory comes limping after. We fall in love and write poetry through understanding and not through reason.

The finest imagination is understanding on the highest level at a height that few ever attain, and those that do never, alas, for long. Reason alone never produces a work of art; though art may be the product of a great intellect, the driving and controlling power is deep emotional and imaginative understanding. The development of ecclesiastical art demonstrates how beauty vanished when reason was enthroned. There are plenty of intelligent people about today but no great art. It may be that the difficulty is quite a simple one; we do not begin the day's work on our knees in prayer.

> '*And would we ought behold, of higher worth,*
> *Than that inanimate cold world allowed*
> *To the poor loveless ever anxious crowd,*
> *Ah, from the soul itself must issue forth*
> *A light, a glory, a fair luminous cloud*
> *Enveloping the earth.*'

CHAPTER 16

The Sketch

—=·»o»(O»(»·=—

The first step is to draw the outline of the window to scale on a sheet of hot-pressed Whatman paper, or Bristol board if very fine line work is desired. Some artists put a thick band of tone either grey or brown or possibly black round this outline to emphasize the brilliance of the coloured sketch when completed. In the writer's personal opinion this is a mistake, but it is not easy to explain why and arguments are apt to be inconclusive. Some people find that the coloured sketch looks more luminous with a white surround than with a heavy contrasting band of colour. In theory the dark surround should emphasize the lightness of the design but in practice this is not always so. The only adequate comparison is that of a water colour painting. This looks best mounted on a wide white or cream board and no one would suggest putting a black or dark band round it to emphasize the colour.

The next step is to put in the position of the bars. There must of course be one at the springing line because a division of the window will take place at this point and the tie bar is necessary for constructional purposes. Some artists do not attempt to plan the position of the bars until they have worked out their design, but in the experience of many this has proved unsatisfactory as it leads to a lot of unnecessary difficulties.

The soundest point of view is that the bars should be placed in accordance with structural requirements. The shape, height and width of the window have to be taken into consideration and the design planned accordingly. The bars are essential and should obviously be placed where they are of most supporting value and the design arranged so that they give no interference. Normally the bars are not noticeable in the completed window. A personal anecdote may emphasize this point.

When I was working in partnership with Karl Parsons, formerly Master for Stained Glass at the South Kensington School of Art and the Central School of Arts and Crafts we used to leave the positioning of the bars until the design was completed. On one occasion Parsons had completed a design for an east window and had not indicated the position of the bars. We both tried our hand in arranging a satisfactory placing but failed to find a solution that pleased us, and in the end decided on a compromise that neither of us liked.

Soon after the window was in position the client kindly asked us to lunch after we had inspected the window. In the train on the way down we were both considerably worried about those bars, and I think that perhaps our main purpose in going was to find out what aesthetic damage those bars had done. I think that our first impression of the window as a whole was that it was a success, but I happened to notice that due to halation from the face and the chest, the neck of Our Lord in the rose tracery appeared to be shortened. As I had painted it this worried me considerably. Parsons on the other hand was upset about the blues. He thought that they had intensified in position, which this colour can very easily do. However the Vicar, the client and all the congregation were quite pleased. Parsons did not worry about the neck and I thought he was making an unnecessary fuss about the blue.

The lunch was superb and it was not until we were half-way back on our train journey that we both seemed to remember suddenly that we had not noticed the bars. The truth is that you do not normally notice the bars though of course they can affect the design to some extent by passing across some important feature. I first got the idea of putting in the bars at the beginning and settling it once and for all from Carl Edwards who had learned this method from James Hogan which shows that at least in practical matters tradition is of real value.

For a window of from 2′ to 2′ 6″ in width bars should be 1′ apart. For a window three feet or more in width the space between the bars should be reduced to 9″, whereas for a window less than 2′ wide the bars can be 18″ apart, or for a narrow window even 2′ apart. It is simply a question of giving the leaded window the necessary support to withstand stresses.

One other routine matter is best settled before the design is begun, i.e. whether or not to have a $\frac{1}{2}$″ fillet of white glass round the contour of the window. In a full-coloured window this fillet is desirable. It not only helps to keep the design two-dimensional and to preserve the outlines of the mullions and traceries but it also enables the window to be removed if necessary without damage to the glass, except of course for the white fillet which is easily repaired. There is no need to use a fillet for a quarry window. It does not help the design and so may be discarded as an unnecessary expense.

With regard to the design itself, and its technical execution it cannot be too strongly emphasized that slickness is the hall-mark of the trade hack. It might perhaps be called the occupational disease of the craft. The slick technician is the smart-alec of the art world, and, just as in daily life, his company soon palls. Probably more designers and cartoonists founder on this rock than from any other cause, particularly where firms are concerned. Slickness, like the smart-alec, only appeals to the ignorant. The danger is that in concentrating on technical dexterity, the designer is apt to forget the mood and subject that he is attempting to express. On the other hand to get some particular depth or subtlety of emotion or to realize some especial beauty, a certain spontaneity of technique may be lost. In a really fine stained glass design it is the whole conception that delights and any dexterity of technique will hardly be noticed.

Examination of the technique of Fra Angelico, Botticelli, El Greco or in fact of any of the masters will show not the slightest sign of slickness. A fine sensitive and expressive line is quite another matter. It is the difference between depth and superficiality. Most clients are cultured people and will appreciate the sincerity and dislike the superficial.

There is further the question as to the amount of finish that should be put into the design. Much depends upon the particular circumstances. It may be a matter of personal choice in the case of small windows, but where a large window is concerned, for which inevitably several assistants will be required, a high degree of finish is advantageous. Obviously a large window calls for unity and cohesion in the execution. The more precisely the detail is stated in the sketch, the less is the danger of misunderstanding and divergence. Line and tone and colour are determined whilst the whole conception is fresh in the mind. It must be remembered that as a rule months elapse between the completion of a sketch and the commencement of work upon the actual window. Martin Travers, undoubtedly one of the finest stained glass artists of his time, complained about this time lag: 'Very often, by the time I get the sketch back again I have forgotten what it is all about.' This is very understandable because in the interval the designer will certainly have been working with equal concentration on some entirely different project. It seems that the question of a highly finished sketch is not so much a matter of pleasing the client as of making a detailed statement that will completely recall to mind the designer's original plans and ideas.

No one can dogmatize about this. It is possible that as a work of art the sketch that is indicative and suggestive may have the greater aesthetic appeal, but the point is that it is the window that matters and not the sketch. The sketch is the means to an end. Unfortunately it is only too true that a fine design does not necessarily lead to a fine window, but it would seem obvious that everything should be done to promote the possibility of a fine window by a full exposition of the theme while this is clear in the designer's mind.

The actual method adopted is not of primary importance. When the design has been pencilled over carefully it may be gone over in black indian ink with the object of trying to get a balance of strength and delicacy in the line work which conveys a feeling of unity. The water colour may then be applied. Some craftsmen have experimented with touches of luminous paint but normally the only foreign matter used is occasional touches of red ink in the rubies.

If it is felt that the pure indian ink is too harsh and black it can be diluted with distilled water or again a sepia ink may be used. Any of these methods is satisfactory, and, providing the finished window is constantly kept in mind, it is a matter of personal taste and probably of what one considers will find most favour with the client.

This raises the question of presentability or showmanship. Probably nothing so impresses a client as a coloured transparency. From a practical point of view, except for showmanship, transparencies are a waste of time. The designer has depicted his colour scheme in the sketch (indeed the transparency will have been made from this) and the cutting of the glass is carried out by the cutter from the coloured design after consultation with the designer as to the correct interpretation of the colour values.

A transparency can be made on glass, celluloid, cellophane, perspex, or on a photographic film. Windsor and Newton supply bottles of the most suitable colouring medium for this process. The colour does not seem to be very durable but it will certainly last long enough for the transparency to be exhibited or submitted to a client.

Most sketches are carried out to an inch scale, but if the window is a particularly large one, $\frac{3}{4}''$ scale is more convenient, whereas if it is a question of a very small window or panel $1\frac{1}{2}''$ or $2''$ scale is advisable to prevent the result from looking too insignificant in size.

It is always worth while mounting a sketch. This not only shows the work off to the best advantage but it helps to ensure better treatment from the various hands through which it may pass in the committee stage.

CHAPTER 17

Cartooning

—————=•○•◇◇◇◇◇○◇◇◇○◇◇•○•=—————

The cartoon can be prepared as soon as the design has been finally approved and any necessary faculty has been granted. For windows other than rectangular a template is necessary to ensure the accuracy of the shaped heads. The templates can usually be taken during the period when the design is being passed through its various committee stages.

It is best to have the template taken by the glazier if possible so that should there be any mistake in the size when the window is fixed there can be no dispute as to the responsibility for the error. If this is not convenient or if the window is to be situated abroad, any builder or competent carpenter can supply the template. Sometimes it is carefully cut out from a thin sheet of wood or hardboard but brown paper templates are quite satisfactory.

If the window is rectangular no template is required because the shape can easily be determined by measurement which should always be taken sight or daylight size; that is, the shape of the window opening as seen against the daylight. The depth of the rebate or groove should be ascertained.

An architect's $\frac{1}{4}''$ or $\frac{1}{2}''$ scale elevation of a window is all that is needed for making the coloured design but it is certainly not accurate enough for drawing out the full-size cartoon. This needs to have exactly the same shape and measurements as the actual window opening and there is often considerable, though not observable, difference between the masonry when built and the architect's full-scale drawings. Architects seldom care to admit this, and yet it is this very fact which adds to the quality of their work.

For example, it is possible to make well-proportioned Gothic windows in cast iron and to colour them to resemble stone. The effect is harsh and mechanical precisely because it lacks those slight inaccuracies which give a quality to craftwork. This is why the idea of prefabricated standardized churches is a modern blasphemy and obeisance to mammon rather than to God. Architects are usually among the first to appreciate the beauty of hand-made tableware in contrast to that made by mass production methods in moulds, yet in modern architecture they often seem content with the aesthetic standards of a Woolworth's store.

It is because of these variations in the masonry made by craftsmen that it is necessary for an exact template to be made of the heads of each of the lights and the tracery openings. The template of the head of the light is taken from the springing line. Then the length from the springing line to the base of the window is carefully measured and also the width of the light.

The height from the springing line to the apex of the window should be measured and added to the length from the springing line to the base. This gives the overall height of the window. A separate measurement, ignoring the springing line, should be taken from the base of the window to the apex to act as a check. If the measurements do not agree, they must all be re-taken until complete accuracy is achieved. It is often necessary to take each measurement three or four times to make certain that there is no error. This may seem rather tedious but it is nothing compared with the trouble that can arise through inaccurate measurements.

A steel six foot spring rule is most useful. By this means a height can often be reached that would be inaccessible to a two foot rule, and time saved in searching for a possibly non-existent ladder.

Ordinary brown paper or white lining paper is quite satisfactory for taking the template or pattern, if the window is not too wide. A simple method is as follows: cut a piece that is just a few inches larger than the opening in the masonry. Then place this centrally in position against the glass, having cut a few gores to prevent creasing or wrinkling when the edges of the paper are forced against the shape of the masonry. Carefully run the finger round the shape of the glass and when the paper seems to fit accurately run a pencil round it. Cut the pattern carefully to this pencil line, removing the surplus paper and then, having apparently made an entirely accurate pattern of the window opening replace it in position to see if it fits.

The chances are that it will be an $\frac{1}{8}''$ too big in one place and too small in another. Where it is still too big the extra bit can be removed, but where it is just a little too small, a note on the paper to this effect will enable the necessary correction to be made on the cartoon and cutline. If the error is considerable a fresh attempt must obviously be made. A pattern that is, say, $\frac{1}{4}''$ too big all round will be much easier to fit into position, and if it is accurately pencilled round, on cutting out an exact fit should be obtained.

It is important to mark on the template not only the particular light to which it belongs, but also which is the inside of the template. As has already been suggested the shaped head of the light may not be symmetrical, so that if the glass were cut to the reverse shape it might be impossible to fit it into position.

If, as is often the case, the templates have to be taken from a ladder, it is helpful to use a little gum to stick the brown paper in position on the glass—not all over but just a spot or two to hold it up temporarily. This leaves both the hands free for manipulating the edges of the paper carefully into position.

With this information the exact sight size of the window is drawn out on a large piece of cartoon paper. The template of the head of the light should be placed on the cartoon paper and carefully marked round the outline in pencil, exactly marking the

The Nativity.   The Good Shepherd.

Cartoons by Burne-Jones, Whitefriars Studios.

P<small>LATE</small> 65.

ANGELVM ASCENDENTEM A
ORTV SOLIS HABENTEM
✠ SIGNVM DEI VIVI ✠

Cartoon by
Marjorie Walters.

Cartoon by
Colwyn Morris.

Whitefriars Studios.

PLATE 66.

springing line which must be accurately drawn at right angles to the perpendicular sides. The length from the springing line is measured down the paper, and the sides of the window and the base pencilled in. The position of the bars and divisions should be clearly marked by pencil lines drawn across and just outside the outline of the window, and an indication should be made as to where the sections are to be cut. This may be a help when cartooning to prevent any important detail in the cartoon from being obscured by a bar or cut. All these operations are best carried out with the paper on a flat table.

There are various methods of enlarging the sketch. Probably the most common practice is the traditional one of the old masters, that of dividing the sketch into squares say $\frac{1}{3}''$ in size and dividing the cartoon into squares of $4''$. This is obviously conditioned by the fact that the sketch has been drawn inch-scale, but the method can be employed whatever the scale.

Some craftsmen draw the correct outline of the light on to the cartoon paper, pin the paper up on a wall or screen in the dark room and project the sketch on to it by means of an epidiascope. If a photograph has been taken an enlarging camera can be used. One artist is known to put the cartoon paper on to a glass easel and then work on the opposite side to the rays of light coming from the camera or epidiascope. These methods, are, of course, only used to place the main lines and general position of details.

Other artists have their designs enlarged to full size by photography. All these methods have their advantages and disadvantages. It is doubtful if much time is saved by one method rather than another. The enlarged photograph has the advantage perhaps of keeping to the original character of the sketch which is apt to get lost in the labour and time taken by the other methods, but this enlargement will need working on to make adjustments and minor corrections, and the surface of the paper is not suitable for this purpose. There is much to be said in favour of photographing the original sketch to about twice the size and then working up this enlargement to a clear definition of detail. If this is carefully done the final full-size enlargement made from it will be quite satisfactory for painting from and can be cutlined straight away.

On the other hand some cartoonists ignore all the expedients and merely rely on the position of the bars or on measuring the position of the principal features such as the top of the head, hands or feet and so on. Whichever method is used is only a means to an end and it is obviously the final product that is important.

The amount of finish to be given to a cartoon depends to a large extent upon the way in which the window is to be carried out. For example, if the glass is to be painted by the artist himself, he will only need to put sufficient detail in the cartoon to enable him to trace the drawing on to the glass. He will only need the slightest indication of shading, if any, as he can easily paint this on the glass. To work up the tone work on the cartoon would not only be a waste of time but indeed a disadvantage because if the cartoon is heavily shaded it makes it more difficult to trace the main lines of folds in the drapery etc. on to the coloured glass. It may be, however, that the painting will be done by someone else, in which case it is obvious that the more information that can be given in the cartoon the better. But unless a cartoon is needed for exhibition purposes, once the window has been completed it is stored away and possibly never seen again. Generally speaking a cartoon should be a working drawing, a means to an end and not an end itself.

It is perhaps unnecessary to mention that a figure in a Renaissance or naturalistic style will need much more shading than a figure designed with decorative line work harmonizing with a general pattern.

Everyone agrees that the ideal method of production is for the artist to carry out practically every process of the work himself; certainly the cartooning, the choosing and cutting of the glass and the painting. But in practice, particularly where a large window is concerned, the time factor nearly always prevents this. Nevertheless one of our leading artists does cartoon, cut the class and paint it himself. The result is that the number of windows he produces is extremely limited and his well-wishers are sorry that he will not allow himself more assistance.[1]

One of the more important considerations in cartooning is to preserve the colour pattern of the original design. For example in making the full-size drawing one might feel that by enlarging a particular swirl of drapery the figure would be given additional vitality, but this enlargement of drapery might obscure a piece of ruby background very necessary to the colour background. The perfect cartoon would give the most satisfactory arrangement of line and mass, with a pleasing pattern of colour.

There is not only the danger of adding deliberately to the original design; there is also the difficulty of preserving faithfully the proportions of the silhouettes, which of course make up the pattern. For example, the proportions of a head in the sketch might be something like the diagram marked A.

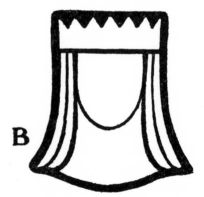

An inexperienced cartoonist struggling with the difficulties of drawing the features might produce a silhouette something like B. Now no amount of skill in drawing the features will compensate for the bad proportions. The figure would never look dignified simply because the proportions of the silhouette are wrong. This may seem very

[1] I think I can speak impartially on this matter as I have carried out every process from cutting the glass to the fixing the window in position myself, and I am convinced that a certain amount of assistance is beneficial. Moreover, there is, I believe, little doubt that some of the masterpieces of the past were carried out by a master craftsman and his assistants.

obvious, but painful experience proves how difficult it is to get some cartoonists to appreciate the importance of the silhouette and pattern values.

If a design is at all successful it is almost impossible to improve on its general proportions in working out the full-size cartoon. This is one of the advantages of enlarging a sketch by photography; the pattern and the character of the sketch is maintained. It is true that a design may sometimes have a generally pleasing effect and yet contain some anatomical impossibility, which, though hardly noticeable in the small scale design, will be quite apparent when drawn out full size. The cartoonist might then rightly complain that the design has not been properly worked out; as a rule, however, the function of the full-size cartoon is the working out of the detail that cannot be so easily achieved in the small scale design.

When cartooning one should control the emphasis of the internal line to support the main silhouette. Most people are familiar with the experiment of drawing two lines of equal length and then making slight additions which will make one appear shorter or longer than the other.

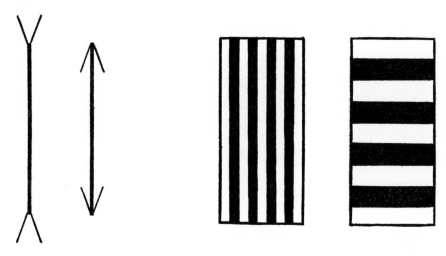

Similarly every woman knows that vertical or horizontal lines can be used to add to the apparent length or shortness of the figure. These considerations are important in the full-size drawing no less than in the design.

The artist may not be conscious of these particular principles at work, but he must constantly take into account what effect any particular line or detail has upon the proportions of the work as a whole. This is helped by judging the work from a distance rather than with the eyes a few inches away from the drawing.

In practically all windows it is advisable to make the figure nine heads tall. This measurement does not seem out of proportion when the window is in position. It will simply give a measure of dignity to the figure which would inevitably look dumpy if the natural proportion of seven and a half heads tall were adhered to. For a figure that is to be seen at a great height, ten heads tall is not excessive as this helps to counteract the foreshortening.

The effect of halation or the spreading of light must be kept in mind, though this can to some extent be counteracted in the painting. If a chequer of black and white squares is drawn with the squares of equal size, from a distance the white squares will look considerably larger than the black. This is simply due to the spreading of white light. Even in a window that is placed in a position near the eye, the light portions will tend to be enlarged and the darker passages correspondingly reduced. It follows that in a window that will be seen from a distance, halation can cause considerable distortion and due allowance must be made for this. For example, in a border of small white circles or pearls it might be necessary to have an inch of black between each circle; otherwise from the distance they would appear as a continuous line.

Similar considerations affect the choice of lead, which should be drawn on the cartoon with reasonable accuracy as to the width. If this is left to the cutlining, important detail may be interfered with and the pattern disturbed.

PLATE 67. Uncompleted and completed cartoon by Aidan Savage, Whitefriars Studios.

SAINT MICHAEL

PLATE 68. Cartoon by Alfred Fisher,
Whitefriars Studios.

CHAPTER 18

Cutline

When the full-size cartoon is complete, the cutline is made from which the pieces of glass will be cut. This is done by placing a large sheet of transparent tracing linen over the cartoon and carefully drawing a line down the centre of each lead shown on the cartoon. The selvedge of the linen should be torn off otherwise it will crinkle at the edges and not lie perfectly flat. Cutlines can be made from tracing paper and other materials but, as a rule, this is not advisable as they will not stand up to the wear and tear of the workshop. The cutline has first to be used for cutting every piece of glass and is finally laid on the glazing bench for the final leading up of the whole window.

First an outline is carefully drawn giving the exact size of the shape of the window opening. When the glass is leaded a $\frac{1}{2}''$ lead will be centrally placed over this outline thus enlarging the window by $\frac{1}{4}''$ all round. This extra $\frac{1}{4}''$ fits into the groove or rebate in the masonry when the window is fixed in position so that the actual shape of the glass corresponds with that of the daylight opening of the masonry.

Tracing linen has a slightly greasy surface and will not take either ink or paint. If the lines are first drawn in pencil it will be found that either ink or paint will mark quite well on top of the pencil line. Another method is to dust the surface of the linen all over with powdered french chalk, rub this well in and then brush off. This will remove the grease sufficiently for the ink or paint to become effective.

Cutlining is by no means a mechanical procedure and is best carried out by someone with an appreciation of design and an understanding of the subsequent craft processes. In ideal circumstances every artist will wish to make his own cutline to emphasize the particular quality of the design. Slight adjustments are continually necessary. For example, in drawing the position of the lead round a hand, care must be taken to prevent the lead from overlapping the contour of the hand. For this reason, the size of the piece of glass will probably need to be slightly increased.

Again, where a dark piece of drapery is adjacent to a white or very light piece, the dark portion should be very slightly enlarged and the white correspondingly decreased. This is to allow for halation.

The main outline leads of the figures are used for emphasis and are usually wider than the secondary type of leads called the arbitraries. The extra width of the outside lead may be indicated on the cartoon but if not, the necessary adjustment must be allowed for on the cutline. The outline or silhouette lead of a figure may vary from $\frac{3}{8}''$ to $\frac{5}{8}''$, but in certain cases, for example where a window is to be fixed at a great height, $1''$ or even $1\frac{1}{4}''$ lead is not excessive.

The arbitraries are usually $\frac{1}{4}''$ or $\frac{3}{8}''$ according to the width of the outline leads of the figures. They cut across the drawing of the folds of drapery etc. and can be skilfully used to quieten certain passages in the design and to build up a pleasing pattern in the cutline itself. It is possible to get a fair idea of whether or not a window is reasonably good merely by looking at the cutline, since this indicates the general proportions of the figures and shows the pattern of the mosaic of glass. In a grisaille or a purely ornamental window any lack of design must be obvious in the cutline; it is just as much so in windows with figure work.

A pencil line indicating the position of each bar should be drawn across the cutline but not inked in or painted in black. Part of this line should be used to form the edge of alternate pieces of glass as shown in the diagram. The alternate pieces of glass should cross the line of the bar to ensure the stability of the window and to help it stand the stress of the wind against the bar.

At the ends of several of the leads, following horizontally the line of the bar, copper wire ties will be fixed. When the window is in position these will be fastened to the bar fixed in the masonry, thus helping to hold the window rigidly in position.

The position of the copper ties should not be shown in the cutline. This can be left to the discretion of the experienced glaziers who often have the additional job of fixing the window and therefore have most practical knowledge. The position of the bars and also the sectional cuts should be shown on the outside outline of the cutline as indicated in the diagram. If in doubt about alternative positions for the cuts it is well to consult the glazier or fixer. Naturally there is the question of weight and convenience in handling, especially if the work has to be done from a ladder.

When the cutline has been carefully pencilled in, all the lines should be gone over cleanly and firmly with black water-colour or poster paint. It is not advisable to use ink, partly because it is liable to run, but chiefly because it is difficult to erase if a mistake is made or some alteration be necessary. The paint can be removed if necessary with a piece of clean rag and a little water.

Whether one is cutting the glass oneself or whether this is being done by an assistant it is helpful to indicate on the cutline the colour of the pieces of glass to be used; Y for yellow, R for ruby and so on. With so many pieces it is at times very easy to make a mistake in the colour. The cutter should have the coloured sketch in front of him and the cartoon should be available if he requires it. This also helps him to avoid a mistake in colour or tone value. He has plenty to think about in concentrating upon following the subtleties of the colour scheme, and any help that can be devised is clearly an advantage.

It is useful to mark on the top and on the bottom of the cutline brief details such as 'St. Paul's L'pool. East window. Centre Light'. This saves the tedium of unrolling to find the particular cutline needed from amongst a clutter of rolls.

CHAPTER 19

Cutting

Cutting the glass is possibly the most fascinating of all the craft processes connected with the production of a window. The material has a beauty and fascination that is captivating. In contrast to water-colour or oil paint one is dealing with scintillating gleams of coloured light. There is excitement in finding an especially interesting and beautiful variation and it is doubtful if anyone except a stained glass artist has such a realization of how many myriads of tints and combinations of tints actually exist.

The cutline completed, it is taken together with the cartoon and coloured sketch to the cutting bench, so that all the necessary information is at hand. The first procedure is to choose sheets of the principal colours used in the design: possibly ruby, green, blue, yellow and madder. These should be placed as near together as possible on a window ledge against the light and various tints tried until a pleasing harmony which represents the main colour scheme is achieved. The particular tint of white to be used for the flesh is then chosen. It may be greenish in hue, or yellow, brown or neutral according to the colour scheme and the position of the window in the church. If it is to be set at a great height darker tones of flesh will be needed to counteract the halation.

It is usual to cut the flesh glass first, especially where, as is often the case, the painting will not be done by the person who cuts the glass. The drawing of the heads etc. can then be traced on the glass whilst the rest of the window is being cut. The cutline is placed on the bench and a sheet of whitish flesh glass is placed over the portion to be cut. A section is first cut from the main sheet so that it just covers the shape to be cut. For figure work an ordinary glazier's cutting wheel is used.

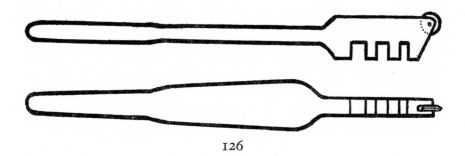

126

A diamond is best for cutting straight lines but it is not satisfactory for curved shapes. The wheel is then run round the form to be cut following the shape of the cutline just inside the line. The piece of glass will thus be slightly smaller to allow for the heart of the lead in glazing. When cutting it is important not to press too heavily on the glass as this merely stars it and makes a crack liable to fly off in the wrong direction. The cutter should penetrate only the surface of the glass. This releases stresses in the structure so that when the glass is tapped along the line of the cut it breaks right through its thickness. On completion of each cut it is important to run the side of the cutter or the grozing pliers along the newly cut edges to remove minute flakes of glass and to blunt the razor-like sharpness of the edge. Otherwise cuts on the finger are bound to happen in the subsequent handling.

The correct technique is to draw the wheel towards one when cutting. To the uninitiated the obvious method would be the reverse, as by this means it is easier to see and follow the shape of the line. In fact excellent cutting has been done by what is generally regarded as the wrong method.

Complicated shapes in a cutline are, as a rule, indicative of bad designing or cartooning. The simple shape has a strength which is frittered away by elaborations. A simple example of this is illustrated. Part of the wing might be cartooned or cutlined either as A or B, and it is at once obvious to most craftsmen that the wobbly line B is unsatisfactory.

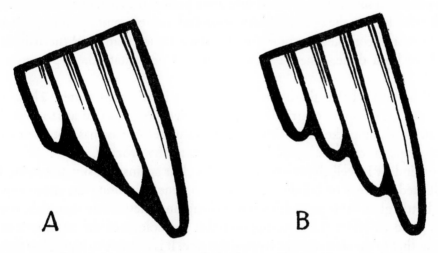

Occasions may however arise when a difficult piece has to be cut, so it is just as well to know how the job should be tackled. If a shape of glass is to be cut as shown in A, the first step is to cut out from the main sheet of glass B the simple outside shape of A. It is advisable to run the wheel over the curved line as well and tap it, so that a clear cut is shown right through the glass. The odd pieces of the main sheet are next tapped and broken off. This leaves the piece of glass A as shown in Fig. 2, having the semicircular piece of glass held firmly in position, although the wheel cut has gone right through the thickness of the glass. The difficulty is to remove this section without breaking off the glass on either side of it.

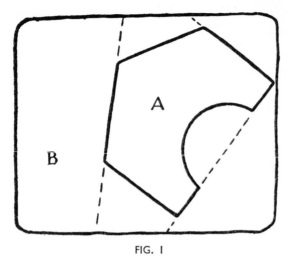

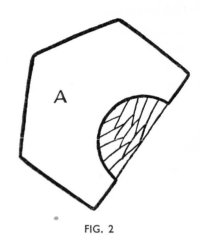

FIG. 1   FIG. 2

This semi-circular section can be removed simply by grozing, i.e. taking off little bits at a time beginning from the centre of the outside edge; but it is safer and quicker to make a series of wheel cuts somewhat as shown in the diagram and tap these gently until the cuts penetrate right through the glass. The small sections may then fall out, though in some cases it is preferable to groze out each small section separately.

When the pieces are out and the edges of the glass have been smoothed, the shaped glass is placed on the cutline to make sure it is a perfect fit. Each piece as cut should be carefully checked on the cutline before being laid out for painting. It is obviously far better to ensure complete accuracy at this stage rather than after the painting and firing have been done, when a breakage would necessitate these processes being repeated.

It will be noticed that there are three notches in the glass cutter. These are for grozing off, i.e. chipping or grinding off small pieces of glass that are too small to be removed by tapping the line of the cut. If the piece of glass has not been cut per-fectly to shape the error can sometimes be corrected by grozing.

If the window is well above eye-level and is clear against the sky, not being in any way affected by trees or buildings, there is no benefit in using the more expensive slab or bottle glass. Antique, which is not cheap but is less costly than slab, will pro-duce as good an effect. This presupposes that the colour of the antique is as satis-factory as that of the slab and this is often the case. It is possible to have glass that is too brilliant or strong in colour. The benefit of slab glass is that, having much more variation in thickness than antique, it acts more like a prism in reflecting and re-fracting a greater proportion of light. For this reason in any position where the light is not as adequate as one would wish there is a definite advantage in using slab or bottle glass.

When cutting white or light-coloured glass it is easy to see the lines of the cutline through the glass, but when darker shades of colour are being used it is impossible to see through the glass when it is laid flat upon the cutting bench. To overcome this difficulty a sloping sheet of plate glass is placed upon a supporting frame against the

Drawing the full-size cartoon.

Cutting the glass to the various shapes.

PLATE 69.

PLATE 70. Painting the glass.

light with a piece of mirror glass on the other side adjusted so that it reflects the light through the cutline which rests on the sloping sheet of glass (See Figure below). The lines on the cutline can now be seen through the piece of coloured glass. The advantage of this type of frame is that it can be folded up and put away when not in use.

The next figure shows a simple workshop table with a sheet of plate glass permanently fixed on the top, and a sheet of mirror placed beneath it. In the table illustrated the mirror can be adjusted to various angles to suit the position most convenient to work in. It can be used for tracing and also for applying Brunswick black enamel paint as described in the chapter on aciding.

Should neither plate glass nor reflecting mirror be available there are two ways in which the problem may be tackled.

METHOD 1. Make a paper template from the cutline just a little smaller than the shape that it is to be cut.

Place the template on the piece of coloured glass and cut round the edges.

METHOD 2. Take a piece of very thin but tough brown paper and chalk it completely all over with ordinary white school chalk.

Blow off the dust.

Place the sheet of glass on the bench and put the brown paper in position on top of it, with the chalked surface next to the glass.

Place the cutline on top of them both.

With a very hard pencil go over the shape of the piece required following the inside of the line of the cutline.

Carefully remove the cutline and the brown paper.

Blow the loose chalk dust off the glass, when a thin white outline of the shape will

I

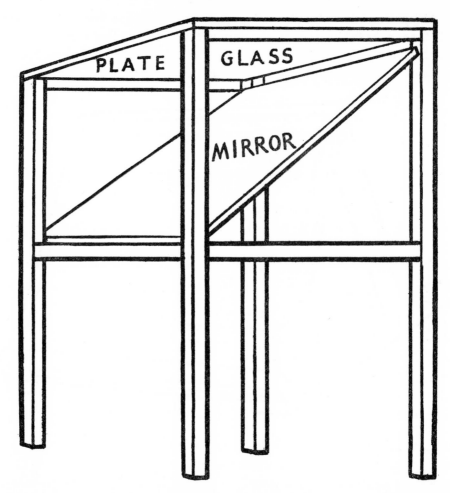

be visible. Care must be taken in handling as the chalk line comes off with the slight-est touch.

Both these methods waste time compared with the more efficient procedure of using the plate glass and reflecting mirror.

The quality of colour in any piece of glass depends largely upon its variation of tint and depth of colour. The unpleasantness of a sheet of uniform blue, seen too often in cheap domestic glass, is due to its even colour. If part of the blue flash is unevenly acided off, this cheap glass can become quite pleasant in appearance. On occasion, if the requisite tint is not available in slab or antique aciding this cheap glass will give the desired effect but it is no economy on account of the time and labour involved.

Some artists resort to plating and even tend to boast about it, but it is best avoided. 'Double plating' is the leading up of two glasses of the same shape, one behind the other. It is unsound craftsmanship. There is always the extra risk of one of the pieces cracking, and there is likely to be condensation between the two pieces of glass. The difficulty of preventing the cement from running between the two pieces of glass can be overcome with due care, but it is absurd to imagine that the beauty of any window can depend upon the practice of plating of which there is no trace in medieval glass.

This is a matter that must be decided by the individual artist, bearing in mind that it is on occasion a necessary evil, e.g. the size of a Union Jack might be too small for the blue and ruby to be leaded separately.

The quality of colour in a window depends not only on the harmony of its main tints but also upon the minor variations in each colour used. The old craftsmen understood this very well. As previously mentioned, in a fine copy of a Ravenna mosaic, the writer counted a dozen different shades of green in the tesserae which from a short distance combined to produce a patch of quiet but refreshing colour. It would be quite impossible to achieve such an effect by using one shade of colour alone, however pleasant it might be in itself. As the pointillist school have emphasized, it would lack vibration. A similar patch of colour recently studied in a pre-war English mosaic showed only four or five variations, which bears out the saying that genius is an infinite capacity for taking pains.

When cutting a piece of flashed glass that has to be acided, possibly for some detail in heraldry, it is necessary to cut with the flash uppermost. To do this one has to turn the cutline over and work on the reverse side, thus cutting the glass on the opposite side to the flash. The reason for this is that the flash is thin and also hard to cut. When the flash is marked with the cutting wheel, the major thickness of the glass is unaffected. If, however, the glass is turned over, the cut is made on the major thickness of the glass which then breaks, where desired, the thin flash being broken off with it.

As each piece is cut it should be laid out on the bench or in a tray in position and a slight tick or mark made on the cutline to show that it has been cut. There are often hundreds of pieces of glass in a window and confusion among them may cause considerable loss of time.

Cutting is a fascinating and exciting job. With an oil- or water-colour painting the value of each colour added can be seen at once in relation to the rest of the picture. With glass there is not this advantage. At best half-a-dozen pieces can be held up, a very small fraction of the whole window, for the effect to be judged. It is not until all the pieces have been cut and waxed up together that the appearance and value of their colour as a whole can be studied properly. A certain amount of recutting will almost certainly be necessary, but this should be reduced to the minimum because most unsatisfactory pieces are found to be too small for use in another window and are therefore thrown away.

CHAPTER 20

Aciding

This process is the only part of stained glass technique that can be described as unpleasant. It is certainly the one that is least enjoyable. If possible it should be avoided but unfortunately there are occasions when it becomes necessary.

Perhaps the most obvious example is in heraldry. For instance, if the blazon of one of the quarterings of a shield is Rouge three lions regardant or, indicating three yellow lions on a red ground, the area of the shield is very small. Indeed, unless the shield is fairly large there will be no room to place even the smallest of leads round each lion and leave sufficient space for the ruby ground to show through.

In such a case all the parts of the glass on which the ruby must be retained are painted over with Brunswick black enamel, Japan black or some similar paint. The glass must, of course, have been cut with the ruby flash uppermost.

If the line is not too delicate and intricate the necessary parts can be covered with beeswax. The advantage of this is that the wax cools at once on application to the surface of the glass and the aciding can proceed immediately. The disadvantage is that the melted wax, even with a fine brush, cannot be accurately controlled.

If Brunswick black is used it must be left to dry very thoroughly before the next process, which is to place the glass in a shallow tray and pour over it a mixture of hydrofluoric acid. This of course requires skilful handling and care must be taken not to get any acid on one's flesh or clothing. If the hand is accidentally touched with acid it should be immersed immediately in water; this dilutes and stops the action of the acid. Even the fumes arising from the working acid are harmful, and many a craftsman has been kept awake at night by the pain in his hands caused only by the fumes from the acid.

Rubber gloves, like those of an operating surgeon, can be worn, but in handling the glass care must be taken not to cause a cut without its being noticed, because if this should occur the acid may pass through the rubber and get well soaked into the hand before treatment can be given.

The safest method is to rub the hands all over with Vaseline before starting work. This is rather a messy procedure but not as unpleasant as the action of acid on the flesh.

Many craftsmen, however, take no precautions of any kind and simply rely on care to avoid contact with the acid or its fumes. Others fix up an aciding cupboard with a ventilation hole and fan that draws all the air away, and this is probably the best method. It is a problem that has to be solved according to general working conditions. The simplest way of all is to do the work in the open air keeping to the windward of the fumes, but obviously this is not always convenient in our unreliable climate.

When the acid is poured onto the glass it becomes coated with a white or grey film. This should be removed so that the acid can continue to work on the uncovered glass. The best way to do this is to fix a piece of cotton wool or cloth on to the end of a piece of stick and use this as a swab.

It is best to work near a water tap in case of accidents. If this is not available then have a pail of water handy into which the hands can be immersed in case of emergency. Strong soda solution or ammonia has the effect of neutralizing the acid but usually the pail of water suffices.

When the acid has worked down cleanly to the underneath glass, and all the ruby has been removed, the acided piece of glass is taken out of the tray and washed thoroughly in cold water. The black paint is then removed by scraping with a flat knife disclosing a piece of ruby glass with the shapes of three lions, or whatever the subject may be, showing in white or yellow. The flash may have been on yellow or white according to the quality of yellow desired.

If the ruby has been flashed on white, it will be necessary at a later stage after the painting and firing, to apply silver stain to produce the required yellow for the lions. This is usually the best method as it allows for a greater variety of colour in the yellow.

There are also occasions when it is advantageous to acid the glass, not to take out the colour from the background for a particular object, but to get variety or quality in the colour itself.

For example, for the reproduction in colour of a red brick wall, it might so happen that the only type of glass which could give the requisite red translucency compared with the colour of the surrounding glass would be, not antique or slab, but simply sheet ruby.

This ruby is not an unpleasant colour in itself but it is uninteresting because it is uniform in colour and texture all over its surface. To draw the brick wall on this would produce a harsh and strident result. It is therefore advisable to acid off part of the ruby flash unevenly, giving the glass variation of tone and quality. When treated in this manner the sheet ruby is aesthetically very pleasing and the only disadvantage in making a practice of using it is the time, trouble and unpleasantness of aciding.

Quite apart from the unpleasantness of the work, from an aesthetic point of view aciding should usually be avoided. People have been known to spend hours aciding sheets of ruby and sheets of blue with extremely careful gradations of colour so that when they are plated and stained yellow in the appropriate places, and with the appropriate strength, they produce a perfect rainbow effect.

Technically this is no mean achievement but artistically it is futile. It produces a far more pleasing and decorative effect if the various coloured glasses are leaded together. In any case the rainbow is not one of nature's major artistic achievements. An aurora borealis is impressive and sunsets and sunrises sometimes superb but at best a rainbow is a pretty affair and if desirable as a symbol is best treated decoratively and not realistically.

Another use of acid is to remove imperfect stain. It is always a highly debatable point when staining has gone wrong as to whether the fault lies in the way the oxide of silver has been applied or whether it is due to overfiring. As the artist more often applies the stain and the firing is done by the kilnsman, it is natural for the designer to believe that the error lies in the firing, but whatever the truth of this, the faulty stain has to be removed by aciding.

A small piece of cloth fastened on to a thin piece of wood is dipped into the acid and swabbed round the stain on the back of the piece of glass until sufficient has been taken off to give the desired effect, or, should this prove unsuccessful, until every trace of stain has been removed so that the process of staining can be begun afresh.

Acid is also occasionally used when it is noted, after firing, that a piece of glass has been overpainted so that the tones are too dark. To save time in recutting and repainting, the piece of fired glass can be placed in a weak solution of acid and the shading thus partially or wholly removed. After being thoroughly rinsed in water it can be touched up with paint where necessary and refired. There are times when it may be expedient to adopt this method, although it must be said that as a rule it is far better to recut and repaint the unsatisfactory piece of glass.

CHAPTER 21

Painting

All the glass has been cut and any necessary aciding completed. The pieces are laid out in trays correctly placed and looking somewhat like sections of a jig-saw puzzle. Indeed it must have been the early medieval glaziers who first practised this modern pastime.

The cartoon is placed on a bench or flat table-top of convenient height in a good light and from one of the trays a piece of glass is selected. If, as is likely, it is dirty and greasy, it must be thoroughly cleaned. The handiest method is to pick up a brush, dip it in some paint diluted with water and dab this on to the glass. Then with a piece of rag or newspaper rub it all on both sides until both surfaces are perfectly clean.

Most craftsmen start by tracing the heads, hands and feet—the flesh as they are called—though there is no absolute necessity about this order of precedence. Usually, however, it fits in best with the general scheme of work.

For example, once the flesh colour has been chosen it can be quickly cut straight-away. There are no further subtleties of flesh tints to search out. It will all be cut in the same tint of glass.

The cutting of the coloured drapery, background etc., takes very much longer owing to the necessity for choosing varying tints of the blue or other colour. So once the flesh tint has been cut it can be traced by the painter whilst the cutter carries on cutting the rest of the window.

The piece of comparatively clear glass is placed exactly in position over the drawing of the head, hand or foot as the case may be and the lines of the drawing on the cartoon carefully traced on the glass. At this stage any shading is ignored.

The tracing can be done either with paint thoroughly mixed with water and a little gum arabic or with the same mixture to which a little vinegar or acetic acid has been added. This mixture must be ground on a sheet of ground glass with a pestle or palette knife until it is perfectly smooth and has a silky sheen. Thorough mixing is very necessary to obtain a fine and flowing line.

It is the practice in some studios to fire this first tracing in the kiln but many sound craftsmen regard this as an inefficient method, wasteful of time and money. More-over, it prevents any modification of the traced line in subsequent painting, and until the glass has been assembled on the easel and the various parts seen in relation to the whole, it cannot be certain that some modification of the traced line may not be advisable.

A more satisfactory method is to add a little white vinegar or acetic acid to the paint. This makes no difference to the smooth flowing of the paint but it has the advantage of setting very hard, and although it can be removed or modified with a stick or needle it remains firm when covered over with a water matt.

When all the tracing has been completed, the outline is fastened to one side of the glass easel which is laid flat upon a bench or trestles so that all the pieces of glass can now be placed correctly in position.

The easiest way to fix the cutline is to make small V-shaped cuts in the linen. These can then be lifted at their points and a drop of melted beeswax dropped on to the glass through the opening. The V-shaped flap of linen is then pressed back flat on to the glass and the cutline is held firmly in position. If this is done at points about eighteen inches apart, the whole cutline will be securely held flat against the glass.

All the pieces can then be laid out, with a slight gap left between each piece which allows for the heart of the lead when glazing. The end of a pointed piece of glass or metal is dipped into a small saucepan containing melted beeswax and a drop of the hot beeswax placed at each corner of each piece of glass so that it adheres to the glass of the easel.

As soon as this process has been completed the whole layout is tested by tapping each piece to make sure that they are all firmly fixed. If the piece is secure the sound of the tap is dull, but if the wax is not holding it firmly a slight crack is heard, and another spot of melted beeswax is dropped to hold it.

The easel is lifted and placed in an upright position resting against two struts of 2″ by 2″ fixed firmly in front of the window. A cord, with weights suitably adjusted, is hooked to each side of the easel which can then be raised to any convenient height for painting. This can, perhaps, be more easily visualized with the help of the diagram.

The cutline fastened to the easel by wax can easily be taken off by a slight tug and the wax removed by a flat-ended knife or scraper.

Now that the work is seen as a whole for the first time against the light it is possible to judge the amount of success achieved in the selection and cutting of the glass. No doubt some pieces will appear either too light or too dark or else the wrong tint of colour, but it is advisable to delay final decisions until the lead lines have been put in.

The process of mixing the paint for leadlining is rather a messy one. It consists in placing some soot on a sheet of ground glass and trying to persuade it to be mixed with water. The allusiveness with which it evades both the palette knife and the water can only be credited by anyone who has made the attempt. Its successful accomplishment is a triumph of mind over matter.

Once a black mass with a consistency of well-kneaded putty has been obtained, a drop or two of liquid gum arabic is gradually added. The effect of this addition is rather astonishing. The unaccommodating lump of material becomes an easily workable quantity of fluid paint with a consistency resembling that of cream.

The black lead lines are painted on the glass of the easel, on the reverse of the side to which the pieces of coloured glass adhere, and these lines approximate to the effect of the actual lead in the finished window.

Some firms and painters omit this process of lead lining and paint the glass with pure white light shining between each piece of glass, but the majority find that it is more satisfactory to use the lead lines.

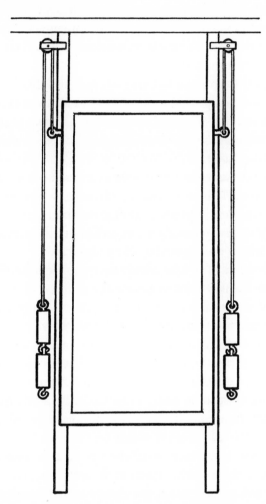

At this stage final decisions must be made as regards colour and recutting where necessary.

A proportion of glass paint is then very thoroughly mixed and what is known as a matt applied to the glass. The process of painting on glass is rather similar to that of drawing with white chalk and charcoal on brown paper.

The pieces of glass are taken one by one, and carefully covered with an even wash of paint applied with a soft sable brush of about 1″ in width. Before the paint has time to dry, it is gently smoothed as evenly as possible all over with a long-haired badger. This brush made of badger hair 3″ or 4″ long is nowadays an expensive part of the painting equipment.

The time that a matt takes to dry varies with the weather but in any case it is only a matter of minutes and if for some reason it is necessary to hurry the process, this can be done by fanning the surface with air by means of the badger. Technical considerations prevent a too exuberant application, since, if the paint is applied too heavily on the glass, it will fry, that is to say when the glass is fired the paint will bubble up into an uneven surface, only partly adhering to the glass. When the glass is taken out of the kiln this partly adhered paint has to be scraped off, leaving an uneven pitted surface which should be sandpapered to make it as smooth again as possible.

All this is a deterrent to work, a waste of time and labour and once experienced is carefully avoided in the future.

There is an important alternative to a smooth matt and that is a stippled matt. This has the advantage of producing minute spots of light all over the glass which tend to make more luminous the final shadows that are left. The stippling can be done either with the badger or with a stippler according to the texture required, the stippler brush giving a much coarser grain.

With a hog-hair brush the paint is removed and gradated wherever a light passage and modelling is desired. This is similar to drawing with white chalk on brown paper, the traced line representing the black charcoal line.

The hog-hair brush is most generally serviceable but other brushes and implements have their uses according to the particular effect aimed at.

A piece of pointed wood, a needle, a palette knife, a quill, in fact almost any implement may be used to secure the desired result.

It is possible to save a firing by the use of an oil matt. The water matt having been applied and worked on in the usual way, some of the powder paint is mixed with oil of lavender or spike oil instead of water. Oil of tar, possibly diluted with rectified oil of tar, may also be used. A matt of this oil paint is then applied to the glass, and being mixed with oil it will not disturb the under painting carried out with water matt. In a few minutes it will have set sufficiently to be worked on, but this time it is advisable to use soft sable brushes as an oil matt comes off very easily.

This method is really only useful when an extremely subtle change of tone is required as it has the advantage of allowing the first modelling to be further strengthened without waiting until it has been fired.

This first painting, being completed, the easel is again placed on the bench, and the pieces of painted glass carefully removed and laid out in large trays ready for the kiln.

After firing they are once again waxed up in their original positions and the second painting is undertaken.

The number of times that repainting and firing is carried out depends upon the type of work that is being produced, but generally speaking two paintings and firings are sufficient.

So much for the technique of painting which anyone of moderate capacity can learn to carry out in a comparatively short space of time. This technical ability, however, is only the beginning, since a stained glass artist has not only to be a sound draughtsman with a knowledge of light and shade and anatomy comparable to that of a figure painter in oils or water-colour, but he has also to gain experience in countering the effects of light and halation.

Anyone who has to hang pictures in living rooms soon realizes that a painting will often look much better in one position and room than in another. But these variations are insignificant compared with the effect of position on a stained glass window in a church.

Not only are the colour values liable to be altered considerably, say by a north or south aspect, the blues and cooler colours being helped by the north light, whilst rubies and warm colours are enhanced by a south light, but the amount of halation, that is the spreading of light, varies with the condition of the light and the height of the window from the floor level, so that a window may easily be entirely satisfactory in the studio, and not at all so when in position in the church.

A considerable amount of argument has arisen in this connexion as to how one should paint windows for New Zealand, the Middle East, South Africa, U.S.A. or Canada, some artists asserting that they should be painted much more heavily on account of the strong light. Others maintain that this is not advisable because although there is a strong light outside, there is a correspondingly and counter-balancing strong light inside.

An artist from U.S.A. has in fact stated that the depth of treatment given in this country corresponded with that used by him in America.

It is very probable that the position of the window in the church and the height from the floor level are more important factors than its destination and it is undeniably true that windows have been carried out by British studios and artists for countries as far apart as Burma, New Zealand, Norway, U.S.A. and Canada and South Africa without complaints of underpainting. Hogan's masterly series of windows for St. Thomas' Church, New York, which are constantly referred to as outstanding examples of splendid colour, are indeed heavily painted, but not because of the local strength of light, rather because they are high up in the clerestory and so would have received similar treatment had they been carried out for a similar architectural position in this country.

Generalizations are apt to be misleading but on the whole it is better to underpaint than overpaint. All the worst Victorian glass was overpainted and the dull depressing result is only too familiar. Nowadays it is realized that a window is made of glass and the beauty of the material is appreciated for its own sake.

Two large windows recently carried out for Canada, one of which was set over the altar in Trinity College School Chapel, at Fort Hope, Ontario, received different treatment in the painting. The College window was painted far less heavily than the other which was carried out to match existing windows. The College window was an immediate success and the cause of much congratulation. Moreover, a visitor from Canada who had seen both windows told me that one was overpainted, and he very much preferred the Fort Hope window. This would seem to bear out the theory that the most important considerations are after all the architectural setting and the height from the floor level.

CHAPTER 22

Firing

There is no particular mystery about firing. The writer once trained a bricklayer's labourer to do this work. He enjoyed it and within a month was firing as well as any kilnsman one would be likely to find. Nevertheless it is a responsible job requiring constant care and attention. A bad kilnsman can spoil much of the work, and a man who does his job well deserves recognition and respect.

It is analagous to the art of cooking. Skill can only be acquired by practical experience of which glasses are hard and need to be put in the hottest part of the kiln, and which are softer and requires less heat. As with ordinary cooking stoves the characteristics of kilns vary, and the best results can only be obtained by experience with any particular types. The fundamental principle is to heat the glass slowly and to cool it gradually. If this is done carefully and the glass watched through the peep-hole in the kiln, nothing can go wrong.

The painted glass to be fired is brought to the kiln room and transferred to metal trays. These metal trays have first to be filled with plaster of paris. It is wisest to buy the best quality and to make sure that it is thoroughly dry before using. One method is to heap the plaster on to the metal trays and then heat them thoroughly in the kiln to remove any possible moisture. It is then removed and allowed to cool ready for use. Damp plaster will cause blisters and bumps on the even surface of the glass, and can easily necessitate recutting and repainting. Most kilnsmen put the bags of new plaster on top of the heated kiln. This is quite a sound method and the whole point is to make sure that the plaster is not damp.

The plaster with which the trays have been loosely filled must be pressed down to form a fairly firm and smooth bed for the glass. Any dents or impressions on the plaster can act as a mould into which semi-molten glass is liable to sink. This smoothing and flattening can be done either with a small trowel, a roller or with a long, wide and flat palette knife.

In the Cummings' Studios in San Francisco it was noticed that the usual metal tray with plaster bedding for firing had been discarded and composition trays requiring no plaster were used instead. This seemed to be an improvement on the traditional method as it saved labour in bedding and changing the plaster. Mr. Cummings explained that the trays were made of Johns Manville marinite and were supplied by Western Asbestos Co., San Francisco, 3. The material is $\frac{1}{2}''$ in thickness and grey in colour when purchased but changes to terra cotta when the moisture is driven out. One of the American studios found that the sheets warped; the Cummings' Studios, however, experienced no such difficulty, being most careful to ensure that the sheets are separated so that air can circulate round each sheet when moisture is being driven out in the kiln. The drying out must be done very slowly.

When arranging the glass for firing it is best to lay out the largest pieces first and then fill in the gaps with smaller pieces. Some glasses are hard and some comparatively soft; with experience it becomes easy to recognize which is which. The hard glass should obviously be placed in the hottest part of the kiln, and the softer in the the coolest. Each kiln varies somewhat in this respect, but again experience is the best guide. Naturally reasonable care must be taken in lighting a gas kiln. It would obviously be folly to turn the gas full on and then apply a match. In most cases there will be a row of jets on each side, and it is best to turn on one jet on each side and light it; all the other jets may then be lighted in turn allowing each one to light up from the one next to it.

The general opinion amongst stained glass craftsmen is that an electric kiln is equally efficient and just as easy to manipulate. The procedure of firing is, of course, similar in both cases.

Above the chamber in which the glass is fired, one tray at a time, there is a preheating chamber which will hold three or more trays. A long-handled tray lifter is placed under a tray which has been carefully filled with painted glass ready for firing, and the tray is lifted carefully and put into the preheating chamber. Whilst this is warming, a second tray of glass is laid out ready for the kiln. The fire box of the kiln will take about an hour to warm up to a satisfactory heat for firing, and during this time the preheating chamber will have been filled with trays of glass.

The door of the preheating chamber and that of the fire box are now opened. With the tray-lifting tool in the right hand the kilnsman pulls the first tray nearly halfway out of the preheating chamber and uses his left hand to place the long-handled tray lifter centrally under the tray. The tray is then gently lifted, removed from the preheating chamber and inserted in the fire box, where it rests on runners. Both doors are then closed.

If the door of the fire box peep-hole is opened it will be seen that the glass on the tray appears to be black, as also the walls of the kiln and the plaster. In about another ten minutes the walls will begin to glow, though the pieces of glass will still look dark. By the time twenty minutes have passed the glass should look red and shiny, indicating that it is sufficiently fired. The whole aim of the process is to fuse the paint into the surface of the glass and it is therefore necessary to increase the heat gradually until the surface of the glass begins to melt. As soon as this has taken place the paint and the glass naturally amalgamate into one even surface and this objective is achieved.

As soon as the tray of fired glass is ready it is removed and placed in the annealing chamber. When a fair amount of firing is being done at one time there will not be sufficient room in the annealing chamber to take all the trays of fired glass. To overcome this difficulty a metal box or cupboard may be made with runners on each side to take the trays, leaving a small space between. This may be composed simply of sheets of iron with an iron door. As the trays are taken from the kiln they are placed inside this cupboard and the door is kept shut. By the time a few trays have been put in, the metal cupboard, standing on a concrete floor, will become red hot. This method is particularly successful if firing takes place in the evening, as, when the last tray has been put in, the door may be shut and the cupboard left until the next day. In the morning it will be practically cool and the glass, losing heat gradually without any danger from draught, will be perfectly annealed, with no danger of fire flies.

Fire flies, or glass breaking or cracking after firing, are due to bad annealing. It is quite a common experience after the fired glass has been waxed up again in position on the easel, to hear, hours afterwards, little cracks, and to find that several pieces have flown. The metal annealing box eliminates the possibility of this misfortune.

As has been explained the object of firing the painted glass is to fuse and incorporate the paint with the smooth top surface of the glass. Firing for a yellow stain is a different process. A paint fire should take from fifteen to twenty minutes; staining should be satisfactorily achieved in two to two and a half minutes. The yellow is produced by chemical action and will be induced by a smaller amount of heat than is required for paint fusion. The depth of yellow colour depends partly upon the amount of silver oxide applied to the glass, partly upon the chemical composition of the glass and partly upon the amount of heat and the length of time during which it is subjected to this heat.

Unless the way in which particular glass will react to stain is known from experience it is wise to fire a sample in the kiln to find out just how it behaves. Different batches of the same type of glass will sometimes give a different reaction. It is impossible to tell by looking at the glass; neither its quality nor its colour will indicate exactly what its staining potentialities may be.

A light lemon colour is produced by using a small amount of oxide and a minimum of firing. For a deeper yellow colour more stain is used and the glass is longer in the kiln. A few glasses such as kelp will give a very deep yellow approximating almost to red. The disadvantage of allowing the staining process to carry on too long in the kiln is that the glass 'metals', i.e. it gradually becomes coated with an opaque film somewhat resembling mother-of-pearl. Occasionally use can be made of this reaction and a rather dull rich yellow produced for some particular effect, but as a rule the more clear the yellow the more pleasing it will be.

Pot-metal yellow, where the colouring is produced in the manufacturing of the glass, has never got quite the same clarity and brilliance as silver stain. It is often excellent in colour and unless directly compared with stain might seem as satisfactory, but a comparison of the two pieces, side by side, will soon show the difference. It is something like the comparison between pure cadmium in water-colour and the same pigment with a touch of white body colour added. It is still quite a pleasant colour but it has lost some of its luminosity.

Besides the excellence of colour, stain gives us the advantage of being able to combine yellow and white on the same piece of glass. It is quite permanent as may be seen by examining stain produced in the fourteenth century.

Although the procedure for the firing of stain is very well known, difficulty is more likely to arise over stain than over paint firing. The reason for this is that the kilnsman does not want the extra trouble of laying out a separate tray of glass for stain firing. He naturally likes to fire a full tray and so is tempted to combine the firing for stain with the firing for paint, and will explain the metalling by condemning the glass when the fault is really in the firing. There are instances when it is necessary to fire paint and stain together, such as when, due to the size or nature of the glass, it might be tempting providence to chance more visits to the kiln than is absolutely necessary. In such cases a weak stain is used to minimize the risk of metalling due to the overlong period in the kiln made necessary by the higher fusing temperature of the paint.

When the fired pieces of stained glass are taken from the tray after firing, yellow discoloration will be seen on the plaster where it has been in contact with the silver oxide. This discoloured plaster must be carefully and completely removed, otherwise any residue left in the plaster may stain a piece of glass in a subsequent firing.

If the yellow stain has come out too strong or if the surface has metalled, the faults can, in both cases, be removed by the use of hydrofluoric acid. This operation is extremely delicate, and great care must be taken to prevent either the acid itself or its fumes from affecting the painted surface on the other side. If this happens it, of course, necessitates the additional task of repainting and refiring for paint. A kilnsman who saves his studio any of these calamities is a valuable craftsman.

As regards the relative values of a gas or electric kiln, both have been used on different occasions at the Whitefriars Studios, and Mr. Steel, our kilnsman, does not seem to mind which he uses. Of course it is not essential that the artist should have a kiln and do his own firing. Arrangements can be made with such expert craftsmen as Messrs. Lowndes & Drury, Lettice Street, Fulham, for the work to be fired by them.

Frederick W. Cole, F.B.S.M.P.G., writes:

Notes on the firing procedure at William Morris Studio

An electric kiln is used with a firing chamber to hold two trays about 14″ × 10″.

The kiln includes a warming rack, pre-heating chamber, firing chamber, annealing racks (12), each with a separate detachable door.

Procedure closely follows that described by you with the difference that any moisture absorbed by the plaster from the atmosphere is dried when the tray is in the warming chamber. The kiln room being a warm dry place, the amount of moisture absorbed by the plaster is insufficient to effect the glass during firing or the quality of the stain in actual contact with the plaster.

Additionally we have a pyrometer which truth to tell is seldom used though it impresses the public. It is often useful when making experiments with new materials in that it makes it possible to complete one's tests at a given and accurate range of temperature.

The eye at the peephole has still to be improved upon when playing with material as variable as glass.

PLATE 71. Wild–Barfield Electric Kiln.

CHAPTER 23

Leading, Cementing and Banding

LEADING

When the glass has been painted and fired and laid out in position in trays, it is taken to the glazing bench ready to be leaded up. The first operation is to lay the cutline smooth and flat on the glazing bench and secure it in position with drawing pins. A strip of wood about $\frac{3}{8}''$ in thickness and $1\frac{1}{2}''$ in width is then placed along the length of the cutline parallel with and $\frac{5}{16}''$ away from the sight size line of the cutline. This should be nailed firmly on to the bench.

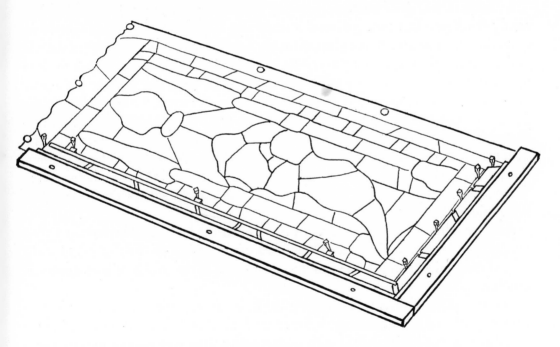

A similar strip of wood is placed along the base of the cutline also $\frac{5}{16}''$ away from the sight size line. This should be at right angles to the strip running along the length or height of the light; it should be checked with a set-square and when accurately in position nailed firmly to the bench.

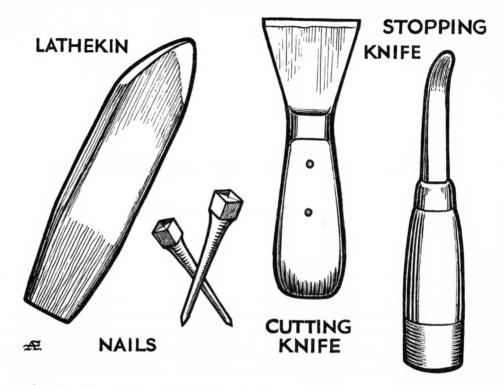

LATHEKIN

NAILS

STOPPING
KNIFE

CUTTING
KNIFE

A length of lead ½″ in width is stretched by making fast one end of the lead in a firmly fixed grip and then giving it a sharp tug. This stretches and straightens it, removing any wrinkles. Many glaziers simply bend over a couple of inches of the end of the lead at right angles, put this end on to the floor, stand on it and stretch the lead upwards. It is just as well not to do this in line with one's face because if the lead breaks an unpleasant blow may ensue. Having been stretched, the lead is laid on the bench and the lathekin run up and down the core or part of the lead between the two flanges and then along each flange or lead to get it perfectly smooth or straight. It is then placed on the cutline against the long length of wooden strip to form the outside lead of the light. A couple of glazing nails—the best kind to use are bootmaker's 'lasting nails'—should then be tapped into the bench at the side of the lead to hold it in position.

Another calm of lead is straightened in a similar manner and a length cut a little longer than the width of the base. This is placed up against the strip of wood at the base of the cutline, tucking one end into the flanges of the length of lead already in position.

The first piece of glass that fits along the base and into the corner of the leads is tapped gently into position in the heart of the lead. This is done with the end of the stopping knife which is covered with lead or solder. It is most important not to proceed with the second piece of glass until the first piece has been accurately placed in its position on the cutline. The short connecting pieces of lead are cut and mitred where necessary to fit exactly against the adjacent lead, but wherever possible, for instance along the length of the border or the outline of a figure, a length of lead is

Glazing the window after the glass has been painted and fired.

Soldering each joint of lead after glazing.

PLATE 72.

left loose and gradually fitted into position as the work proceeds. This gives strength to the leading, a clean silhouette to the figure or line to the border and minimizes the amount of soldering.

With every window the question of the width of the lead has to be considered. For the outside lead a $\frac{1}{2}''$ width is usual. This allows $\frac{1}{4}''$ of lead to fit into the groove or rebate of the stonework. If necessary for a particular rebate $\frac{5}{8}''$ uneven hearted lead can be used; that is to say the heart or core will be so placed that $\frac{3}{8}''$ of the lead will fit into the rebate and $\frac{1}{4}''$ will cover the glass.

The choice of the internal leads will depend partly on the type of design, partly on the size of the window but largely on its position in the building. The higher the window will be placed and the stronger the light to which it will be subjected, the wider the lead that must be used. For an average-size window in a medium-size church $\frac{3}{8}''$ lead round the outside of the figures and round the panels etc. that need emphasis is usually suitable and $\frac{1}{4}''$ lead for the arbitraries or incidental leading.

When a piece of lead has been gently tapped into position a glazing nail should be used to hold it in position whilst the rest of the work is proceeding; it is advisable to place a small piece of lead between the nail and the glass to prevent the glass from being chipped. The process of placing pieces of glass in position and fitting the lead round them, making sure that each fits exactly to the cutline, is continued until the whole section is built up. Occasionally it may not be possible to make a piece fit exactly because of some slight protuberance on the edge which has not been noticeable in laying it out on the easel. When this occurs the piece must be carefully grozed until it fits exactly.

On completion of the section, the end of the outside strip of $\frac{1}{2}''$ lead at the base is cut off so that it measures correctly to the required dimension. A long strip of lead is placed on the other outside length of the panel, making sure that the lower leaf of the lead passes under the surface of all the outside pieces of glass. A second length of batten similar to the one on the other side of the section is placed against the outside lead and hammered carefully, forcing it to fit exactly to the width of the panel. So far there are outside leads placed on three sides of the panel and a strip of $\frac{1}{2}''$ lead is next measured and cut to fit along the top. It should be noted that in choosing the leads consideration must be given to the thickness of the glass that has been cut. If it is thick slab glass a wide heart lead will be needed, but if the glass is antique a lead of narrower heart can be used. There is no advantage in using wide heart lead where it is not necessary.

If the light is a small one, and this last strip of lead completes it, the outside leaf or flanges will be left on ready to fit into the masonry, but if, as is probable, this is merely the first of a series of sections, the outside flanges are removed with the cutting knife or a carpenter's chisel, leaving the heart and the leaf covering the top pieces of glass of the lower section. A fourth strip of wood is laid along the top of the section and again carefully tapped into position, making sure by means of a set-square that it is at right-angles to the side.

The section is then ready for soldering, and the next step is to clean the lead at the joints. This can be done by scraping with a knife or rubbing with a piece of emery cloth, but the most effective method is to use a small scratch card brush made from a piece of 'file card'. It is not necessary to clean the whole length of the lead as this will finally have cement rubbed into it which must be scrubbed off, cleaning the surface of the glass and the lead. The only necessity is to clean the lead thoroughly at the joints to allow the solder to amalgamate smoothly.

A little flux should be applied to each joint. Either of two methods can be used. The joints can be rubbed with a tallow candle or a little powdered resin can be sprinkled on them. Both these fluxes are quite effective and there is little to choose between them. The tallow leaves traces all over the section but they are easily removed with a brush, and in any case the work is thoroughly rubbed over in the process of cementing.

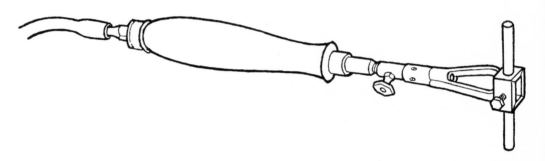

The ends of the copper bit in the soldering iron must be filed to ensure perfect cleanliness. A little powdered resin is placed on a piece of tin plate or into a flat and shallow tin box. The gas in the soldering iron having been lit, it is necessary to wait until the copper bit is just hot enough to melt the end of a thin strip of solder placed against the resin in the tin box. The end of the copper bit is rubbed round the tin plate until the tin and the solder amalgamate and coat the end of the copper bit.

With a thin strip of solder in the left hand and the soldering iron in the right, the end of the solder is touched with the soldering iron bit so that a small drop of molten solder hangs from the end of the copper bit. The bit is then lowered until the drop of solder just touches the lead. The solder should at once flow evenly over the joint, and there is no need for the copper bit to touch the lead. If the bit is too hot and touches the lead, a hole will be formed by the melting of the lead. The art of soldering is to keep the bit just hot enough to melt the solder but not hot enough to melt the lead. When all the solder joints have been made, the work must be examined very thoroughly to make sure that no joint has been missed. However careful one tries to be, it is difficult not to overlook one or two.

The section has now to be turned over so that the joints on the other side can be soldered. Obviously this has to be done with great care to avoid cracking any of the glass. The section should be slid towards the body over the edge of the bench, the near portion being supported with the flat of the left hand. When the section has moved just over half way across, it can be swung into an upright position by swivel-ling it on the edge of the bench, with one hand on its bottom edge to support it and the other hand at the top to keep it vertical.

The panel can then be lifted, still in a vertical position, on to the bench and lowered carefully, supported by the flat of the hand. An alternative method is to hold it against the side of the bench and swivel it on to the top of the bench by a reverse process to that of taking it off. Unless it is necessary to hold it against the light for inspection, when possibly it will be seen that one or two pieces should be re-moved for improvement, the unsoldered side is soldered in a similar manner. If any pieces do have to be removed, it is obviously easier to do this when one side is still unsoldered.

It may be necessary to plate a piece of glass, and although this practice is not to be recommended and should be regarded as unsound craftsmanship, nevertheless at times it cannot be avoided. The following method is the most satisfactory. Run a piece of lead exactly round the piece of plating glass and solder the two ends. Cut off the top outside piece as shown in the diagram. Carefully clean the leads and solder right round the lower leaf to make the joint completely watertight.

SOLDERED

INSIDE OF WINDOW

CEMENTING

The soldering process is followed by cementing which can be done in two ways. The ingredients most often used for the cement are a thin mixture of 5 parts powdered whitening, 4 parts fine plaster of paris, 2 parts driers, 1 part lamp black and $\frac{1}{2}$ part of red lead, although these proportions may vary slightly in different workshops. These are mixed well together, boiled linseed oil is added and the mixture thinned with a little turpentine until a porridge-like consistency is achieved which will brush easily into all the finer crevices of the work. It should be just thick enough to maintain a stick in an upright position.

The second method is to omit the turpentine and to work the mixture into the consistency of well-kneaded putty. This is then well-pressed into the space between the leads and the glass and finally cleaned off and smoothed by running a pointed stick round the glass next to the leads. This is not only a laborious process but is also not as efficient because the consistency of the putty prevents if from really penetrating into the heart of the lead, in the way that the liquid cement does.

In the case of plating however, it is essential to use the putty. If, in this instance, liquid cement were used it would be liable to run between the surface of the two pieces of glass. If this should happen there is nothing for it but to unstop the plated piece of glass, clean out the cement, re-solder and use putty instead of liquid cement.

Normally the liquid cement is more efficient and should be rubbed well into the leads with a stiff brush and the section sprinkled either with sawdust or with powdered whitening which is then lightly brushed over so that most of the superfluous cement is removed. The section is turned over and the process repeated on the other side. It will be noticed that a certain amount of the cement will have already run through the leads. There is no harm in this as it shows that the cement has got well into the heart of the lead.

The section is now put on one side for the cement to harden. It depends to some extent on the weather and also on the consistency of the cement how long it should be left: possibly a couple of hours, but it is important not to leave it too long or the cement will harden on the uneven painted surface of the glass and will be extremely difficult to remove. If taken at the right time, a stiff brush will quickly and easily remove all the cement from both sides of the glass and with a little vigorous brushing the leads will become clean and polished. At this stage the cement will present a slightly uneven and crumbly line against the lead. For some types of work advantage can be taken of this to give a quality of softness to the lead line when in position against the light. But for work to be seen at close range or for polished Rennaissance windows it is necessary to give the lead a perfectly even line by running a pointed stick, or nail fastened in a piece of wood, round both sides of the lead.

BANDING

After the panels have been left three or four days for the cement to harden, they will be ready for the final process of banding; that is, the attaching of copper ties which will be fastened round the saddle bars fixed in the masonry of the church. The position of the copper ties must be carefully thought out in making the cutline; in an average light there are four or five ties, the alternating pieces of glass tending to keep the section firm and rigid under the stress of wind pressure.

The thin smear of cement or oil must be carefully removed from the soldered joint where the copper tie is to be fixed and the joint thoroughly cleaned. Short strips of about 4″ are cut from a length of copper wire that has been stretched to make it perfectly straight. One or more of these are placed on a small piece of plate glass and touched in the middle with a piece of pointed wood that has been dipped in spirits of salt. The spirits of salt should have been previously 'killed' by placing a small piece of zinc in it. This causes it to react violently for a short time but it can be used as soon as the bubbling has ceased.

A touch of solder is placed on the heated soldering bit, and the drop carefully brought into contact with the centre of one of the short strips of copper wire at the point where it has been touched with the spirits of salt. This acts as a flux which enables the solder to adhere easily to the copper. Before work on the leaded light is begun, a sufficient number of copper ties should be prepared to finish off the work. The process of fixing them on to the lead work is comparatively easy. The solder joint of the leaded light is touched with the spirits of salt and the copper tie held at the end in the left hand, is placed so that the centre globule of solder is resting on the solder joint of the leading. With the soldering iron in the right hand the heat of the copper bit is applied to the globule on the copper so that it melts and adheres to the solder joint of the lead, fixing the copper tie in its required position. Banding is rather a satisfying job because with a little care a really neat piece of work can be done quite expeditiously. The two ends of the copper tie are pressed flat on to the glass and the section is then ready for packing.

CHAPTER 24

Fixing

———✦◄O❋❂◗❋◗❂◗❀❂◗◗❂◗◗◗❋◗◗◄O❂◗❋◗◗◗O◗◗✦———

Although experience of fixing a stained glass window is useful, this is not to suggest that it is an essential part of the training of a potential stained glass artist. It is, however, advisable for the craftsman to be acquainted with every respect of the work, particularly if he is ever to be in a position of responsibility or to run his own studio. In practice the job is done by glaziers and fixers in the studio's employ or by an outside firm of expert craftsmen like Messrs. Lowndes & Drury of the Glass House, Lettice Street, Fulham.

Unless the building is a new one, the first task is to remove the existing window or leaded quarry glazing. If the leaded light that has to be removed is of any value and has to be preserved, the operation will take considerable time and care, and to some extent the masonry may have to suffer to avoid damage to the glass. On the other hand if the existing window is of no value it can be deliberately broken round the edges adjacent to the masonry, the leads cut through and the bulk of the section lifted clear. It is then comparatively easy to dig out the lead remaining in the groove or rebate, without damaging the stone. The necessary tools are a hammer, a mason's point, a mason's cold chisel and perhaps an old table knife. The latter is very useful if the cement is especially hard because you can hammer it into the lead in the rebate and gouge out the lead and the mortar. When the cement is hard it is probably best to begin with the bottom section of the light and work upwards, but in cases where the cement is soft it is better to begin at the top and work downwards. The groove in the masonry must be carefully cleaned out, and the lead and cement moved with the use of a mason's point.

Before placing the first section in position, the position of the bars must be checked to ensure that they are in the correct place for the new glazing. For this a bar tape is useful and if the light is a large one, it will probably have been made already to check the position of the bars on the cutline and cartoon. It is simply a long piece of tape or strip of narrow linen, the length of the light, and correctly indicating the exact position of the bars.

When the rebate has been properly cleaned out, a measurement should be taken from the depth of the groove to the sight size of the masonry opposite. By checking this with the width of the new leaded light it can be seen whether it will be possible to place one side of the new section of leaded light deep into the groove, and have sufficient space to bring the other side of the leaded light opposite to the groove on the opposing side of the masonry and flush with it. If the size is correct when the section is placed into position, it can be moved slightly to one side fitting it into the groove on the other side of the masonry.

Should the width of the leaded light be a little too great to allow for fixing in this manner, it can be slightly bent and sprung into position, but this is a dangerous game to play and not worth the risk. Quite apart from the possibility of cracking some of the pieces of glass, the rigidity of the whole section is weakened and the cohesion between the glass cement and the glass and lead is interfered with. It is better to spend time on deepening the groove.

It may be that the artist has designed the window to fit the existing bars. Alternatively the position of the bars may have been changed, and if so the existing bars must be chiselled out with as little damage as possible and new holes made to slot bars into their new positions. This is done by a process similar to that described below for fixing the section of leaded light with the obvious difference that in the case of the bar there is little chance to bend it and spring it into position.

When the first bottom section is in position, the second section is placed above it and then eased down, making sure that the saddle lead on the bottom of the upper section fits correctly, overlapping each side of the top lead of the lower section. A little soft putty placed on the top lead of the lower section will help to ensure a waterproof joint where this overlapping junction occurs. The top and final section of the light is the most difficult to place into position because it has to be passed not only sideways into the groove but upwards into the groove as well. The grooves in the top of the light must be deeply cut to allow sufficient upward movement to allow the top section to be passed over the section beneath it, and then lowered down on to it again with the saddle lead in position.

As the sections are placed in position the copper ties are passed round the saddle bars, brought together and twisted once or twice to make a temporary fastening in case for some reason the section has to be removed or readjusted before the work is completed. When all the sections are correctly placed, all the copper ties are twisted into a neat fastening and the end bits of the two pieces of copper wire snipped off to make a neat finish.

The most awkward sections of leaded work to fix into position are the traceries, particularly trefoils, quatrefoils and so on. With the quatrefoil it will probably be necessary to fold over the lead flanges on the two lower foils and deepen the grooves into which the two upper foils have to fit. With patience and manipulation each section can be eased gradually into position.

The final process is to point up all the space between the stone and the leadwork. For this, a mixture is made up of one part of the best Portland cement and two or three parts of sharp, clean sand. The correct portion of sand is measured on to the mixing board, the cement is added and the mixture turned over until it is thoroughly combined. This very thorough mixing in the dry state is most important. The mixture is then shaped into a heap and a hollow made in the centre to take the water as if it were being poured into a bowl. The water is poured in and sprinkled with mixture taken from the outside of the heap very carefully so that the water does not break through and start to flow away. The process of mixing is continued until all the mixture is impregnated with water, and the desired consistency for working is obtained, not too stiff and not too fluid.

With an old brush dipped into a pail of water, the stonework is now thoroughly wetted on each side of the lead, and the water swished well into the crevices so that the whole surface is damp. A small heap of the cement is placed on to the mortar board with the pointing trowel and the spaces between the lead and the stonework filled in, beginning with the bottom of the light. Care should be taken to force the cement well into the crevices so that the groove behind the lead is filled up.

It is advisable to begin on the outside of the window first as this forces the leaded light against the saddle bars and flush with the inside face of the rebate. It is necessary to keep on wetting the stonework as work proceeds and to smooth off the cement flush with the surface of the masonry. When the outside is finished a careful scrutiny should be made of the glass and leadwork, and any cement that may have dropped on to them by accident removed. The inside of the window should be treated in the same way.

The work has been described as if the saddle bars were fixed on the inside of the window which is nearly always the case and is of course the proper construction. Occasionally, however, it is found that the bars have been placed on the outside. This is altogether wrong because obviously in a gale the copper ties will have to take all the stress of the wind, whereas if the bars were on the inside they would be giving most of the support. Moreover, when the bars are on the outside they are exposed to the weather and certain to rust badly. If it is not possible or convenient to reposition them on the inside, then the process of fixing must be the reverse of that just described and the pointing up must begin on the inside.

For drilling fresh holes for the bars, a job which is best carried out after the old leaded work has been removed, an ordinary cold chisel can be used, preferably one that is slightly wider across the cutting edge than the bar which will have to be inserted into the hole. If available, a wall drill having four cutting edges is, however, much more efficient, and enables the work to be done more quickly. It should perhaps be noted that the action required is not one of continuously revolving the chisel or drill as when using a bit for boring wood. It is more a matter of pulverizing or chipping the stone with the edge of the chisel. The chisel should be struck with the hammer and allowed to rebound slightly with each stroke. A hole of, say, two inches deep should be bored on one side of the masonry and one inch deep on the other.

The inside of the holes having been thoroughly wetted, the bar is slotted into the two-inch hole and then moved back so that the opposite end slots into the one-inch

PLATE 73. The method of fixing glass at Canterbury is very unusual. The leaded panels are fixed to iron frames and these are fastened to the permanent iron work by means of wedges, and so are removed quickly.

hole. Cement is now forced well into the holes and round the bar and again pointed off neatly, flush with the stone surface.

The illustration from a photograph by the late Sidney Pitcher shows an unusual way of fixing glass at Canterbury Cathedral. The leaded panels are fixed into iron frames and these are fastened to the permanent iron work by means of wedges and so can be removed quickly.

CHAPTER 25

Slab Glass and Concrete

━━━━━━━━━━◦•◦◇◌◊◦◉◦◒◦◌◇◊◦◌•◦━━━━━━━━━━

In recent years a new technique has developed, using pieces of slab glass, one inch or more in thickness, held together by cement instead of strips of lead. Like so many things that are very new it is really a reversion to something which is very old.

Sir Giles Gilbert Scott, R.A., has expressed the opinion that this method is particularly suitable either for very ancient buildings or for very modern buildings. It is appropriate in very old buildings because it is, in fact, a reversion to the primitive form of window, which consisted of fixing small pieces of glass into openings made in clay, adobe or mortar.

It harmonizes with the most modern architecture in that it lends itself readily to abstract design, and its very limitations prevent any ill-conceived attempts at photographic realism, misplaced perspective or three-dimensional chiaroscura. It is essentially decorative and two-dimensional.

As the surface of the glass is faceted by chipping, it gives the maximum brilliance by refracting the light, as does a cut diamond, and it is therefore more effective than ordinary stained glass under conditions of comparatively poor lighting when the window does not receive direct light from the sky. For this reason it has unlimited possibilities of use in town buildings and particularly in congested areas where daylight is partially obscured by adjacent houses.

Its effectiveness can be seen in the church at Dovers Green, near Reigate, architect E. F. Starling, B.A., A.R.I.B.A., where the Whitefrairs Studios have carried out two small square windows in the sanctuary, one on either side of the altar, symbolizing the Bread and the Wine. The designs were by Fourmaintraux.

Another interesting example of this new technique is the series of tall narrow windows carried out by the same studio in the John Knox Church, Stepney, architect F. Goldsmith, A.R.I.B.A. These designs, also by Fourmaintraux, consist of abstract symbolism, four motives in each light, blended into a harmony of line and colour which adds warmth and significance to the impressive architectural setting. In this particular setting it is doubtful whether the usual stained glass technique would have been so successful.

One advantage of this new technique is that it almost rules out the banal. On the other hand it is likely to trip up the novice by appearing so simple. It is true that any pieces of glass picked up haphazard from a cullet box and placed in juxtaposition would almost certainly achieve a pleasant or interesting effect but the result would probably need all the theories of neo-abstractionism to endow it with any possible significance.

It is of course not necessary that a piece of beautiful decoration should have meaning. A pattern of black and white tiles may be entirely satisfactory but not necessarily expressive of meaning unless some abstractionist suggests the ups and downs of life.

A grisaille window is an obvious example of beautiful decoration without meaning though it should be designed in scale with the architecture. Nevertheless some significance is usually expected of the design for a church window. This can be achieved within the limitations of the new technique and it should particularly appeal to those who believe in Herbert Reade's dictum that the object of Art is to brighten things up a bit.

Although in some ways this type of window is cheaper to produce, since, for example, no painting and firing are required, there is great wastage in the cutting, and this kind of thick glass is understandably expensive.

It is usually made in squares of about 6″ or 8″ and is from 1″ to 1¼″ in thickness. For successful execution hundreds of different tints are needed and these necessitate considerable storage space.

The first step is, as usual, to make a design to scale, one inch to a foot usually being the most convenient. In making this design it is well to remember that the sections must not be larger than about 2′ 2″ by 2′ 6″. Obviously a decrease in one dimension allows one to increase the other but this is roughly the largest size that can conveniently be handled owing to the weight.

TOP WIDTH
1¼″

SIDE WIDTH
1⅜″

BOTTOM WIDTH
1¼″

1¼″ THICK

SIDE WIDTH
1⅜″ ″

The above diagram will give an idea as to the space that must be allowed on each side of the panel and also at the top and bottom where the panel has to fit into another one above and below. Some artists use reinforcing wire but this does not appear to be absolutely necessary. In fact the experts of the Cement Manufacturer's Association advise against it.

Copper wire should be used, if any, as the metal is too near the surface to be safeguarded from oxidization. Another disadvantage in using wire is that it may interfere with the even flow of cement, when it is being poured into the narrow partitions. If, however, it is intended to use the reinforcing wire this should be allowed for in the design and a thicker outline made where the wire will go.

The finished design has to be enlarged full-size and this can be done quite satisfactorily by photography. Where this is not convenient the enlargement can be done by hand with the usual method of squaring up.

From the completed cartoon two cutlines have to be made. One on fairly thick paper or linen to be used for the cutting, and the other on thin paper. On this the cut pieces of glass are placed and the cement poured between them. Thin paper is necessary because it minimizes the size of the wrinkles caused by the cement when poured upon it. If thick paper is used the size of the wrinkles becomes comparatively enormous. On this thin paper, the position of the reinforcing wires should be marked in red.

On the thick cutline paper it is advisable to indicate the colour of the different pieces of glass. Some artists then cut out the shape of each piece of glass separately and use these shapes as templates from which the glass can be cut.

If reinforcement is being used, the next step is to make a frame of wire which will go all round the panel or section, and to bend into shape and tie in position with very thin wire the reinforcing wire that runs across the panel. This must exactly coincide with the red line drawn on the thin cutline paper. A small piece of lead should be placed under the reinforcement wire at each of the four corners of the panel so that it will be in the centre of the thickness of the panel and the cement will be able to run below and above it.

A wooden frame is now fitted round the four sides of the panel, the wooden sides

(a)

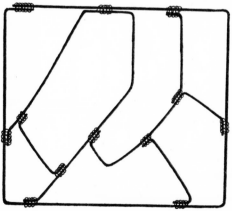
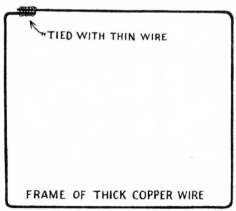

TIED WITH THIN WIRE

FRAME OF THICK COPPER WIRE

PLATE 74. Slab glass and concrete panel by Colwyn Morris, Whitefriars Studios.

at the top and bottom being shaped to give the requisite bead and groove as shown in diagram (*a*). This grooving is of course only necessary when the panel has to be assembled with others as part of a large window. The four side pieces of wood should be screwed together so that they can be unscrewed when the cement is hard.

For cutting the glass an ordinary steel wheel or diamond is used. To cut a big slab in two, a line is first traced with the wheel or diamond on both sides of the slab, then, held in both hands, the slab is brought down hard on the upright chisel just where the cut has been made. The slab should split cleanly along the line.

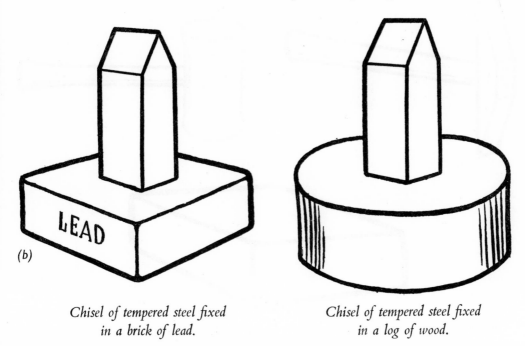

Chisel of tempered steel fixed
in a brick of lead.

Chisel of tempered steel fixed
in a log of wood.

The smooth side of the glass always faces outwards and this is the side which rests on the thin paper when in position for cementing.

If it is necessary to cut pieces with narrow angles, the glass should be put on the chisel and a wooden hammer used. To cut other shapes, especially small ones, the glass should be cut on one side following the outline of the shaped piece of paper with wheel or diamond point just as if cutting a piece of antique glass. The piece is then placed on the chisel and with the steel hammer chipped until it takes the right shape. For this it is useful to have a brick of lead on which to place the glass whilst finishing it to an exact shape.

A chisel fixed in wood is also useful. The vibration is not the same as on lead and in some cases it gives better results. It is entirely a matter of vibration of the glass, and the skill that comes with practice. Some craftsmen fasten rubber round the handle of the hammer to lessen the vibration on the hand.

When the piece of glass has been cut to shape it should be hammered on the edges thus flaking off facets to make it sparkle. This faceting of the top surface of the glass gives the sparkle and lustre which is so characteristic of this technique. It can be alternated with pieces that are not so treated to achieve a quieter and contrasting quality where desired.

As soon as a piece of glass has been cut to the exact shape it is placed carefully in position on the thin tracing. It is as well to fix it by means of a small piece of putty or plasticine on the bottom corners or better still by 'Durafix' to prevent it from being displaced as the work continues. This especially applies to the small pieces of glass. When all the pieces have been placed correctly in position the cement can be mixed.

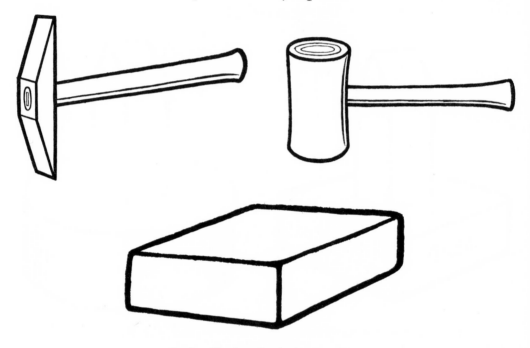

Brick of lead to finish shaping glass.

(c)

Glass chipped on top surface from the sides.

A fairly quick drying cement should be used with very fine sand in the proportion of one part of cement to three parts of sand. The mixture must be liquid enough to pour. This operation is best carried out by two persons, one keeping the bucket of cement continually stirred, and the other pouring on the cement from a jug with a pointed spout.

The correct amount of cement needed for the whole operation should be mixed beforehand, so that it is not necessary to stop in the middle of pouring it. As soon as the jug is nearly empty it should be replenished from the bucket which has been kept on the stir. Should some of the pieces of glass be very much lower in height than the rest they should be carefully built up flush with the rest with plasticine, to prevent the liquid cement from running over the surface.

As the cement is poured on, surplus water runs off and a final smooth and even surface of cement left in the spaces between the pieces of glass. The panel is left in position for three days, when it will be hard enough for the wooden panels to be removed. Should any cement have run on to the surface of the glass this can now be carefully removed before it sets too hard.

This done, it is best to leave the panel to set for three weeks, after which the outside should be painted over with a waterproofing mixture. There are various brands, which can be obtained from a reliable builder's merchant, all having a base of silicate of soda.

As in all craft work, each individual develops his own variations of method which best suit his particular temperament. It is a question of sound craftsmanship, practice and the aesthetic appreciation of the material combining to produce a work of art.

The above description is the method as practised on the continent, and does not allow for the setting up of the panel against the light to judge the effect before it is finalized by cementing.

At the Whitefriars Studios, the pieces of glass are always fixed on to a sheet of plate glass, resting upon an easel against the light, the cement spaces being painted in just as when putting in lead lines.

Admittedly this takes much more time and labour but on the other hand, it can easily be seen how, as is more often than not the case, the finished window will be improved by the recutting of one or two pieces, though indeed it may be argued that in medieval days there were no sheets of plate glass to enable a preview to be taken.

Slab-glass windows are at present a novelty. Compared with traditional leaded glass they have a crudity which in itself impresses some people, while rebuffing others. As with every form and period of art, some creations are more interesting for what they attempt than for what they achieve.

Nevertheless works of great beauty have already been produced. A visit to the newly built church at Lèves, a few miles from Chartres, is sufficient evidence of this. The architects are Messieurs Pichon and Redreo and the windows are entirely filled by designs in Dalles de Verre by Gabriel Loire. Coming straight from the glories of the Cathedral to view a modern window is about as severe a test as one could imagine. It is really remarkable that these windows do not suffer by comparison. The colour is equally vibrant and exciting and utterly refutes any suggestion that windows today cannot compare in beauty of colour with medieval glass. It is remarkable also that almost the whole of the south wall of the nave is made up of glass and concrete, giving, as M. Gabriel Loire says, a tapestry effect, embodying scenes from the history of the Church. In these windows one feels that the artist has not been trying to impress by a new technique but to create something beautiful and significant, and that, moreover, he has succeeded.

When the Whitefriars Studios first started to experiment with slab glass and concrete windows, a serious problem had to be solved. It is comparatively easy to make concrete panels, but it is not so easy to guarantee that they are going to last.

Lead is a material which is known to endure but architects are aware that concrete is another matter altogether. It can be made to last as is proved by the Roman and even pre-Roman remains today, but so much depends not only on the ingredients, but also on the proportions and conditions of mixing and application.

The problem was put to the technical staff for experimentation in the laboratory, and advice was obtained from the technologists of the Cement Manufacturer's Association. For weeks the coefficients of expansion of concrete, glass and copper were subjects of daily conversation, until finally it was generally agreed that on the scale of even the largest stained glass windows the differentials were infinitesimal and could not have any harmful effect.

There was also the question of the various qualities of sand. After prolonged experiment several of these proved quite satisfactory, though in the interest of perfection it was decided to use granite chips, powdered granite and cement in the proportion of 2, $1\frac{1}{2}$ and 1, so that to say that the completed panels sets like granite is not a mere hyperbole of speech.

In spite of all this it was still not felt that a guarantee of durability could be given to clients. How could it be definitely asserted that in pouring in the cement every interstice of the glass had been completely filled to ensure perfect cohesion?

Finally a vibrating table was constructed. The simplest way to do this seemed to be to fix a small motor on the underneath part of the table top. When this is running a gentle vibration is set up throughout the whole structure. The cutline with the outside boarding or shuttering is placed in position on the table top, the copper reinforcing wire running round the panel fixed, and the glass carefully stuck to the cutline.

The cement is then mixed by two operatives, one mixing whilst the other applies it freshly mixed to the spaces between the glass. The motor is set in motion and the cement automatically flows evenly into every crevice of the glass, with the result that a definite assurance as regards durability can now be given.

CHAPTER 26

Art Schools

It is doubtless platitudinous to say that the lessons of history are never learnt, yet the plain fact is that in any period or country when the greatest art was produced art schools were unknown. In such days the craftsman was regarded as an intelligent member of society, with a status ranging from artisan to courtier according to his personal abilities and experience. The whole of the modern system of so-called art schools is artificial, and thousands of young people waste the formative years of their lives in an atmosphere of false values and make-believe. Graduate students with national certificates for every possible aspect of art are so often found to be unable to produce work of any reasonable standard of merit. Some of them should never have been allowed or encouraged to waste their time attempting a career for which they had no true qualifications. Too many art schools would admit a blind horse if it could sign the register. In some cases, the amount of remuneration depends upon the number of students which obviously encourages the accumulation of deadheads.

On the other hand no artist or craftsman is going to pay an inefficient assistant, at least not for long, and this, of course, is to the beginner's advantage, because if he or she is not likely to make the grade the sooner he leaves and commences to gain experience in a profession that suits him so much the better for him. But with all the modern jargon about self-expression the art student becomes only too easily convinced of some precious quality about his work which only remains unrecognized through the mental and aesthetic blindness of the world in general and his would-be employer in particular. It is a very significant fact that the people who have most in them are usually the most genuinely modest about their achievements. If they have any reasonably worthy ideals this must be so.

It may be asked what is the alternative to art schools, and the answer is simple. As Ervin Bossanyi says, a craftsman can only be taught in the workshop of a master. This is very true and it is far wiser to regard all forms of art as craftwork which becomes art when carried out by someone of fine aesthetic appreciation.

Take the case of some promising youngster with the intelligence and character that suggests the possibility of a future master craftsman. If he is interested in stained glass he would be wise to join a studio in which every branch of the craft is carried out. He

164

would, if the master craftsman were sufficiently wise, be taught to cut the glass, glaze it and cement it. Even if he were not given the opportunity to carry out this work himself he would at least see the work being done and understand the various processes which he would practise in his spare time. As soon as he was reasonably proficient he would be sent to the painting room to learn to trace. It would be folly to attempt to teach him painting at this stage because his knowledge of draughtsmanship would not be sufficiently advanced, but as soon as he was reasonably competent at tracing he would go to the drawing studio helping to cutline, draw out the sketch forms, start to space out the lettering and help to rough out the full-size cartoons. He could soon be put on to cartooning heraldry, doing research work and making drawings at museums and libraries of particular information needed. In his spare time and over the week-ends he should be developing his draughtsmanship.

From the beginning he has been able to see the whole process of production and to understand the object and necessity of his own training. Moreover, all this time he has, to his own advantage, been serving some useful purpose, a statement that could not possibly be applied to the thousands of students in art schools.

His seniors will be only too anxious to make use of whatever talents he may possess and sooner or later, through illness or rush of work, he will be given the opportunity of attempting more advanced tasks, always providing that he has the necessary ability. If he shows no promise, this fact will soon be apparent and instead of his being encouraged to pursue a hopeless aim, he will be advised to tackle some other profession for which his natural abilities are more suited.

The truth is that a very small proportion of the young people entering art schools today would suffice to meet all the national needs for craftwork, once the blind-alley occupation of art teaching was abolished. The majority would do better for themselves and their country by becoming, perhaps, surgeons, mechanics or finding some occupation in which manual dexterity or their particular abilities would prove of use.

All the leading stained glass artists of today learned their craft in the studio of a master but it should not be thought that this applies only to this particular craft. For example, a few years ago an intelligent young lady apprenticed herself with a premium to one of our best illustrators. She had had no art school training and yet, after only one year acting as his bottle washer and general assistant she was able to earn a modest living with her own work.

The truth is that the national needs as regards art production in all its forms can be gauged by the number of craftsmen earning their living by their craft. Any successful craftsman can make very good use of at least one assistant, and if all art schools were abolished the necessary recruitment of new master craftsmen could easily be met by these assistants. The only possible excuse for art schools is that they may possibly have some national value as therapeutic institutions but this is a matter for the British Medical Association to decide.

Perhaps it might be beneficial to keep some schools open in the evenings to act as centres where amateurs might interest themselves in some form of craft as a hobby. Evening life classes might be advantageous but admission should generally only be granted to those who were actually engaged in the day in some form of craft work, using the term to include illustration, commercial designing and so on.

The futility of art schools became very apparent not so many years ago when innumerable students were studying to acquire Art Master Certificates. Successful candidates then proceeded to teach other students how to teach other students how to acquire Art Master Certificates. It took some time for it to be generally recognized that this had no relationship with craftwork and still less with art. Finally inflation set in; the A.M.C. had to be devalued and an attempt made to correlate supply and demand. It is probable that even today there are far too many students studying, not for any creative purpose, but primarily to obtain a safe teaching job with a pension attached. For those about to marry, ignoring Mr. Punch's advice, this is understandable, but again it has nothing to do with craft production or the advancement of art. It cannot be sufficiently stressed that there is no such thing as a teacher of art; there can only be a craftsman teaching his craft by knowledge acquired through practical experience.

Theoretically the best students are awarded a scholarship, a misfortune from which many of them never completely recover. This statement is not a mere expression of prejudiced opinion but the result of having seen students of undoubted promise return from a two or three years sojourn at Rome with a portfolio of utterly slick and commonplace work. That fine sculptor, Jagger, told Rupert Moore, A.R.C.A., that it was only the world war that saved him from the effects of his scholarships. This seems too high a price to pay even for the sake of art.

The reason that such scholarships are so harmful is because they further prolong the period in which the student is debarred from the realities of life. It is not possible to study with any really beneficial effect until the purpose of the study is understood, and this knowledge cannot be acquired without participation in the activities of a real world. No doubt this was why Arnold Bennett and H. G. Wells were always antagonistic to academical institutions and would therefore have included these scholarships among their abhorrences.

Creative ability either in literature or the visual arts does not germinate in any scholastic curriculum. It is ludicrous to suppose that any school or university could have produced a Cervantes, a Dostoyevsky, a Shakespeare or a Bernard Shaw. To imagine vainly that such men would benefit from an art school training or a Rome scholarship is to descend from the sublime to the ridiculous.

Nevertheless scholarships can be and, in fact are, awarded in circumstances that help young craftsmen. The Worshipful Company of Glaziers and Painters of Glass each year invite anyone up to the age of twenty-six who is actually working under a master in stained glass, to submit one panel of stained glass entirely carried out by the applicant, together with the design and full-size cartoon. These are assembled under nom-de-plumes and judged by a panel of the leading stained glass artists of the day. The first prize is £200, the second is £100 and the third £50, together with consolation awards. The money is paid half-yearly for two years with no restrictions as to its use, so that it can be spent on travelling, buying any necessary reference books, or in any way that the recipient chooses. This is an excellent way of encouraging talent, and it is specially helpful because, instead of causing a delay in his real training, it aids the young craftsman whilst he is actually continuing with his real work in life.

It is to be regretted that the appropriate authorities do not scrap the academical and artificial scholarships and devote the money instead to young craftsmen who have already proved a definite ability and interest in some form of creative work. There is difficulty in avoiding the uncomfortable suspicion that the object of academical scholarships is not so much to encourage art as to bolster up the attendance at art schools.

If the lives of the great artists are studied it will be found that they all had their training as assistants to artists who were earning their living by their craft. In many cases, the masters were practically unknown or accepted as second-rate, but they were quite competent to teach the craft, and this, it must be emphasized, is all that can be taught. An interesting experiment has recently been carried out to introduce reality into the curriculum of the Royal College of Art, South Kensington. The master and two former students of the stained glass school were commissioned to carry out the windows for Coventry Cathedral in the school studios. Naturally this raised difficulties of administration as public funds and facilities must not be used for private gain. These difficulties were finally overcome but the arrangement is not regarded with any great enthusiasm by the world of stained glass artists generally. The experiment with the Coventry windows is interesting but it is not the complete answer. The solution is better expressed in a letter by Mr. Terence Mullaby in the *Daily Telegraph*:

'Sir,

How right Mr. Claude Muncaster is to acclaim the past achievements of Venetian Art, to note the continuance of a great tradition, and to lament our own artistic poverty.

But is not the sorry state of the visual arts in Britain due in part to the art schools? They are no substitute for the old master-pupil relationship.

However much sympathy one may have for certain art schools, they are inevitably cold and impersonal when compared with a studio in which the pupils and assistants work alongside the master and are in continual contact with him.

I believe that as a first step towards regaining the artist's responsibility to eternity of which Mr. Muncaster speaks, we need more pupils in the old sense of the word, not more art schools.

This is an impatient age. The young artist of today learns the bare rudiments of his craft and then rushes out to try to get a one-man show. Those of us who frequent the London Galleries will remember a surprisingly large number of exhibitions of the work of very young artists.

How much better it would be if, as in the past, the young artist served his apprenticeship under an established master, and how much the better, too, it would be if at first he prepared the canvas or panel to be used by the master, ground colours, and swept the studio, rather than squeezed paint out of a tube on to a lifeless synthetic board of a standard size. We might then have fewer cracks in recently painted pictures.

It may be objected that a revival of the old master-pupil system is an economic impossibility. But I cannot help feeling that if the art student were prepared, in return for his keep, to work for an established master, and thus really to learn his craft in all its facets, there would be many more established artists than there are at present.'

The following unbiased opinion is a quotation, by kind permission, from Mr. John Betjeman's delightful and instructive book *First and Last Loves*:

'Where shall we send the fellow? To an architectural school of course, where he will meet a lot of other healthy minded youngsters and learn to turn out prize medal drawings to be judged by Mr. Maufe, and learn to make letters in all the latest face-types, and elevations in all the latest mannerisms, and to cast lovely shadows down his elevations.

Are you surprised that with such people as this, frightened on the one side by the "dry-as-dust" antiquarian, tickled to death on the other by all the jolly tricks of a rebellious moderne, futurist, Swedish, cubistic, yet tasteful nature—are you surprised that architecture in England is what it is? With an Ealing veneer of antiquity or moderne-ity.

The time-honoured system of apprenticeship and practical experience, of being articled to an architect who either repulses you so much that you react against him as Bodley did to the elder Gilbert Scott, or evolve from him out of admiration as Soane did from the younger Dance—that system is over. That system created individualists, great men of whom Comper, Voysey, Ashbee, Lutyens, Baillie Scott and a few others survived.'

That system also created the old masters, in architecture, painting and stained glass.

These opinions are further substantiated by those of a distinguished architect, Mr. Louis Osman, M.A.(Arch.), F.R.I.B.A., who remarked, in his lecture to the Royal Society of Arts on Wednesday, 14th November, 1956:

'Clearly the holes in the creative artist's time should be filled by arranging that he should teach—that is education—and so we have between 1954 and 1955—I have the figures from the Ministry of Education—10,958 full-time art students under their "tape"—that is not counting the universities or part-time art students, or music or poetry or ballet—and 1,260 full-time and 4,727 part-time teachers—a frightening prospect. And what is happening: sometimes these institutions of learning have to carry out work of their own—but the artist is very rarely allowed to apply those standards in his work which his teaching taught him to consider essential. The universities have schools of architecture, decoration, fine art and history of art, and yet they often house their students in hostels from which any artistic expression is eliminated—often the work is done by commercial firms whose standards are utterly opposed to those which the schools themselves are teaching. Many artists of fame and promise, who would be creating, are either teaching a majority of students who will become teachers to teach more students to become teachers, or if they are not so serious, are using a sinecure to provide background security and to establish contacts and distinction and a ready call on a source of lightly-paid staff to carry out the works to which they will attach their name while they are at Royal Institute, club or charity ball, or giving talks on Children's Television or taking part in a panel game. "I don't bother much about commissions" said a silversmith to me the other day "I've got a well-paid job teaching—and the director bothers even less because his job is even better paid".'

PART 3

Modern Practice

Introduction to the Collation of
Contemporary Work

The craftsman and the connoisseur, when studying the stained glass masterpieces of past ages, often wonder what was in the minds of the men who created them. To what extent were those efforts deliberately planned and how much was intuitional or accidental? Were they due to technical necessities or have they been produced as a result of weathering, breakages, re-leading or restoration? No doubt all these influences have been at work and it would be interesting to know the thoughts that guided the masters of those days in the creation of their windows.

For the benefit of posterity as well as the modern student, most of the leading stained glass artists of today have been approached and have kindly consented to write a short account of the principles and considerations that guide them in the creation of their work.

They have also kindly supplied an illustration of one of their windows. This, of course, presents an insuperable difficulty, because no single example can fully illustrate the scope of a craftsman's work. It can only give a slight indication, and, even then, the photograph cannot give the full aesthetic effect of the actual window in its architectural setting.

Again, as regards the articles, they probably need to be read with some understanding and reservation. For example, it may be noted that the stress all the time seems to be on material and craft with little or no emphasis on the guiding spiritual motivation. This lack of spiritual declaration is of course a characteristic of the present age which no artist can entirely escape, and it must be remembered that the modern individual is extremely reticent about his innermost feelings and convictions, any expression of which, in an age of sophistication, might be regarded as rather bad taste. There is also the fact that the finest characters hesitate to express ideals and high spiritual motives which they feel are too seldom even moderately realized.

I mention this as it is my conviction that a comparison between medieval work and that of later periods shows an aesthetic decline which generally seems to parallel the decline in spiritual consciousness to that of a prosaic individualistic materialism. Whilst the conditions of life enabled or even impelled the medieval individual to gaze at the stars, a constant reminder of the immensities, the view of modern man is obviously too often restricted by the neon lights in Piccadilly Circus.

In the earliest practical treatise on glass painting, written in the twelfth century by Theophilus, alias Rogerus, priest and monk, we have an indication of the medieval spirit at its best.

> 'God knows that it is neither from the love of man's applause nor the desire of earthly reward that I have written what is here contained, and I have kept back nothing valuable out of jealousy or envy, but that I have endeavoured to supply the wants of many, and have considered their advantage for the increase of the honour and glory of His Name.'

Dom Charles Norris, O.S.B., writes in the *Buckfast Abbey Chronicle*:

> 'No considerations of any medieval art are of much value if they do not take into account the vigorous intellectual and religious background of the artists, the strong traditions and the eminent social respectability of the craft guilds. The inspiration of Art was religious, its appeal was chiefly intellectual, and its expression, like the official liturgical worship, was impersonal in character. Historians and archaeologists who as a race are not expected to manifest much sentiment seldom leave their studies of medieval art without giving expression to their respect, even of awe, in presence of something which they can hardly understand, much less express in words.'

Professor Lethaby writes:

> 'They are more than buildings, more than Art; something intangible was built into them with their stones and burnt into their glass.'

I believe that the majority of my fellow-craftsmen would agree with that distinguished author, Mr. T. S. Eliot, when he observes in his book *Notes towards the Definition of Culture*:

> 'The artistic sensibility is impoverished by its divorce from the religious sensibility.'

And further:

> 'Aesthetic sensibility must be extended into spiritual perception and spiritual perception must be extended into aesthetic sensibility and disciplined taste before we are qualified to pass judgement upon decadence, diabolism or nihilism in Art. To judge a work of Art by religious or artistic standards should come in the end to the same thing; though it is an end at which no individual can arrive.'

It may not be inappropriate to remind the youthful student that technical abilities are not in themselves sufficient, a fact so well suggested in this further quotation from Mr. Eliot:

> '. . . the apprentice (ideally, at least) did not merely serve his master, and did not merely learn from him as one would learn at a technical school—he became assimilated into a way of life which went with that particular trade or craft; and perhaps the lost secret of the craft is this, that not merely a skill but an entire way of life was transmitted.'

PLATE 75. Glasgow Cathedral. Grisaille window designed by E. Liddall Armitage,
Whitefriars Studios, in collaboration with Sir Albert Richardson, P.P.R.A.

M. C. FARRAR BELL

Guiding Principles

What are the principles by which one works? Until asked such a question I suppose most designers and craftsmen take them very much for granted, like handwriting or riding a bicycle. One just sets to and the work grows, usually ending by looking rather different from what began in the mind's eye. Therein lies a large part of the fascination of a designer's work. Clearly there must be principles otherwise the cyclist falls off, and the design, whether it be stained glass or anything else, has no meaning; secondly, these principles inevitably have a strong bearing on the development of an artist's style.

I believe windows were placed in walls to let in light. That being so, I think, stained glass should enhance that light and decorate the opening without obscuring it. It follows that I like my windows to contain some clear glass, which accentuates the colour used by contrasting with it. Naturally there are exceptions, such as some east windows and very small lights where the main source of light is drawn from other windows. Even so, I like a window which is entirely filled with stained glass to be translucent without being heavy; by this I do not mean it should be pale and anaemic.

Strength is a quality I try to aim at. That is to say a boldness of the line drawing, a depth of colour, and a firmness and balance of composition. The leadlines in which all glass painters must work should not become shackles but should be worn easily and turned to the advantage of the design by way of emphasis to the line. When this is done satisfactorily the eye will accept them as part of the window and is scarcely conscious of them. I abominate the type of window which is so heavy with lead that it appears to be half black. Nevertheless the leads should be arranged in such a way that they will preserve the composition even if every painted line and shadow were removed. In short they should be a form of skeleton or foundation to the design and no more.

Glass is a translucent material. Its whole beauty depends on the light which passes through it. It is necessary, in places, to control this light by means of a little tone and texture, but I believe very strongly that the paint used for this purpose should be applied with a very light hand. The late Maurice Drake said of my father, Reginald Bell: 'He has realized the vital fact that he is most the master of his craft who paints his glass the least.' I can think of no words which express better what I mean. I can see no point in using a transparent material if one is going to make it opaque with a heavy, muddy film of paint. I have seen recently some windows destined for a modern cathedral in which part of the glass has been rendered literally black, so thick an impasto of paint had been applied to it. I wondered why the glass painter had not sent for a carpenter or a blacksmith who could have achieved obscurity with more efficiency.

Was ever artist born who could claim his work to be entirely original, save perhaps the first cave artist? We are all influenced by the work of our predecessors and sometimes by our contemporaries, and indeed it is only common sense to see how someone else has tackled a problem before having a go oneself. No one worth his salt has any desire to be a mere copyist, nor will this happen—for when did two people ever have the same handwriting? We can only strive to be original, but we cannot help being individual.

For myself I look to the fifteenth-century glass painters for translucency and to the fourteenth for depth of colour, and for sheer all round merit I need go no further than the work of my own father. No one could have had a better master or examplar; he drew with consummate ease, with lightness, power and strength. He never used a curved line where a straight one would serve better and was a complete master of portraying form by means of line. I never saw him make a drawing to which modelling or shading was a vital adjunct; the merest touch to suggest the shadow of an eye socket, the bridge of a nose and the like was all he ever used. I try my best to follow his lead but am too well aware I never do better than approach his excellence.

BO BESKOW

'The ideal of the stained glass artist must not be a picture made transparent, but a window made beautiful.'

I do not remember where I picked up this quotation: maybe from the kind Dean of York, smoking his pipe among the riches of his wonderful workshop; but it is a good and useful statement in discussions about glass. Stained glass is rapidly becoming a fashionable medium for younger painters; there is much talk about it and consequently much confusion. The material seems to inspire an ambition to create something 'new', something never done before. But glass is not an easy medium, and as in every field of art you have to learn the laws and limits before you can move freely within the boundaries and on the strength of this knowledge.

'A window made beautiful', that is the meaning of stained glass: to beautify the room and underline its architecture, to shine like a jewel set in the wall. That is how the first pieces of primitive glass were used in the temples of the Far East, and that is what we want to do today: adorn with jewels—a mass of pearls and diamonds as in the famous Sisters of York, or the heavenly blue of the Jesse window in Chartres, or gold and rubies in the churches of Gotland.

To choose the right jewellery for a fair lady is not an easy thing. When rightly done, the result is of staggering beauty. Could anything be more appropriate to Our Lady of Chartres than the harmonious falling scale of mostly blue, less red, some green, and very little yellow and white? And who would change the silvery robes of the sweet Sisters of York?

The 'story' told by the windows is of secondary importance. In the Jesse window of Chartres it is the blue space between the figures that makes it live and sparkle, and the Sisters of York tell no story but the story of beautiful pieces of glass put together by a good craftsman.

I do not underrate the windows' role of a *Biblia Pauperum*, the poor man's bible. A stained glass artist, working for a church, must know his bible by heart and find his

PLATE 76. University College Chapel, Kingston, Jamaica.
East window designed by E. Liddall Armitage, Whitefriars Studios.
Commissioned by Her Royal Highness, Princess Alice, Duchess of Athlone.

PLATE 77. St. Leopold Church in Luneville (Meurthe-et-Moselle) France, 'Christ In Glory', by J. Barillet.

PLATE 78. Soulbury Church, Leighton Buzzard, Bucks.
Designed and made by M. C. Farrar Bell, 1956.

inspiration in it. But if the strange processes of creation lead him to express his love in abstract or realistic form, it is of no importance, as long as he finds the right jewels and the right settings for this particular church.

I could write a long, more or less learned treatise on the subject of my windows for the ancient, Gothic Cathedral of Skara. They have taken me eleven years and will take eleven more at least. Each window means twelve square metres filled with five thousand pieces of stained glass. When I see the result so far, I feel no personal pride, only a little tired and surprised, and eager to go on with the work. I feel no need to talk about how I approached and planned this huge task, and others may judge the result. But I do like to talk about glass, in the hope of reaching others doing research on the same line.

For many years I have been looking for glass with the qualities of the earliest glass in Chartres and Canterbury. The glass in the market is far too clean and uninteresting to be used as it is. I have had to treat it in various ways and burn it at high temperatures to give it life and mystery. This is slow and tedious work, and takes away some of the colour and brilliancy of the glass. The blue glass in the Jesse window of Chartres has no aftertreatment; it has come right out of the pot, clear and fresh and full of fun, and ready to be cut and leaded as it was.

I have been trying to find the way back to the primitive glass, and together with a Danish artist I have worked out a very simple method of treating the glass taken directly from the melting pot. The result is very satisfying. I have now a stock of glass, where every piece is individually full of all the small blairs and irregularities that make glass interesting, make it sparkle and break the light. The range of colours is partly built on pieces of medieval glass, collected through the years. This glass is my palette, I can work directly with it.

There is great satisfaction in handling a glass you have made yourself—it makes me feel in closer contact with the timeless art of stained glass. I have used it in a newly-finished window to The Virgin, the patroness of the Cathedral of Skara.

Dulcis in memoriam
favus mel destillans.
Fiat tua gratia
firma mens vacillans.

ERVIN BOSSANYI

To try to comprehend what can only be felt, is an endeavour as understandable as it is futile. It is only human not to renounce success as long as life lasts. No failure, be it your own or someone else's, is a good enough deterrent. Man will always attempt to translate one element into another though in his very being he knows that to explain light in terms of shadow is just as impossible as to make the sun experience darkness.

Much has been spoken and written about music yet it vibrates unequalled in its inviolable dimension. Much has been explained about stained glass, yet its appeal to the special sense and special men is so unique that it remains, even in the sphere of painting, gracefully, self-sufficiently, ever lovably alone. None of its sister arts needs less illustrating words and none defies more subtly and more decidedly the literary approach, the monochrome and to a high degree the polychrome reproduction.

Far from venturing to substitute the seeing of original glass, i.e. the sensual recognition by words or intellectual construction (which endeavour must, I imagine, give the feeling of trying to put a giant oak tree back into its acorn shell) I give a few ideas about the approach to making stained glass windows.

We are the children of light; naturally we owe to it a kind of filial love and veneration.

Entering a room on a sunny morning one would first draw the curtains in order to let the flowers have their due of light. The mother when she opens the nursery window to the sun obeys the same instinct. We lean aside in order to avoid casting shadow over a book that is being read. Our gesture to maintain nature's life and health-giving conditions is spontaneous and its lack forms criterion of poor response.

When starting on a design for a window I must ask myself 'Have I sufficient reason for excluding any of nature's light and am I able to compensate my fellow men for that loss by what I give them in merely human values?' This is the necessary, the right, indeed the only approach and promising start for an artist who paints with light.

In a way it means to compete with the sky, nay with the superior of our celestial bodies, the sun. This admitted, the exigencies of painting with light become evident. The glass painter must possess unusual abilities in addition to those implied generally in the making of a work of art, for his medium, glass, is of enormous strength and durability.

This celestial palette is fuller than any other and demands a fuller range of talents. 'Paint what you love' is a propitious axiom for every artist but for the glass painter it is the *sine qua non* condition, together with this addition that he must paint for the given architectural setting.

To satisfy the demands of this art one must acquaint oneself with its peculiarities: the materials (glass) and its strong colour effect in transparency. To know the glass one must work with it and go through all the various processes to get a thorough knowledge of the technique. To design a window one must train oneself to make use of its peculiarities. To be able to do this not only is a highly developed colour sense necessary, with a feeling for translucency but also a sense of space and an appreciation of 'the spirit of architecture'. There is no better way of preparing a design than by making a small-scale transparency. The transparent model should be made accurately to scale using $\frac{1}{4}''$ plywood for the walls and $\frac{1}{8}''$ perspex for the window. The perspex can be fixed on to the plywood with very small screws.

The design should be drawn on the perspex with opaque fluid paint mixed with gum arabic sufficiently strong to resist wiping but not to resist scratching with wood. When the design has been carefully worked out on the front surface of the perspex in a distinct black and white drawing, the colouring can be commenced on the back of the perspex. Of course the colour scheme should have existed as a mental picture

PLATE 79. Skara Cathedral. The Virgin, by Bo Beskow.

PLATE 80. Canterbury Cathedral, south transept.
'Unity and Peace' window by Ervin Bossanyi.

PLATE 81. 'Angel brings blessings to washerwomen' by Ervin Bossanyi. Tate Gallery, London. Made 1939–41, erected 1948.

PLATE 82. 'Rafael', by Jan Brazda.

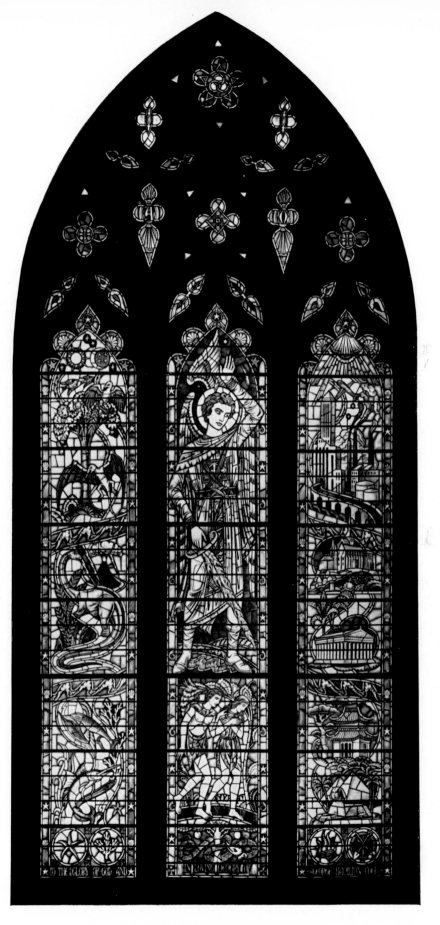

PLATE 83. Washington Cathedral. Choir clerestory window, Garden of Eden, by Wilbur Herbert Burnham.

from the start of the work and the colouring is now an attempt to realize this dream on the perspex. Winsor and Newton's Transparent Colour Paints can be used, or those of Herman Proll, Nuremburg—1. Lasur Rot, 2. Lasur Blau I, 3. Lasur Blau II, 4. Lasur Gelb.

JAN BRAZDA

Lumen de lumine

When working with stained glass I have tried above all to learn from the great epoch of the eleventh and twelfth centuries with its primitive glass and its few—but strong and pure—colours. The current demand that the material should produce its own effect has led me to a pure, unpainted glass, i.e. a glass that is not overlaid with a lead oxide film, the method which has been generally employed until now.

In my method of procedure without this patina, the gradation of light is achieved not through the application of paint to tone down the material, but simply through the simultaneous contrast of the mutual combination of the colours and the extent of their surfaces. Their power of radiation is hereby enhanced, subdued or extinguished. This cumulative blending of colours, where several excitations of light, each of which in itself causes different impressions of colour, simultaneously strike one point on the retina, creates the impression of a completely new sum of colour. One can say, therefore, that this dynamic process ensues in the space between the glass and the observer, where light is in a perpetual activity of the interference between the various sources of light. I try to limit my scale to a few colours, and by not applying a light-absorbing coat of black, they can pass their maximum strength and become saturated. The kinds of glass which exist are prepared for so-called 'antique treatment' and have a structure which did not satisfy me. I therefore sought the technical co-operation of my colleague Bergholtz. We have experimented with a 'ceramic' treatment of the glass. The glass is heated to melting point and is given a rough structure with an incomparable, greatly increased lustre. In its grained surface prisms are formed which break up the rays of light, thus creating an aureole. By this means one can eliminate the transparency of the glass without limiting its translucency. To my mind the function of glass is to present not a surface on which to paint but rather a 'pictorial material'. The essential thing is no longer the figurative or non-figurative 'picture' on the glass: the stream of light as a whole becomes the medium for the artist's message. More than any other form of visual art, this medium is able to make a direct appeal to the human spirit.

WILBUR HERBERT BURNHAM

The Middle Ages has been rightfully called 'The Golden Age of Stained Glass'. It was then that the Cathedrals of France and England were glorified and enriched by beautiful windows of coloured light in a most perfect art form. In no other art is colour so alive as when the light of God streams through a glorious pattern of primary hues, each colour giving value to the others.

M

For centuries artists and craftsmen have striven to recapture the same beauty of colour and deeply devotional character of the masterpieces of the Middle Ages, not always with much real success. In the Middle Ages, the Church was the chief patron of all the arts. A wave of religious fervour spread all over Europe. Artists and craftsmen became inspired to create works of art. Groups worked together keenly competing on a qualitative basis to glorify the House of God with beautiful stained glass, sculpture, and painting.

Unfortunately, in the periods that followed the basic principles upon which great windows were made were almost entirely forgotten with disastrous results. Ugly, sentimental pictures in a medium wholly unsuited for pictorial effects became the vogue, and the art went into a serious decline. Evidences of this decline and bad taste are still cropping up here and there, and all too frequently.

Fortunately, however, we are in the midst of a revival of stained glass all over the world. There are artists and craftsmen today with ability and imagination who are making windows to rival those of the Middle Ages. Radical changes in architecture to meet economic needs make it necessary for artists to search for new methods of making windows, and although they may borrow from the past, they are expressing their own ideas and emotions in straightforward and simple terms. They fully realize, too, that stained glass must always remain as a component part of an architectural whole. Many of their contemporary experiments are exciting and stimulating. In the years that lie ahead, all great windows whether traditional or contemporary, for churches or secular buildings, will be those in which the principles of the early window makers will be followed.

The 'Garden of Eden Window' is installed in the choir clerestory of Washington Cathedral, now slowly but surely rising in the Nation's Capitol. Because of its lofty location, scale became an important element to insure its carrying power. But the first consideration was to glorify the Cathedral with a beautiful pattern of translucent colour and to create a spiritual atmosphere to heighten the sacredness of a hallowed place.

ARTHUR E. BUSS

The technique I employ in making a design for a stained glass window is as follows:

Having previously visited the church, viewed the position of the window, discussed the subject of the window with the parson or architect and ascertained as much of the history of the church as possible and finally had the templates and sizes taken, I set out the window to inch-scale and ink in the outlines with indian ink. I then decide on the type of background to be used; this I usually discuss with the architect, as it is often required to carry on a scheme of glazing for the church, or to match an existing pattern. Normally these patterns are either quarries or squares or variations of them. Having, therefore, determined a suitable size of pane and arranged the bars as near as possible to twelve inches apart, I then proceed to sketch in the design, keeping all figures within the mullions even where the subject of the window is spread over two or three lights. The only exception to this is where the figure of Christ is drawn to a

PLATE 84. St. Angel's Church, Munich, Germany. Archangel St. Michael.
By Professor Bürkart, F. X. Zettler, Stained Glass Studios.

PLATE 86. St. John's Church, Hillingdon, Middlesex. Window designed by Arthur E. Buss. Godard & Gibbs.

PLATE 86. Aisle window, Christ Church, Bronxville, N.Y., U.S.A.
By Wilbur Herbert Burnham.

larger scale than the rest of the figures, when it is often necessary to allow the arms to extend into the side lights. I think it is quite wrong to disregard the stonework of a window, by letting the design run over the whole window space, making the stonework look as if it had been superimposed or was actually secondary to the design.

Before going too far with the pencilling in of the design, I place a sheet of tracing paper over the sketch form and carry on with the drawing; this prevents the surface of the water-colour paper being roughened by rubbing out the pencil too many times.

The rules I try to follow are:

1. To keep the drawing as flat as possible; that is, two-dimensional with as little perspective as I can manage.
2. When colouring the drawing with water-colours to keep the effect as heraldic as possible, counterchanging the tone, i.e. light on dark and dark on light, this will often necessitate making alterations to the drawing in order to get a balanced design or better colour shapes. If this rough design appears well or pleasing, I take the opportunity of showing it to the architect or parson first, for their criticism, before making the finished design.

Having now decided that the rough design is right, the outline of the drawing is transferred to the original sketch form. When this has been completed and the drawing corrected, I ink in the leadlines keeping the sizes of the pieces of glass about the size of the background shapes or smaller, leaving the actual heads of the figures as the largest pieces of glass.

When the inking has been completed I clean off the pencil lines leaving only a faint trace to help me when the detail is added. Next, the colours are washed in getting as near the rough design as possible. The final details are then pencilled in on top of the colour, keeping them as simple as possible and trying not to dull the colour in any way, and I then finish off with a wash of colour over the lines to fix them.

Naturally, each window has to be designed for its special position with a different set of problems to solve each time. I would, therefore, like to take an actual window to show how this technique works.

Plate 85, which will serve as an illustration, shows a portion of the east window of St. John's Church, Hillingdon. When I visited the church with the architect and Rector I saw that the window had been glazed with sheet quarries. This had given the congregation a very pleasant view of the park beyond with its fine trees, although the light coming through the window was too bright for the congregation facing it and the altar. It was felt that it would be rather nice to retain some of this clarity so as not to lose sight of the trees altogether and this was borne in mind. The main subject of the window was to be Our Lord in Glory and flanking this on the left the Virgin and on the right St. John the Baptist, as the two Patron Saints of the two altars in the church, whilst in the two extreme outside lights I included a series of shields depicting some of the persons and institutions that have played an important part in the history of the development of the Parish. During the course of my talk with the Rector he mentioned to me an old document he had found. This was a twelfth-century foundation document of the Vicarage when the living passed to the Bishop of Worcester in A.D. 1247. In this I was able to find an idea for a frieze for the base of the window; thus by placing a small figure of the Bishop of Worcester on the extreme right and one of the Bishop of London on the extreme left, I was able, between the two, to show the 'two carts of hay each drawn by two horses' payable each year by the Bishop of Worcester and tithes of calves and lambs, of fowls, of curtilagers and gardens, of young pigs, of milk, geese and cheese, of wool and wax and of the vine keeper. All this passes across the window in a long line, to be received by the Bishop of London. It will be easily understood that by the time I left the church, the window was more or less designed as a mental picture; all I had to do was to get all these ideas down on paper. Following the technique I have already described, the rough design was therefore prepared. The only thing that I added to the original ideas was to link the whole design together with the Tree of Life growing from the foot of the centre light and spreading throughout the whole window with foliage appropriate to each subject. Thus in the panel of Our Lady, lily leaves are to be seen, and in that of St. John, bulrushes, while in the historical panel a sturdy oak is growing. Certain colour alterations were made to the rough design, as it was desired to harmonize with a scheme of re-decoration being carried out by the architect.

Thus a combination of ideas, colouring and figure subjects were fused together and took shape in the finished design.

MARGARET CHILTON

My aim is to keep glass clear, to use light and bright colours with a good deal of light background. I am interested in the churches and try to make my compositions simple and understandable to the usual churchgoers: especially, as far as I can, I aim at drawing a good type of person to suggest something above the everyday figure. I would like to make a heroic type to attract children and young people, and at the same time keep to the limitations of glass.

In our workshop we use only antique and slab glasses (no sheet or other mechanically made glasses). We cast and mill our leads.

I try to make each part of the work good, as I believe that even the cutline should be beautiful in line, for well planned leadwork is an attraction from the outside of the building. I do not leave anything to an assistant: I make the design and draw out the cartoon to the last detail, plan bars and divisions, choose and cut the glass. This last is the most important of all because it is impossible for two people to see colour alike, and if the designer cuts his own glass he puts something of himself into it. I believe that all artists have a colour rhythm peculiar to themselves, as a musician has a sequence or phrase of sound; and if only successful designers would not give way to the temptation to turn out more work by employing more craftsmen, we should have more worthwhile windows to look at.

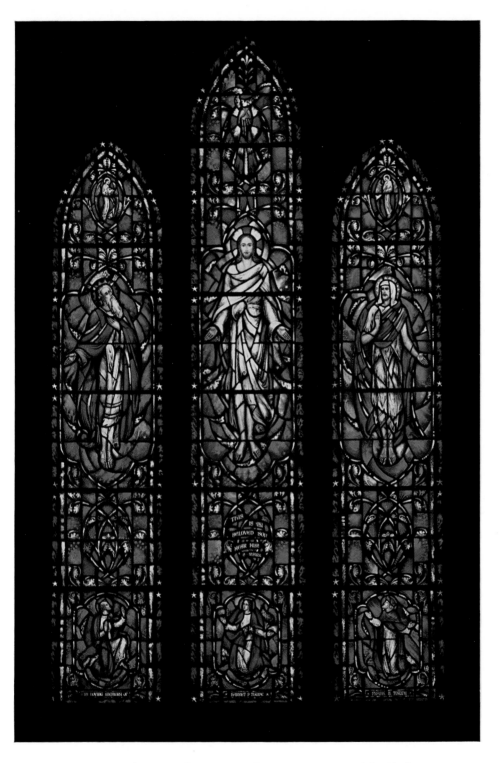

PLATE 87. The Transfiguration. The Towne Memorial Window.
In the Second Congregational Church, Holyoke, Massachusetts, U.S.A.
Designed and made by Charles J. Connick Associates, Boston, Massachusetts.

It is possible to add interest to the leadwork, varying the thicknesses at will. In painting I prefer light matt and strong line and a good deal of solid painting out.

Another important point is scale. One must study the building one is working for and get the right scale for the proposed ornament. So many windows dwarf the building by the size of the figures, which of course look larger than they are owing to the spread of light.

FREDERICK COLE

The first essential is to keep clearly in mind that a stained glass window is a form of architectural decoration in glass. It is a window, the purpose of which is to admit light. It is not a painting on glass and its narrative or picture value must always be subordinated to these dominant factors. At no time must the former functions be sacrificed in an attempt to achieve the latter.

The designer is subject to responsibilities and disciplines. The disciplines are imposed by the structure of the window, the architectural style and setting and most of all by the materials with which he works. Where the artist has a sense and appreciation of material, his designing will be influenced accordingly and sound work will result. The very limitations of material can be exploited to the ultimate and lasting beauty of the result. The overriding desire of the designer to express his personality through the medium of glass should be firmly suppressed; the church is a place of worship not an art gallery.

His responsibility is to the architecture which will receive his work, since it will be seen for good or bad for centuries to come, long after all who were associated with its conception have passed on. The whims, follies, fashions or insincerities will be forgotten and the work will be judged on its inherent qualities or weaknesses as a work of art.

Stained glass is not only a craft, it is an art and as such it is, to a large extent, the expression of an individual's conception of how his material shall be best used to solve a problem in architectural design and composition.

Some designers avoid as far as possible the use of lead, regarding it as ponderous and unsightly. They use large areas of glass, applying their interest and detail by the use of a semi-opaque pigment and planning the leads only where made necessary by consideration or constructions.

I do not subscribe to this school of thought. If a stained glass window has beauty, it is contained in the use and quality of colour. A large range of glasses of every colour and combination of colours is available, and if the whole range is to be exploited lead must be used to bond these colours together into a compositional whole. Lead is a material which can be likened to the setting for jewellery; without the setting the jewels must lose much of their quality of beauty.

It is not suggested that lead should be used to construct a kentish-rag pattern of glass. Its use should be planned in the design stage; the subject should be drawn in lead and painted in coloured glass.

This method makes it possible for any area of colour to contain an infinite variety in that colour; for instance, a robe can contain blues ranging from turquoise green to purple.

The use of paint can be reduced to a minimum. There is no beauty in paint, a brown opaque material with unfortunate powers of light resistance far in excess of coloured glass. It is used extensively by some artists in an attempt to make pictures out of windows. Paint should only be used to elaborate and clarify the sense of composition conceived primarily in colour and lead.

A stained glass window should always be designed in two dimensions. There should be no striving after effects of perspective or distant landscape for such effects are seldom convincing and stem invariably from a confusion of mind as to the purpose and function of a window.

One should never allow oneself to be persuaded into basing a stained glass window upon a painting such as the Light of the World or The Good Shepherd. To be guilty of such insincerity in one's work can result in sensations of frustration and certainly in loss of reputation. Such commissions should be spurned with a good heart.

Where light windows are required methods will vary but principles still apply; glass is still the material, beautifying a church is still the object using narrative or illustration to that end.

Colours should certainly be lighter when seen against pale-toned or white backgrounds. A wide and varied range of pale-toned glasses is available. Leads should be fewer and of smaller section. Silver stain with its wide tone range can be used extensively.

The designer and artist must always retain the power of self-criticism. It is not sufficient to experience gratification at completion of a commission. He must recognize that each window is full of faults and resolve that successive works shall be without those faults and so on in endless pursuit of the perfection he will never achieve. He may, however, achieve wisdom and humility, together with a curious and rare satisfaction.

CHARLES J. CONNICK ASSOCIATES

Colour has a way of expressing emotional ideas beyond the reach of words, and symbolism is the poet's way of expressing spiritual visions. Thus, the craftsman in stained glass possesses the means of setting forth high ideals in patterned form and colour.

Colour and light come first in our thought of windows. Our most successful designs have always been made to take full advantage of light, as the arrangements of great musical composers deal in sound.

Colours cannot be separated and placed in a vacuum. In our daily work we are constantly reminded that no colour lives in itself alone, but in its relation and association to other colours, just as the notes of a musical composition gain significance through association. The composer of stained glass scores must work with 'Brother Sun' in changing skies, to gain the deciding spirit of his movements and moods of colour.

PLATE 88. Westbourne Church, Glasgow. Centre of three lights, by Margaret Chilton.

PLATE 89. St. Mildred's Church, Lee, London, S.E. 12.
One pair of five two-light chancel apse windows,
by F. W. Cole, Messrs. William Morris & Co.

As in colour, so in form, stained glass finds expression in symbolism. It is the underlying ideal, not the surface appearance, the inner reality rather than the exterior manifestation of nature that we seek to represent in design and pattern. We strive to convey the essential image in symbolical form.

Although we have tremendous admiration for the ancient glass, we do not follow tradition beyond what we believe to be the natural idiom of the medium.

We believe that good stained glass is not fundamentally a question of style or period, but is related to inherent qualities of the material itself and its use in architecture. Recipes for beauty in terms of law destroy the creative faculty. And so we keep in mind the broader aspects of stained glass in original and contemporary feeling directly related to the individual character of the surrounding architecture. We believe that the design and detail of windows should be established, not only by the character of the structure, but by its exposure and distance from the eye of the observer. A window should become a harmonious part of the very wall surface.

Our figures and designs are stylized, but we make use of present-day knowledge of anatomy—designing in expressions of our own times.

We deal in terms of glass and lead. We may cut the glass in large or small pieces, and paint it lightly or heavily, or use no paint at all, but no matter how we manipulate our material, we do not lose sight of or conceal its inherent character.

While our windows cover a wide range of design, we feel there are certain qualities that are characteristic of all. Perhaps first is the purity and clarity of colour. Our palette is quite primary, and we do not use paint to shut out colour and light, but rather to pattern and enrich it. Areas of clear unobstructed glass are left in every piece, even where the pattern and texture are most obvious.

All of our designs are built on a geometric and rhythmic foundation, much as music is written; and this basic structure supports even the most complicated design. We like a continuous flow of line and form, but we feel that subjects should be contained within medallion shapes, with no truncated figures or objects cut off in mid-air that might be supposed to continue beyond the confines of the medallion. Unity and integrity of design and form, and an ethereal rather than earthly aspect is our objective.

Our group has been working together for so long that we function almost as one mind and one pair of hands. Each can just about anticipate what the other is going to think. We are, in the truest sense, a co-operative.

Our work is symbolic rather than realistic. As great music does not copy the actual sounds of nature, we do not follow her actual forms, but interpret her pattern and significance in terms of symbolism. We strive to use pattern and colour in light to express the high emotion of praise to God, much as the great organist uses keys and swell shutters for the same purpose.

The stained glass craftsman may be likened to the builder and harmonizer of Aeolian harps, grouped together on a large scale to voice in a volatile fashion, the shifting winds of praise and prayer of multitudes.

CUMMINGS STUDIOS

We are all familiar with the progress of an idea through discovery or re-discovery (as in the case of stained glass), slavish imitation, and eventual emancipation into the creative stage of fresh concepts, all the while adhering to the basic principles of the old. In the United States stained glass experienced a re-birth around the turn of the century, and for decades followed well the traditional patterns of design. In the last few years, however, another significant step seems to be occurring: the emergence into the creative stage, alive to adapt itself (as is becoming to the 'handmaid of architecture') to the dynamics of modern architecture.

Here in the West is this particularly true. The contemporary influence is seen in basic design, materials and techniques.

While the abstract in design is by no means new in stained glass, new uses have been evolved. For example, in the now famous little First Church of Christ, Scientist, in Belvedere (Marin County, California), stained glass has been used in vertical shafts of coloured glass on clear glass fields together with native redwood to form the walls of the church. The shafts themselves vary in width, and there is a play in the widths of the leads used as well. The coloration runs the spectrum, with celestial blues leading out from the high apex of this kite-shaped building.

The development of the technique of thick faceted glass in concrete (which we call 'Vitrolith') has been considerably forwarded technically, overcoming many of the early problems of fabrication. This challenging medium has been most effectively used in modern concrete buildings where it speaks with power and forthrightness.

Another technique perfected and proven is Lucent Mosaic, a cast process in which very small tesserae of glass are used with sparse or no painting. This method is especially effective where detail is important and has been used mostly in secular buildings.

Everybody's problem is one of cost, but often this leads to inventive thought, such as in the case of Sierra High School (Catholic), San Mateo, California, where a tremendous window area was covered by a background of variegated bronze, sherry and honey-coloured glass, on which a bold cross was imposed together with a free form band in primary colour and heavy lead, depicting the missionary travels of Father Junipera Serra establishing the Pacific Coast missions.

There is presently some movement toward the use of large sheets of coloured glass without benefit of tracing, matting or lead came in some ultra-modern buildings. However, it is usually the expedient of the limited budget, although when inherently beautiful glasses are used and colours are sensitively chosen, dramatic effects are sometimes obtained.

The photograph submitted for this book is one of a series of stained glass windows for Mission San Jose, California, and is an example of a modified style designed to compliment a modified type of architecture. The geometric background harmonizes with the rectangular form of the window opening, and a freer approach to matting

PLATE 90. Westminster Abbey. Triforium east window by Sir J. Ninian Comper, 1951.

PLATE 91. Window in the Dominican Convent.
Motherhouse and Novitiate Mission, San Jose, California, U.S.A.
Designed and executed by the Cummings Stained Glass Studios, San Francisco.

is used. The stylized figures, the even more untraditional colour (witness a blue donkey for St. Joseph), and the general dynamics of design meet the challenge of an architectural form breaking away from the old but not fully embracing the radically new.

Technically, the increased use of electricity in this country has brought a threat to the old gas kiln in which the successful firing of all the glass in the kiln was by no means a foregone conclusion, the glass on the outer edges of the trays often being imperfectly fired, only to be discovered during a later process in the making of the window. In the electric kiln, increasingly used here, heat is not only controlled but distributed evenly by a blower so that the many trays of glass being fired simultaneously are fired reliably regardless of their position in the kiln. We regard the use of the electric kiln as one of the most useful advances in the actual making of stained glass, eliminating disappointment, and labour that must be duplicated because of breakage or imperfect firing.

As we all know, lead creeps; that is, it expands more than it contracts. This partially accounts for some of the bulging of old stained glass windows. We observed through the years that chemical companies lined their acid tanks with lead and they found that the addition of a little tellurium increased the life of this lead to the extent that the relining of the tanks was not necessary nearly so often. We are able to have made lead came with a little tellurium in it; this greatly reduces the bulging previously mentioned, and we also find that this lead does not seem to oxidize so rapidly when held in stock.

Our government has interested itself in the problem of training stained glass apprentices along with those for other crafts and trades, and in co-operation with the Stained Glass Association of America, standards for training are set up and enforced. Apprentices are required not only to fulfil their time with the studios to which they are indentured, but they are required to attend school, studying specifically outlined subjects. Arrangements for this training are worked out with local school authorities and classes are held at night either in a technical high school or in one of the local glass shops where special equipment is available for the teaching of its use.

One of the most thrilling facts about the stained glass craft in the United States is the 'grading up' of the calibre and training of young men and women entering the craft. In recent years newcomers offer increasingly excellent background and training and the real feeling of craftsmanship. This was evidenced recently by the Third Apprentice Competition conducted by the Stained Glass Association of America in which were submitted, on the whole, by far the finest exhibitions of promise for the future of the craft yet seen.

Stained glass is indubitably in a true renaissance. Many of the medieval traditions which were the glory of the craft in its inception are no longer applicable to the demands of today. 'Time makes ancient creeds uncouth.' But cherishing the *principles* of this old and revered craft as its life's blood, the craftsman now starts again where the first craftsmen started, in the need of the hour to glorify the architecture of its own time, to create fitting atmospheres, and to inspire.

CARL EDWARDS

(Excerpts from a paper read to the Royal Society of Arts by Carl Edwards.
The Right Hon. Lord Mottistone, F.S.A., F.R.I.B.A., D.L., in the Chair.)

I believe that it is our duty as craftsmen to co-operate closely with architects . . . if we are to achieve a sense of unity and congruity in our churches. Alberti, the great Italian architect and scholar of the fifteenth century says, speaking of architecture: 'The business of congruity is to put together members differing from each other in nature in such a manner that they may conspire to form a beautiful whole.' It is, therefore, reasonable for a craftsman to subject himself to the architect's concept of a building so that there may be harmony in all its parts. . . .

Too often people confuse stained glass with picture painting. They will discuss a panel of glass in an exhibition on the merits of the techniques employed, on the type of draughtsmanship and other abstract qualities which may please them. They do not always appear to be aware that all these qualities are but a means to an end. That the panels would look entirely different in a building such as a church does not occur to them. Indeed the architect of the Temple Church, Mr. W. H. Godfrey, on seeing one of the east windows erected recently in the church suggested to me that I should keep people out of my studio, because the window looked so different when he saw it there.

One imagines a painter taking endless pains on the choice of a frame for his picture, and if his work is exhibited great trouble is taken to ensure that his work may be shown to advantage. A picture painter may paint, in any manner he pleases, whatever subject may interest him personally. How different it is for a stained glass artist or for that matter a mural painter or a sculptor, who works on the fabric of a church. The setting is there. It cannot be altered. The technique applied to the work must be adapted to the height or position which it is to occupy. The position might not be satisfactory. I have at the moment a commission on hand which is a series of windows behind which is a brick wall, three feet away from the glass, obscuring half of the windows. The problem is to unite the brilliant light at the top with the dullness of the bottom so the onlooker may enjoy the windows as a whole. One hears much of Chartres and rightly so. There the windows are marvellously placed so that they have clear and unobstructed light. But the glass of Chartres is not a yardstick for comparison with all other windows, nor indeed is any style of window absolute and proper for all buildings. An artist making his first window may have a love for rich vibrating colour, only to find that his first commission is a window which needs to be as light as possible because of the site of the building. He may find that his window receives so little light that he may not even be able to use colours at all. His window, however, especially if he is well grounded in his craft, can still be made to be very interesting.

Viollet Le Duc, the famous French architect, understood that there must be some order in the use of colour in windows. He knew that the medieval artists had great method in their planning of colours. He was able to point out that the decoration

PLATE 92. Cairo Cathedral.
Eighth Army window
designed by Carl Edwards, Whitefriars Studios.

16   19

GOD'S GIFT

S·STEPHEN

S·PAVL

PLATE 93. St. Stephen's Church, Dulwich. Cartoon for west window by Moira Forsyth.

and ornament had a function in controlling the colour and light, besides giving pleasure to the onlooker.

In order to understand stained glass one must consider it in connexion with light. A coloured glass window will appear to be quite different in key in the afternoon light and in the twilight; the intensity of colour in glass varies according to the power of light behind it. Not only do the colours vary in intensity according to the light but they also spread beyond the actual areas and affect other colours.

Because colours radiate one into another the effect, unless carefully considered, can in some cases be most unpleasant. Blue and red, if placed next to each other, can intermingle and cause a very distasteful violet effect. To avoid this, white glass must be introduced to control the radiation. On the other hand, the fact that colours do affect one another is not always a disadvantage and a designer will learn from experience that by placing various colours in close proximity to one another, it is possible to obtain something that is very beautiful. There can, however, be no firm rules on the use of particular colours because so much depends on types of glass used, the position of the window and the methods employed by the artist.

To illustrate how colours spread I must mention the east windows I designed for the Lady Chapel of Liverpool Cathedral, and also the high-up north-east transept window. Here is was stipulated by the architect, Sir Giles Gilbert Scott, that they must be deep blue in effect, and that warm colours, particularly reds, were to be avoided because of the warm-coloured stone from which the cathedral is built. The difficulty of such a commission is that a good rich blue is a very powerful colour in itself; it will spread and dominate other colours. It is at its best in a dull or cool light. The danger therefore was that if pure blues were used they would have been too intense to be pleasant or that the windows would have been depressing, or dull and monotonous on a bright day. These difficulties were overcome by introducing bands of other colours and warm colours at decent intervals, but in such a manner that blue was allowed to dominate the colour scheme. By this method the area of pure blue used was not more than 25 per cent to 30 per cent of the total area of the windows; although at first glance from the floor the windows appear to be almost entirely blue and, which is important, the overall colour blue is very different in appearance from the blue glass that is actually used. It is a fact that light sets up all kinds of optical illusions in colour and detail. A tremendous number of pieces of glass were used and the effect in the studio was rather like a large mosaic of transparent colours. The amount of lead in the windows is enormous, but such is the effect of light spreading, or halation as it is called, in diminishing the value of the black lead, and so powerful is the effect of the blue spreading from one area to another, that one is not unduly conscious of the pattern values of the window.

I have mentioned this example in order to emphasize that ornament and colour patterns have a function in glass. I also have in mind a theory which maintained that a window could only be successful if it contained colours similar to those used in Chartres or other early medieval windows; that the colours also ought to be proportionate to each other. What the percentages were I forget. But all conditions are not equal, and there are early windows which do not conform to this rule, among them the windows in Burgos and Leon in Spain. Besides, modern colours, methods, materials and conditions make the question of design somewhat different from the medieval period.

It is impossible, I am glad to say, to make lasting scientific rules about art and each commission for a stained glass artist, particularly if he is true to his medium, is always an adventure and an experiment.

The artist must consider the height, light, materials and balance of colour in his work. The farther away the window is from the eye, the greater the apparent effect of the spreading of light. It follows that the strength of details must be increased in relation to the distance from the eye. Some types of glass radiate light much more than others, so that if different sorts are used in a window the details must be modified, or increased accordingly. Again, different colours do not radiate light equally. White glass tends to become firm and harsh at a distance. Blue is a heavy colour. Large areas of blue with equally large areas of red can get out of balance with one another, and it can appear that one colour is receding and the other coming forward quite considerably—a most disturbing effect, especially if these two colours are very rich in character. All this, however, can be controlled by the details painted on to the glass. If the jewel-like quality of the window is to be preserved, then the proportion of detail on each piece of glass will vary from colour to colour. An artist, if he has a good knowledge of abstract value of pattern, can transform an uninteresting piece of glass to something really brilliant, particularly if it is in its proper relationship with other colours.

I have endeavoured in this lecture to draw your attention to everyday problems of a stained glass artist; to emphasize that the life of a window is light, controlled jewelled light; to show you that the effect of wonderful colour is obtained by using fine pure colours and considering them in relation to one another; to remind you of the great difference between a picture painting and a stained glass window, because the details are not only painted on the glass to tell a story or show fine ornament but also must be considered in the abstract as a means of controlling colour and light, and finally, to show that there must be some kind of unity between the window and its setting. That is, variety but with harmony and thought of proportion.

HUGH EASTON

The following paragraphs show my method of working out the designing and execution of my windows.

I like to develop the design as I go on and not tie myself down to a scale drawing. Many artists prefer to put everything into the scale design and never depart from it; some even go as far as to have the scale drawings magnified by photography into full-size cartoons. I prefer to do the roughest of small drawings, sufficient to indicate to my client what can be done with the window. Then, I consider the design and its possibilities in my mind for as long as possible, turning over and working out different ways of treating the subject. Then I like to work out the whole window full-size

PLATE 94. Window by Hugh Easton from Rolls Royce Works, Derby.
(*By courtesy of Rolls Royce Ltd.*)

in a drawing, instead of spending time on small designs and drawings, and I am prepared to make several full-size drawings until I get what I want.

As for the work itself, I have been most fortunate in having Robert Hendra and Geoffery Harper who for many years have understood what I wanted in my work and have always been able to interpret my slightest drawing in paint. We have worked together for a long time and they came to me first when I was young and they were very young. Latterly, they have been doing their own work as well as mine and their technical knowledge and experience is, in my opinion unrivalled. Although I painted my earliest windows myself, I soon found that if one was fortunate enough to discover an artist who could paint and interpret one's drawings, a far greater technical mastery was achieved, when one had to spend so much time on the designing and drawing and carrying on the business of dealing with clients and committees. As far as the cutting and glazing of the windows is concerned, I have also been lucky in finding two perfect craftsmen, father and son: T. G. and Denis Harris, and they have glazed practically all my windows. I am a great believer in having as large a stock of raw glass as means can command and this is the only real argument for doing a large number of windows. I have done a great many and thus have a large stock of glass that gives me a very extensive 'palette', but as the years go by I feel it is better to do fewer windows and take longer and longer over them.

MOIRA FORSYTH

To work in the living and vibrant colour of stained glass, which changes with every mood of the weather and the play of light through the varying thicknesses and angles of the glass, is to realize that here is probably the most exicting of all the mediums of the artist—and the most difficult! The intense radiating power of light makes the art of glass-painting one of netting and filtering the light so as to enhance the beauty of the colour without dulling its brilliance. Medieval glass was not only a good deal thicker and more variable than most of ours, but with far greater depth and happy accidents of colour. Our over-purified oxides give us a much clearer glass, which usually needs more paint than the strong and vigorous line of the early medieval work. That vigour of treatment and sure understanding of the nature of the medium was lost in later developments, when the painting became more important than the glass; and though the work of the sixteenth century was often most interesting, the decadence of the craft had set in. Today, a healthy reaction against the pious platitudes and elaborate pictorial realism of Victorian windows has taught us to understand the essential soundness of medieval methods. Our technique differs very little from theirs, except in the most recent development; that of setting nuggets of glass in concrete, which is a reversion to the very beginnings of stained glass, when the Mohammedans first set jewels of coloured glass in screens of alabaster.

The limitations on the freedom of the artist in glass are, as in most arts, his most valuable assets. The ingredients of a window—glass, lead, and iron bars are capable of building up into massive size, but it is of primary importance that they should be used architecturally and related in scale and character to the building. The permanence of the materials, the laborious processes of the craft (and today, at least, their cost) make it a medium which is not suitable for empty trivialities, sketchy impressions, or merely fashionable stunts. Stained glass should have something to say which is of permanent value, which can be said with absolute sincerity, combining sound technique with a real love of the medium. Given respect for all these factors—the superb qualities of live, vibrant, joyous colour, of architectural dignity and of permanence, we have a medium capable of expressing the loftiest of human conceptions in positive terms. There is nothing negative about stained glass: its singing colour has a tremendous power of affirmation. It is no wonder that the medieval world seized upon it as the perfect medium for a strong and living faith. 'Sursum Corda' can be said more directly in glass than in any other medium, save that of music.

Perhaps the most difficult problem an artist can be given today is to make a window for a Gothic church, where comparison with past achievements is most immediate and failure most disastrous. It is a fatal mistake to imitate the old glass or produce a self-conscious pastiche of medieval naivety. Only one possibility of success is open to him, to work sincerely in his own idiom, but in harmony of mind and spirit with the builders of the past. If, when we look at some of our own productions, we reflect rather sadly on their comparison with the windows of the Middle Ages, we can, I think look back profitably over the factors which made them great and decide whether we have failed in vision, in technical ability, or in faith.

FOURMAINTRAUX

The designing of a stained glass window must be first of all dependent on the architecture. I strongly believe that, when designing a new church, the architect should think out exactly what the windows will be like. He must decide in advance on the colour and theme, and not leave it till the building is finished. He must from the beginning contact the stained glass designer, so that they can study the work together.

In modern churches, with the new technique of slab glass and cement, the window is part of the wall; it is, in fact, a transparent wall.

I think that liberty should always be given to the artist about the composition. There is nothing more annoying for an artist than to have to follow the ideas of a so-called client who often has no artistic experience.

Designing a stained glass window is great fun, but it is hard work. I often begin a design again more than ten times before I am satisfied with it.

I always try to be as simple as possible. I use a minimum of colour. I think Van Gogh's theory on colours is a great help. But in glass one has to deal with light; the problem is more difficult. Blacks are very important and give sometimes very good effects when well employed.

A stained glass window is not a picture, and I am against everything which gives this sensation. It is the reason why stained glass was decadent for several centuries. But now, since the last war, especially in France, we are trying to go back to the real art of stained glass, and the so-called St. Sulpice art is a thing of the past.

D. MARION GRANT

The principles which I believe to underlie the designing of stained glass windows are these:

1. *Architecture is the Dominant Factor.*

Failure to understand the intention of the architect produces conflict; the limitations set by the architect must be appreciated at the outset. Donors must choose artists whose work is likely to be suitable for the building, and artists must ask themselves whether it is the building that asks for the ideas they have, or whether it is they who wish to put their ideas into the building. A window that identifies itself with the building in effect, and with the teaching of the church in idea, is worth ten that identify themselves with any individual.

Although each period of architecture and each architect within that period sets limitations, the scope for new work within those limits is ample. Keep within them and you may enjoy the fullest liberty.

For this reason it is never necessary to imitate old styles. On the contrary, every building should be regarded as a tapestry for the ideas and current work of artists of each succeeding generation. But each generation must realize that it is responsible, not for creating a new idea for a building, but for developing the original one.

2. *The initial character of a building develops with additions to fabric and decoration, changes in its surroundings and its parochial history.*

No two buildings, even if built from the same plan at the same time, will remain similar in character and influence for long. Character develops with use.

A study of the architecture will show what the building was intended to be, and a design which took full account of this alone would stand a good chance of being 'right'. To get a successful answer you must appreciate what that building has in fact become.

Architecture alone will answer the question of what is required for general effect, whereas a study of the present character of a building will greatly influence the question of how you are going to set about it.

3. *The object of a window is to admit light.*

Let it do so; this does *not* rule out full colour. A treatment that covers a window with paint where it is not necessary, destroys the quality of glass which is one of the greatest assets of the glass medium. There can be no good reason for substituting brilliance and glory by gloom unless you are one of those people who believe gloominess and godliness to be akin.

4. *The position of the window in the church determines the list of subjects to choose from.*

The layout of a church follows, by tradition, a logical sequence which is not only practical but which corresponds to the milestones in the Christian Faith.

The font and main entrance are found at the west end. People are accommodated in the nave. The obvious subjects are Baptism and things of practical secular help taken from the Old and New Testaments, the parables and miracles of Our Lord being popularly chosen. Near to the pulpit where the Church's teaching is given, may be found the Transfiguration, and the Screen is the right place for the Crucifixion, so hat the chancel is free for the events following the Crucifixion.

Failure to appreciate this simple connexion between the building and its decoration often results in the Crucifixion being represented alone in the east window. So far as decoration is concerned, this means that the Christian Faith stops at Good Friday whereas the building does not admit any such thing.

It must be remembered that church decoration originally formed a plan for unfolding the teaching of the Christian faith, in an age when there were many who could neither read nor write, and when the church was the only source of learning.

5. *Subjects should be timeless.*

To pin the subject to a moment in history is to be avoided. It must be something as vital to future generations as to the present, and it will not be that if it dates.

St. Francis of Assisi when shown in the poverty of his calling to illustrate or develop some major subjects already displayed, as in a multi-light window, represents all the many qualities of which his life is an object lesson. Those qualities are timeless and so is his life, and a representation of it is being used to amplify what we want to say in a way which we can readily understand. But by himself, chosen as a subject as a memorial to some kind-hearted person called Francis, he means to the congregation in fifty years . . . what?

Recording current affairs and making too much of things local is to be guided by sentimentality which, however justified and understandable at the time, is lethal to good decoration since it will not last. All major subjects are timeless.

6. *Subjects must be clearly stated according to orthodox theology.*

When a specific subject is chosen it must be clearly stated, if it is to be recognized. The best chance of achieving this is to invite other peoples' minds to follow the best known route which is the orthodox teaching of the church.

7. *Subsidiary subjects and detail should be used to carry the mind on to further meditation and*
    enquiry.

The bigger the main subject, the more it is taken for granted and, like all things that are beyond our full comprehension, it will tend to be thought of almost too objectively.

The subsidiary subjects and detail may often be usefully used to bring the great line of thought of the main subject into our common experience.

8. *There is nothing against having a purely decorative window.*

Although this is true where space is sufficient, it is unhappily not often that such windows are considered practical. There is, however, generally an opportunity to get something into the detail of a window which is put there for no better reason than that it looks nice.

PLATE 95. Dovers Green Church, Reigate, Surrey. 'Bread' (*left*) and 'Wine', by Fourmaintraux, Whitefriars Studios.

PLATE 96. Window by Emil Frei, Inc., St. Louis, U.S.A.

PLATE 97. The Church of St. Andrew, Arcton Gifford, South Devon.
East window by D. Marion Grant.

QVID VIS REGINA

PLATE 98. St. John's Church, Norwich.
Panel from the Queen's window in the north transept,
by the John Hardman Studios.

PLATE 99. The Church of St.-Pierre d'Yvetot, Normandy. Part of the 10,000 square feet of glass by Max Ingrand. *(With acknowledgements to L'Art d'Eglise Abbaye St.-André, Bruges 3, Belgium.)*

PLATE 100. The Church of St.-Pierre d'Yvetot, Normandy.
The Crucifixion, by Max Ingrand.
(*With acknowledgements to* L'Art d'Eglise *Abbaye St.-André, Bruges 3, Belgium.*)

MAX INGRAND

A stained glass window is not only a collection of lead and glass of different colours or of different values. It is, indeed, by its very nature, a wall, translucent certainly, but nevertheless an enclosure made of materials of light, and, as such, the glass will not allow any 'holes' and should not dissociate itself from the rest of the architecture of the building of which it forms a part.

It has, moreover, an extremely important role to play: that of a creator of atmosphere, and on this subject I should like to quote a personal testimony.

Whilst a prisoner of war in Silesia, I took refuge in thoughts of Chartres Cathedral; for me a 'spiritual escape' and a means whereby I could forget the noise of the barracks and live again in quietness and the atmosphere of prayer and meditation that one feels as soon as one enters this wonderful cathedral.

Alas, when I attended mass on my return and because the stained glass had been removed, I found just a huge, white, dismal church, deprived of 'life' and its 'character' of pious meditation, and that extraordinary unique atmosphere that had preserved me during captivity from the burden of the incessant din.

It is the glass worker who makes a church 'prayerful', who makes it gay or dull, cold or warm, and who is the direct and most important collaborator of the architect, because he makes the building live and reflect the hours and the seasons—the sun and the night.

I believe that the craftsman in glass must, first of all, understand the building and serve it—its character and its size will determine the scale of the glass and its colour value. The colour of the masonry must also be taken into account. This is extremely important because it is the colour and the texture of the stone that will appeal to the glass worker, and will awaken in him that sensibility without which nothing valuable, or at any rate, vital can be created.

I believe, moreover, that the glassmaker must absorb the atmosphere of the building; and it is only when he has done so completely, that he will be able to seek his 'dominant colour' in relation to the amount of coloured light that he must allow to enter in order that the stone may retain its value.

I now come to the effect of the masonry on the glass, its effect on the value, the framing and consequently on the intensity.

It is difficult, extremely difficult, for the craftsman to foresee this. I confess that for my part, the more I go on, the more I feel myself incapable of doing it; and I now find it necessary to place a window once, or even several times, in position to be able to judge the colour intensity of the glass.

Moreover, it is necessary to make these trials in the best conditions: it will not do to put up a single panel. Pay attention to any face light—to any holes of light; as a small spot of white light destroys the value of an entire window.

And when you make this trial you will nearly always find that the effect of the masonry, the effect of the framing is considerable.

I can quote the example of Strasbourg. This window which, in keeping with Les

N

Monuments Historiques, I had kept very dark in the studio, proved to be too light when placed in position and it was necessary to change countless pieces, and place 'blacks' so that the window would 'hold' in its architectural settings.

Ageing of the glass must also be taken into account. Anyone who has examined old glass knows what a patina it has, and what unity this gives to the whole work.

Another consideration guiding the craftsman in the composition of his windows is the theme to be illustrated. There are, as we well know, windows without any iconographical theme which we call 'abstract' to use current terminology—although for me there is no abstraction in glass windows: abstraction does not exist when one works with light, filters it, plays with it—light is not abstract. But to come back to our theme, the glass designer does not have to adopt subjects which would lead to imagery with disastrous results. Nothing is more contrary to glass pictorial representation as most members of the clergy imagine it: 'to describe a scene'. I willingly give as my own view, the well-known definition of Maurice Denis: 'A picture is a flat surface covered with colours assembled in a certain order.' What better definition could you give a window, which before representing a saint or a scene, should be the tapestry of glass that I have tried to define at the beginning of this article: creating atmosphere and radiating unusual colours which are reflected in every stone on the pillars and the ground.

Moreover, the craftsman must take into account the position of the window he is composing, not to mention the orientation of the glass. According to its height, the design will vary. In the great windows of the nave of Notre Dame in Paris, it has been necessary to increase the size of the head of the saint in proportion to the rest of the body, so that from the nave the proportions appear correct.

Finally, the craftsman is often confronted with the problem of incorporating a window which he has to make into a building already containing old glass. This is always a delicate problem, and the assistance of the Monuments Historiques Français has, thanks to a man with a pre-destined name—Monsieur l'Inspecteur Général Verrier—helped craftsmen in this most difficult task by his very great understanding and grasp of the situation. For Monsieur Jean Verrier and his staff there is no question of making a cold and academical sketch; on the contrary, it is a question of bringing to the building a contemporary testimony, which, while respecting unity of colouring and scale, will permit the artist to keep his personality and affirm his writing.

In this way stained glass should be 'true' in its expression. It should also be so in its technique, in its matter, and if it is connected necessarily and intimately with the building for which it is intended, it should also be a sincere reflection of the artist.

THE J. R. LAMB STUDIOS

The value of tradition is exemplified by the history of the J. and R. Lamb Studios in the United States. Founded one hundred years ago, in 1857, by Joseph and Richard Lamb, upon the principle of sound craftsmanship and appreciation of fine design, as

PLATE 101. The 'Victory' window
in the Protestant chapel at Camp Lejeune.
Designed and executed by the J. and R. Lamb Studios.

well as of the requirements of church architecture, the Studios are now carried on by the third and fourth generations.

The basic principle upon which the studios have always worked is that there are certain fundamentals which must be considered first. These are:

1. The type of architecture of the church—whether Gothic, Romanesque, Byzantine, Modern, etc. One so often sees church windows which are completely out of harmony with the architecture of the church or with its size or location. For an example, it would seem quite out of place to design the type of window which should go in a cathedral and place it in a small Parish church where simplicity would be much more in keeping. Here again the question of colour enters. It would also be out of keeping to use the rich blues, reds and golds, which are so suitable for the Gothic edifice, in a Byzantine church for example, and when it comes to the church of modern architecture the older schools of glass, as found so beautifully exemplified in the Middle Ages, would again be entirely out of harmony with the modern feeling of the architecture. In fact the church of modern architecture has developed an entirely new concept of stained glass window design and the use of many new types of technique, craftsmanship and material. So, therefore, the architecture of the church is probably the first thing to consider.

2. The type of light and exposure. A study of both of these factors is essential because, as every one knows, a window which has a southern exposure should be designed using a different colour scheme than if the same window was placed on the north side of the church where the light is much colder and where sunlight, as a rule, does not hit. Another thing which is very apt to be overlooked is the strength of light. For example, the light as received in the latitude of London is quite different from the light received in the latitude of New York which is approximately the same as that of Rome. And, of course, as we go farther south toward the equator, the strength of the sun increases. Therefore it is essential to know the latitude of the church if a really careful study is to be made of the type of glass needed.

3. If an old church, to have the window harmonize (if possible and if consistent with good design) with older windows in the church. By this I do not mean that bad glass should be copied, but it is possible, even if there is bad glass in the church, at least to make the new windows good in design and, above all, harmonious in colour. If this is not possible it is better to forget the old windows and still make fine new ones. If it is a new church you should co-operate with the architect. The architect naturally wishes his building to be as fine as possible, but usually he is not an expert on stained glass and will welcome the suggestions of the stained glass artists and craftsmen as to what is most suitable for his particular building. It must be remembered that the building is his brain child, and therefore, it is not only wise but tactful to talk the matter over with him.

4. The denomination of the church must be considered. In the United States, possibly more than in Europe, this becomes a very important factor, not only as to

the subject matter selected, but also as to the character of the design. In the New World there are many newer denominations with much younger tradition than those found in the Old World. Therefore, in the New World particularly, this becomes an important matter to be considered and discussed with the minister, pastor or rector. This is both advisable and really necessary. In this connexion, however, one must be very careful not to be swayed away from good design and fine colour by an ecclesiastic who may not have the training or experience that the stained glass artist has.

As mentioned above, although many churches are architecturally of 'modern' or 'contemporary' design, and these churches are being built more and more frequently, a note of warning should be issued, which is that even though it becomes necessary to study and develop contemporary design, one should use only the best and discard the bad, because there is much of both.

After the above are studied it then becomes a matter of long training in drawing and design, a good eye for colour, a knowledge of the best of the older periods of stained glass, and of the various 'schools' of stained glass, as found in different countries; and trips to study the glass in the old cathedrals of England and the Continent are also more or less essential if the best traditions are to be followed.

The well trained, sincere stained glass artist will understand the above statements and will try to continue to develop in the best traditions of his ancient craft.

LAWRENCE LEE

Studio organization

This centres round the factor of *personal control*: that is, my control of the processes between the scale design and the finished window inclusive. It differs from most studios that I have seen in that I appear to take a hand in all these processes far more than the usual practice—particularly that of the so-called trade firms. This idea of control is, for me, a legacy of my association with Martin Travers, to whom I unreservedly acknowledge my debt. We are still too near to gain a proper estimate of his true worth in the stained glass world, but I believe he will come to be recognized as a most significant artist. His extraordinary ability to clear away the clutter of purist theories and legalistic nonsense and come directly to the root of the matter put me on a firm path: a path which I have travelled far from his own limits (as he always said I would) but still directly connected with its origin.

What did I learn from him in practical matters?

(*a*) The absolute insistence on first-class finish of scale designs coupled with many sound ideas on making these designs appear *like* stained glass.

(*b*) The heraldic principle in the use of simple schemes of colour based on the idea of metals (cold colours) on colours (warm colours) or vice versa.

(*c*) The commonsense use of leading—always your servant and not, as in so many cases, your master.

(*d*) The rejection of all types of painting which served to promote only natural-

PLATE 102. Christchurch, Port of Spain, Trinidad. 'The Living Christ', by Lawrence Lee.

HANNAH
ST ELIZABETH
TOBIAS
ST ANNE
RUTH
FOR THE GOOD ANGEL WILL KEEP HIM
ENTREAT ME NOT TO LEAVE THEE
HORACE & ELIZABETH ANDERSON
HANNAH ANN ANDERSON ALICE & SUSAN WOOD

PLATE 103. Cathedral Church of Saint Luke, Portland, Maine, U.S.A.
Designed by Rupert Moore, A.R.C.A., Whitefriars Studios.

istic effects in favour of a simple direct (but not easy) method of line and tone to express the essentials of face, hand or drapery: always with a sure understanding of, and a provision against, the tricks that light can play with one's efforts.

(*e*) Dependence on (*d*) the use of photostats rather than hand-drawn cartoons in order to preserve the 'freshness' of the sketch and insure that no assistant can deaden the original at this stage.

(*f*) The patient selection of colour to give the necessary break-down of large areas a richness derived from several hues or tones. This means holding a large stock of off-cuts and an iron determination to wade through them many, many times while cutting. This selection is perhaps the most vital of all the processes.

(*g*) Finally, however, much had to be left to assistants, the need for constant personal checks and often active working on any one of the processes.

This, with very little modification, is my own method. I have one senior assistant who is my second pair of hands and sometimes my second brain. He is responsible for the day-to-day working out of jobs. He is expert in interpreting the colours of a sketch in glass so that after a day's cutting I often need alter only one or two pieces. He drafts cutlines for the photostats, and does a good deal of initial matting on the glass as well as tracing, lettering and such hard and fast things as heraldic details and symbols. Every day we discuss the work together and I take over cutting and painting whenever possible, as well as checking and sometimes re-drawing cutlines. We never regard the sketch as absolute, trying always to maintain a fluid attitude to the lessons the actual glass can teach. This might mean quite drastic revision at times. When work is pressing, I use students or 'improvers'. The onset of the Coventry job simply meant that I duplicated this system, endeavouring to organize things so that I could maintain personal control at both studios.

Design

If I have any theories about good stained glass, I would say that it ought to follow the straightforward commonsense methods of the fourteenth- and fifteenth-century glaziers with the use of one's personal images, no matter how 'modern' they appear at first glance, provided they are in the authentic language of our own times—not just fashionable—and always with absolute regard for the two-dimensional limit of a window. In this sense all good glass must be abstract or have qualities of abstraction. What I have said in the foregoing paragraphs on my methods tries to insure this. My use of the word 'abstract' is a workshop one (not critic's verbiage) simply to define those qualities of glass and lead which go to make up a glassy extension of the surrounding wall. If, on this flat, richly coloured and patterned surface one finds figures and symbols that are quite intelligible *within those limits,* so much the better.

GABRIEL LOIRE

As I have been working for thirty years close to the Cathedral of Chartres, I have had ample opportunity to study its superb windows with profit, in all seasons and at every hour of the day.

Keeping to the pure tradition of stained glass which, in my opinion, is simply the combination of coloured glasses, and without breaking with the past, I have striven passionately to develop this great tradition to the utmost of my capacity.

The St. Just Glass Works manufacture glass of colour and beauty hitherto unequalled, and I have tried to make successful combinations of these glasses. The glass is about twenty-five millimetres in thickness and the pieces are held together by cement instead of the usual lead.

I have tried, by studying the proportion of black in the ancient glass of Chartres to obtain an equal sumptuousness by emphasizing in places the blacks in the drawing and cutting into the pieces of glass used.

By chipping the surface of the glass and by dividing up the figures, draperies, and landscape into small pieces, it has been my aim to retain in contemporary glass its modern expression of youthfulness and variety, and through the uneven chipping of the surface of the glass, the rays of light, unceasingly different in intensity and direction, give the utmost life to the work.

Thus, using a superb material and without resorting to any trick effects, I can maintain a purity and freedom of technique in stained glass. The thickness of the glass, held together as it is by reinforced concrete, allows for all kinds of innovations and in this way the craft goes on developing.

Using this method I have been able to design and construct a cupola made up of small panels, all different, following the ancient methods of vaulting (Chapelle du Carmel d'Avranches) and to erect in an elliptical apse, a large figure of Christ in Majesty (Chapelle des Oblats de Marie à Portmain-Mayenne). Recently, at Casablanca, I have put in the Church of Our Lady of Lourdes two immense walls of glass to the glory of Our Lady. (These panels are 45 metres in length and 5 metres high.)

Remembering that stained glass is an integral part of architecture, I think that, now more than ever, it is possible for it, with this new technique, to fulfil its role of dispenser of light and mysticism.

C. RUPERT MOORE

What are the salient points of designing a stained glass window? There are two which come to mind at once, and without which a window could not be a success. The first is that the design should be architectural and should be an extension of the architectural theme of the building itself. Secondly, the scale of the figures and treatment should be in keeping with the architectural setting into which the window is to go.

At the moment this cannot be too strongly stressed to the student, as the emphasis seems to be on personal expression in most of our art schools today. A window, unlike an easel picture, is not a space into which one pours one's 'liquid soul', whether one be a 'modern' or a 'traditionalist'. A window, in fact, is a very complex object with two very definite sides to its character. It has to perform its mundane functions

PLATE 104. Saint Yves Le Justicier (Private Collection), by Gabriel Loire.

PLATE 105. Detail of the B.P.M. (Shell) Jubilee Window, by Max Nauta.

PLATE 106. All Saints Church, Ebbw Vale, Monmouthshire.
Window in west end by Joseph E. Nuttgens.

PLATE 107. St. George's Church. Falk steel works.
Sesto San Giovanni, Milan.
The Annunciation, by Professor A. Panigati.

PLATE 108. East Liberty Presbyterian Church, Pittsburg, Pennsylvania, U.S.A.
Great Apocalypse window, by Reynolds, Francis and Rohnstock.

of keeping out the wet and letting in the light. It is this *light* which the designer should control to produce the desirable background to the functions to be performed within that building. His job, especially for church windows, is almost always impersonal, in direct contrast to the egoistical self-assertion which appears necessary in contemporary secular art. It is not enough to develop one strong personal style, even if that be an excellent one. Each architectural setting requires its own individual solution. The delicate tracery of a 'perpendicular' window demands a delicate treatment and delicate drawing, whereas a Norman window, or modern concrete church, would require powerful drawing and vigorous colour; the latter would possibly be better with the thick contemporary glass set in concrete which is devoid of drawing in the sense of line and tone painted in pigment on the surface and fired in. A designer's mind should be broad and elastic enough to be influenced solely by the architectural problem before him. He should be capable of designing delicately or boldly as required for each particular job.

The modern designer is at a decided disadvantage to his medieval counterpart. The men who produced the glass at Chartres had to contend with the style of, at the most, two centuries, whereas we have to deal with five extra centuries of tradition after they had finished their great work. How much easier it would be to have only one way of doing a window as they appear to have had. We may be called upon to design for any period of building including Renaissance or modern. We may be called upon to design for churches in the tropics where the *light has to be kept out,* or again in the southern hemisphere where the lighting problems are reversed, the windows in the north side being on the sunny side of the church. The example of my work chosen for illustration is of the 'light kept out' category and is consequently full colour with considerable painting. Of course, full colour need not keep out the light if it is kept light in tone and the drawing is kept to line with little or no shading.

This is a very important point in Britain. There is a prejudice against full colour on the ground of keeping out too much light. I have been into churches where it is necessary to turn on the electric light in order to carry on a normal morning service because of the 'dim religious light' from the stained glass. Surely this is the absolute hallmark of failure of design, cutting and painting.

Summing up, stained glass should control the quantity and quality of *light* entering the building. It should be designed in treatment, scale and colour in such a way that it is part of the fabric of the church. The purpose of a window is not to command attention at the expense of its neighbours, but form part of a harmonious whole. A window is *glass* and any treatment which ignores this fact must be bad.

When and only when he has satisfied the above requirements, is the designer free to do what he likes.

J. E. NUTTGENS

In stating the principles and ideals which are at the back of my mind when making a stained glass window, it is necessary to give a brief account of the influences which have moulded them. Starting as a draughtsman under Arthur Orr, I came under the spell of Christopher Whall and his pupil Karl Parsons, and stimulated by their pioneering movement towards the integration of artists and craftsmen, began to work on the glass itself under the latter. The most formative influence, however, came during the years I spent with Martin Travers, whose superb sense of design was matched by an instinct for suiting his work to the building. Later, the clarity and boldness of Eric Gill's philosophy of art affected me greatly. Under these influences, my approach was and is 'traditional'.

Primarily my aim is that a stained glass window should 'tell its story'—of subject, form and colour—simply and clearly. If all art is 'communication', then of all the arts, stained glass has the most to communicate. But in the communication of the story, the design and colour must inevitably be such that they could belong to no other medium; a window should never be merely 'leaded up' drawing. I dislike mannerisms and 'abstract' oddities of form made for their own sake. I think that any distortion of form is permissible only when it gives emphasis or point to the subject matter or is necessary for clarity of design, as in the conventionalized and attenuated forms in twelfth- and thirteenth-century glass.

At the same time, although I do not agree, because of its obscurity, with much of the 'abstract' character of contemporary stained glass, there is no doubt that it is a healthy and liberating influence; and we of the 'traditionalist' school should not allow prejudice to prevent us from understanding its principles, even though we question whether they can ever represent the final aim of any art. Although myself a 'traditionalist', I do not consciously use any forms derived from traditional sources. I believe that ultimately all forms are derived from Nature. Yet I do not advocate 'naturalism'; for it is the business of the stained glass artist to be true to the nature of the materials he uses and to integrate his forms with them, having regard to the limitations they impose: so that finally one can say, 'This is a stained glass window and nothing else.'

Another important point is this: I think that a stained glass window must bear some relationship to the structure and shape of the building for which it is designed. This does not involve the use of stylistic motifs; that would be as absurd as trying to imitate another person's handwriting. But it does mean that one should try to understand the necessary proportion one's work should have to the building. And though they may seem arbitrary, there are certain rules of suitability by which one is bound: the shapes of mitres may vary, but one would not expect a bishop to function in a bowler hat! And it is a waste of time to ask, 'why not?' Even so, this problem of suitability is a difficult one, and I can only hope that my own efforts to solve it have not suffered too badly from a good intention!

I find my general aims concisely expressed in two statements which I would like to quote in conclusion. One is by Lionel Johnson (1867–1902), who wrote, 'So long as art proceeds from, and appeals to, men of a whole and harmonious nature, art must express that wholeness and harmony.' The other is Eric Gill's dictum, 'Look after Goodness and Truth, and Beauty will look after herself'; and this last perhaps holds more true for the art of stained glass than for any other art.

JOSEPH G. REYNOLDS, *President*
Studio of Reynolds, Francis & Rohnstock, Boston, U.S.A.

To the young man who is considering the possibility of entering the field of designing and making stained glass windows it may not be presumptuous for a veteran of fifty years of working in this art and craft to set down a few principles and ideals which are worth striving for. Also it may be helpful to the beginner to realize the demands which will be made upon him if he is to be successful.

First of all stained glass is, or should be, a fine art. But all too often the owners of studios are not and do not claim to be artists. They are merely business men whose chief aim is to make money. They sell windows at so much per square foot and constantly underbid their competitors in order to land a commission. Such studios should be avoided by the beginner. He should serve his apprenticeship in an artist craftsman's studio, and there are such if he will search for them.

The demands upon the artist designer are great. First of all he must love and delight in colour, for stained glass means glass stained with colour in the making. Other necessary qualifications are creative imagination plus; the ability to draw the human figure; to work in pencil, water colour, pen and ink and charcoal; familiarity with the Bible, for most of the important work always has been and still is for churches, cathedrals and other religious edifices; a knowledge of work done in stained glass through the centuries and this knowledge gained by seeing the windows in place; a love of research, for his themes may be drawn from history, science, literature and all human activities; and whether or not he is a member of any church he should be spiritually minded and an idealist. Add to these qualities the ability to meet clients and committees and convince them that he knows how to design and make a distinctive and characterful window.

And this is not all. Stained glass by its very nature is a co-operative art. He must gather about him trained artists and craftsmen and inspire them with his own ideas and ideals. He should be able to design and make a window all by himself but he cannot hope to accomplish much with his own two hands alone. As soon as he has employees he is in business and has a payroll to meet, so he must be a business man also.

Stained glass has well been called the most elusive of the arts. Being able to design and make a window is not enough for a window is made for a particular place as a part of a building. Certain specific problems must be met and solved. These involve the location of the window, the distance from which it will be seen, the scale of the details and the quality of light it receives. A window may look beautiful in the studio and all wrong when it is installed in the place for which it was designed. No formula can be worked out which will solve every problem of light and scale. The ability to achieve something approaching the ideal is gained only by experience.

We hear much today about style. Everyone admits that the windows of Chartres are magnificent. Should we therefore copy Chartres? Certainly not, but the principles of light and colour so evident there cannot be ignored.

FRANCIS SPEAR

When asked, 'What are your principles when making stained glass?' my first re-action is to say: 'I have none, I just make stained glass.' But after consideration it appears that perhaps my first principle is that I just make stained glass.

There was a time when, as a pupil assistant of Martin Travers, and an art student at the Central School of Arts and Crafts, I felt that I was leading a double life, but I can remember the occasion clearly when this dilemma was cleared up by a visit to an exhibition of paintings of Matisse. For there I found an artist who saw things as a pattern of shapes and I realized that I could by his approach blend my two worlds to-gether. It was later when I was a student at the Royal College of Art under the guidance of Professor Travers that I discovered another most important part of the stained glass designer's equipment, a knowledge of Christian iconography, and from that time onwards I have remained a student of art (a different thing I believe from an art student) and a student of symbolism. I feel that these autobiographical details are important in our explanation of my approach to designing and making stained glass.

When I am asked to design a stained glass window I do not like to form the idea of what I am going to put on paper too quickly. I like to meet everyone concerned with the proposed work for both the building and the people give the atmosphere or 'feel' of a particular job. Students and young stained glass workers have said to me, 'Why don't you do what you want to do and take no notice of these people?' The truth must be told, that I have no special type of design that I am itching to make. The stained glass that I want to make is what I believe they want, in terms of my integrity as an artist.

As to the actual treatment of the stained glass itself, I know that every window that I design is reminiscent of the type of stained glass of some past period, but I discreetly use the pictorial language of the contemporary painter, although I have to bear in mind that much of this idiom—the forms and shapes used by the modern artist—is for the purpose of expressing contemporary ideas such as the Freudian inevitability of the Surrealists and the hopelessness of atheistic existentialism, and these forms and shapes do not suit the hopefulness of the Christian Faith.

So far I have only talked of designing. When I come to get a design made into stained glass, if I have made a detail sketch I have this enlarged to full size by photo-graphy, but more often I work more into the design by making full-size drawings usually using ink line and wash. For the last few years I have not painted glass myself but I hand the cartoons to an assistant whom, while I have been full-sizing, I have had in mind. I employ three to four assistants: at the present time two men and two women. One is a glazier who does all the glazing, some of the cutting but at times turns his hand to simple painting. The others are painters, who all help with the first setting out of sketches and designs, but as each is responsible for a particular job, he or she usually cuts the glass and so is also responsible for the colour. Each of my assist-ants is given freedom in the interpretation of the cartoon into stained glass. My part in the painting of the glass is to put in appearances at the workshops to say a word

PLATE 109. Highbury Grove, Christ Church, transept window.
The Last Supper, by Francis H. Spear.

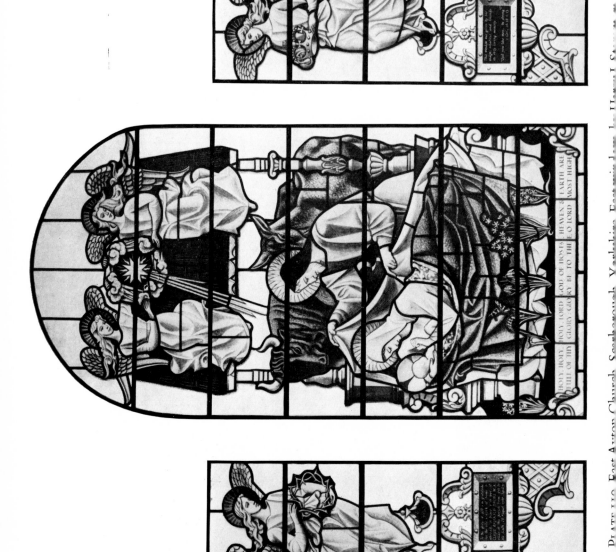

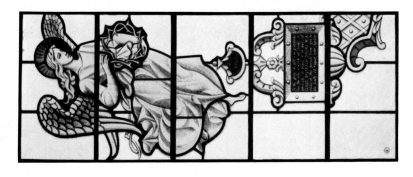

PLATE 116. East Ayton Church, Scarborough, Yorkshire, East window. James Ley, Harry J. Stammers

PLATE 111. L'église St. Lambert, Bonnine, Namur, Belgium.
One of a series of aisle windows by Steger.

PLATE 112. Part of Resurrection window.
Heckershausen Bezirk Kassel, Western Germany, by Richard Süssmuth.

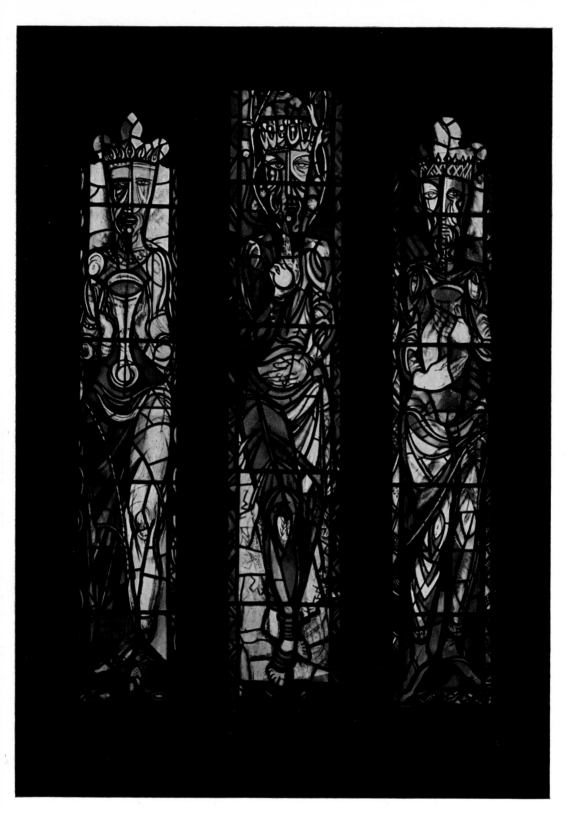

PLATE 113. Oundle School Chapel.
Central window designed by John Piper, executed by Patrick Reyntiens.

here and throw in a suggestion there, but as far as possible after the cartoon is handed out, the window is from then on the assistant's.

STEGER

The use of stained glass in places of worship has caused it to be generally but erroneously regarded as an art that belongs exclusively to the church.

What is certain is that, except on rare occasions, it has followed the tendency which has characterized the decline of sacred art, and if today it is treated as a poor relation, this is due to the fact of its having lost touch with the realities and tendencies of contemporary art. This is the cause of the uncertainty and hesitation which is apparent in modern craftsmen who ignore, often deliberately, the unsuspected resources which glass offers, whichever the technique that may be employed.

The need is to re-establish this broken confidence, and at the same time to strengthen it with a more healthy understanding. The draughtsman and executant must seize the opportunity of discarding all prejudices and clearing away the whole arsenal of accessories and other obsolete symbols, particularly in the case of the church, and give the problems a simple and essential solution without any compromise—even at the risk of failing.

The connoisseur of glass must be made to understand that he is not being offered an *objet de luxe* or a palliative to an error in the architectural order. Glass must be given its own *raison d'etre*, and not used as an attempt to mask an architectural mistake which must be ignored unless it proves itself to be indispensable. Everything must be discarded to become transparent, luminous and simple as glass, without any compromise, and accepting all the risks. But what humility is needed for the rediscovery.

Coloured light can contribute to our way of life just as much as any material, but its judicious use needs to be controlled by an artistic sensibility. Here simplicity and a palette reduced to essentials will have most chance of succeeding. As for the execution, this will then adapt itself to the material and economic conditions of existence.

In short, glass must be freed from a complex which seems to exclude it from the inquietudes and researches of an epoch in full evolution. Why should it not participate totally and courageously?

RICHARD SÜSSMUTH

Painting with glass, and with transparent glass only, is the true method of glass painting. The contour is formed mostly by the leads, and only such details as the eyes, the line of the nose or mouth, the drawing of a hand or a fold in a garment should be painted on with black ceramic paint and fired in the kiln. This is the way it was done a thousand years ago and we cannot do better today. The craft went through a period of decadence when enamel colours were used, thus obscuring the natural translucency of the glass. The stained glass windows of this period were an attempted imitation of the effect of oil painting on canvas; the light and sparkle, and the severity and clearness of the composition and the colouring were lacking. It is my endeavour, when working on windows to use the material as it should be used, following the traditional technique of medieval days.

Besides this ancient method of working with glass, I also make transparent glass mosaics. The coloured picture is made up of many small pieces of glass cut to shape and fixed in position upon clear white glass by means of a transparent adhesive. There is no leading and the clear transparent adhesive allows the light to show in the small space between each piece of glass. Windows made in this way give a much more transparent effect than those in which leading is used.

A third kind of artistic glass work that I carry out in my workshops is the grinding and cutting of glass. Ornaments and figures are cut out from flashed glass of two different colours and this method produces excellent effects in modern buildings. Such windows have an interesting appearance when the thick glass slabs are cut to varying depths causing a graduation of colour giving not only a plastic but also a fine aesthetic effect. The work is also carried out in glass of one colour only.

CHRISTOPHER WEBB

Stained and painted glass is essentially a product of Gothic architecture, and when it is sometimes asked whether there is any place for stained glass in modern ecclesiastical architecture, we would do well to remember that had there been no Gothic Revival early in the nineteenth century there would have been no revival of the glass painter's art as it was practised in the Middle Ages.

Like the sister craft of mural painting, the development of glass painting in this country proceeded from simple geometrical grisaille with little if any colour used entirely as architectural embellishment, to the highly detailed representation in colour and stain of biblical scenes or Legends of the Saints—in short the glass became the *Biblia Pauperum*. The point to remember is that painted glass was a part of the architectural decoration of a church from the beginning: in an age when few were able to read, the enormous possibilities provided for teaching the Faith pictorially in window openings of an ever-increasing size were quickly seized. The great days of stained glass covered the period from the beginning of the thirteenth century to the first quarter of the sixteenth century, some two hundred and fifty years. Although with the coming of Renaissance influences from abroad we find classical motifs taking their place with great charm in the glass of the period, yet both in England and elsewhere in Europe the coming of the Classic Revival spelt the end for the art of the Glass Painter. In England the process was hastened not so much by the Prayer Book Reformers as by the Puritans after them, when almost all colour work whether upon walls, carvings, or in glass disappeared from our churches.

It is perhaps difficult for people at the present day to realize the effect of a great medieval chancel in which everything had been designed as an architectural entity to focus attention on the altar, yet this was in fact the ultimate aim. From the Civil War

PLATE 114. St. Francis Church, Ashton Gate, Bristol. East window, by Christopher Webb.

PLATE 115.
Borton
Grammar
School,
Lincolnshire.
One of ten
panels of
Oriel
window,
by Alfred L.
Wilkinson.

until the Gothic Revival colour practically disappeared from our churches, and we have to thank the Revival architects for the re-introduction of colour into public worship. The desire for colour is a natural instinct that has to be taken into account in our modern churches: it cannot always be satisfied in our northern climate except by the translucence of coloured glass. Although coloured glass either painted or unpainted is being used in the decoration of churches of an untraditional style of architecture, it is possible that the glass painter is, contrary to the intentions of his predecessors in the Middle Ages, inclined to forget the purpose of stained glass in a desire to be above everything original. Another matter for reflection is the temptation for the glass designer to treat his work in the manner of an easel painting—that is without considering that the glass should be a part of the general architectural treatment. It should be remembered moreover that the first purpose of a window is to admit daylight and that once this is shut out and artificial lighting has to be resorted to a coloured window defeats its own end.

Most people would regard the deliberate exclusion, on grounds of anachronism, of stained glass from a modern church as constituting a real artistic loss, and as a confession of failure on the part of the architect and glass designer. For artistic reasons, and in these days on grounds of economy as well, there is much to be said for restricting painted glass to one particular window in a church designed with this treatment in mind; when the traditional plan is adopted the window would properly be at the east end above the altar where it would form an important part of the altar composition. Yet the designer cannot get away from the fact that no improvement on a purely medieval craft and medieval technique has yet been discovered, and it is perhaps due to a desperate effort to forget this as much as the deliberate avoidance of producing anything at all like medieval stained glass or Victorian copyism that has led to the production of so much unsuitable and unintelligible glass.

ALFRED L. WILKINSON

I suppose one has a guiding principle when designing and making stained glass. It usually lies hidden in the subconscious, active yet undefined until some question or event demands its definition; and definition is exceedingly difficult if an artist has a lively sense of the feeling of the extremely varied styles and requirements of different buildings.

Firstly it is essential to retain and enhance the beauty of the material, glass. Secondly it is vitally important to subordinate one's work to the building. This subordination is a discipline within which an artist is free to develop his own personality: it requires no essay in plagiarism, though it should prevent an artist from using a whole building as a frame in which to display a window: it dictates the use of a scale of proportions relevant to the fabric and existing ornamentation. Thirdly the colour must vary with the aspect and position of a window as well as to accord with any scheme already set in the building: some colours may be bright and joyous while not garish, others may be deep and rich, some even dull in tone when glare needs to be mastered.

Fourthly the work must be designed and made as decoration. Lastly, I emphasize a desire to uphold the sense of chastity which is a feature of much English stained glass, a feature which gives scope for strength nevertheless.

It is essential to retain the virtue of humility, which is easily lost in the atmosphere surrounding a student in his final year at College. A client may have firm views about his requirements and these views are not to be ignored lightly. It is important to realize that the object of a window is not to revolutionize the art world, but to express ideas and feelings which your client cherishes, and, if for a Church, to further the worship of God. So do not debase your art, but raise it after a computation of the client's wishes and the aesthetic necessities. This is what the true artist achieves.

You may learn to draw at a college or privately: you learn to make good windows only by working in a studio where you are faced with a plethora of requirements which differ from one order to another. It is by facing the various problems that you assimilate knowledge and learn how to apply it, and to rise superior to any fallacious dictation of style imposed, perhaps unwittingly, by a college or school or club.

Never scorn to mend a broken window: rejoice that you have an opportunity to study the work and technique of another man. Be careful that your new pieces do not stand out in a different plane from the older glass. You may have a good technique; even so, you may be able to improve it after assessing and trying other methods.

'You strive to teach yourself? You have an ignorant tutor.' This gruff comment from an aged man was kindly meant. Such direct statements can be corrosive or cleansing according to one's ability to discern the true meaning.

Do not overlook the value of black; examine Kempe's work—no matter what you think of it, whether highly or the reverse—and see for yourself.

EDWARD WOORE

The Chairman, at one of my lectures, once promised the audience that they would now learn how to distinguish between a good window and a bad one. I might have quoted those lines of Browning, 'Who's to arbitrate? Ten men love what I hate.' All we can do is to state our point of view and perhaps give our reasons for liking or disliking the particular work or style of work. To take the craftsman's point of view: there are certain rules he lays down for his own use. The window must admit light, but this light has to be tempered or modified at times. For instance, an east window is expected to be less bright, though my own opinion is that the west window might have some consideration too if it is a large window. There should of course be some authoritative planning wherever possible, to ensure a balanced order in the design and colour and tone of the window. The designer has to relate his design to the surrounding windows—not to follow the colouring tone or even the spacing or proportions of the adjacent work—but to avoid a discord. Certainly, in regard to tone and colour, he should not indulge his taste for rich and deep colour if the adjacent windows are light and delicate, and of course the converse holds too.

The next important fact is that the window should have a distinctly architectural

PLATE 116. Salisbury Cathedral 'David and Goliath'.
One of six panels in the chancel, by Edward Woore.

PLATE 117. The Church of Heverle, Belgium. 'The Adoration', by Eugene Yoors.

character. The design should have a severe and rigid construction with an insistence on verticality and straightness of line and mass.

The artist will appreciate that he is being helped in this by the bars and stanchions that already exist. He will add to this effect of rigidity by borders or by the use of geometric forms to frame up the various units of his composition. Further, he may echo these by some verticality in the figures and fall of the drapery. I am not suggesting that there can be any sort of formula, ready made for the designing of a window, but that the artist may combine the rigid formality essential to his decorative purpose with the less formal pictorialism that his patron usually expects of him. There are two opposing views about the purpose of the stained glass window. The one I have already put forward is that the window should be looked on as an architectural enrichment with of course a didactic purpose. The other view is that it's purpose is mainly pictorial. The latter view is nowadays less prevalent; in fact, quite a number of people look with suspicion on any window that is well drawn or that resembles anything on earth.

I should take a midway course between the two extremes of the purely pictorial and the purely ornamental. I would choose a course parallel to the medievalists. All the good things you may think of seem to have been done before at one time or another. Why not frankly borrow, beg or steal? Originality or plagiarism are almost synonymous. I've never seen much between them. Have I any space now for a few words about colour and the problems of tone and halation? These are problems that face the practising craftsman. I have already mentioned one fact, namely that while one artist has a taste for rich colours and deep tones, another identifies himself with light tone and perhaps slenderer leads. You may say that the heavy colouring is inspired by mid-thirteenth century glass and the paler colour scheme by the fifteenth century. Actually this is not a very true description of these periods, for corrosion, the penetration of dirt and a great accumulation of leads has added tremendously to the depth of tone. The glass of the fifteenth century was thinner, lighter in tone, and this period has been taken as the inspiration for much of the work of recent years. I think that an artist who works in a light key may face the danger of a thin and papery effect. This I think is due to a kind of doctrine absorbed in art schools that glass should be unpainted. Of course, you should use no more half tone than is necessary to prevent halation. You may dispense with pigment entirely if you wish, but take notice that you may find it wise to use a tinted white in places instead of the purer white you had planned.

GLOSSARY

ANTIQUE — A glass made by flattening a muff or cylinder of glass, and having qualities similar to antique glass.

BANDING — Soldering in position 'ties' of copper wire by which the section of the window is fastened to the supporting bars fixed in the masonry.

CAME — A strip of lead, three to four feet long, used for leading up the glass.

CARTOON — The full size drawing of the sketch.

CORE — The cross bar of the 'H' section of the lead.

CROCKETS — The ornamental bosses sculptored at intervals on any architectural member.

CULLET — Small pieces of glass discarded in the process of cutting.

CUTLINE — A sheet of tracing linen marked with the outline of the shapes of glass from which the glass is cut and leaded.

DALLES DE VERRE — Slabs of glass.

EASEL — A large sheet of plate or sheet glass, usually in a wooden frame, upon which the pieces of glass are held in position for painting.

EUTECTIC — A substance which melts easily.

FLASH — A thin veneer of coloured glass fused on to a white or different coloured glass in the process of blowing.

GROZE — To bite off or grind off very small pieces from the edge of the glass.

HALATION — The spreading of light which causes white portions of glass to appear larger according to the distance from the eye.

LATHEKIN — A small piece of flat shaped and smoothed wood used for opening and straightening the lead when glazing; doubtless old English 'little lathe'.

LEAF — The two uprights of the 'H' section of lead.

LEHR — Chamber for controlled cooling of glass.

MULLER — A piece of granite or glass, flat at the base, for grinding pigment or stain.

PATINA — A film produced by chemical action, oxidization or sulphurization, during the course of time.

PLATING — The placing of one piece of glass of the same shape on to another and leading in position.

QUARRIES — Square or diamond shaped pieces of glass.

REAMY — Wavy or streaky glass.

SCRATCH-CARD — A wire brush to remove tarnish from lead prior to soldering.

SIEGE — Floor of furnace for glass making.

TEMPLET — A piece of wood, cardboard or brown paper cut to fit exactly to the shape of the window opening.

BIBLIOGRAPHY

Angus-Butterworth, L. M., *The Manufacture of Glass*, Sir Isaac Pitman & Sons Ltd., London, 1948.

Aubert, Marcel, *Stained Glass of the Twelfth and Thirteenth Centuries*, Batsford, Switzerland, 1947.

Baldry, A. L., *Henry Holiday, Walker's Quarterly*, No. 31–32, London, 1930.

Betjeman, John, *First and Last Loves*, John Murray, London, 1951.

Boutell, Charles, M.A., *English Heraldry*, Reeves & Turner, London, 1889.

Day, Lewis, F., *Windows. A Book about Stained and Painted Glass*, Batsford, London, 1897.

Eden, F. Sydney, *Ancient Stained and Painted Glass*, Cambridge University Press, Cambridge, 1933.

Eliot, T. S., *Notes Towards the Definition of Culture*, Faber & Faber, London, 1948.

Eve, G. W., *Heraldry as Art*, Batsford, London, 1907.

Fox-Davies, A. C., *Complete Guide to Heraldry*, Nelson & Son Ltd., London, T. C. & E. C. Jack Ltd., Edinburgh

Harrison, F., M.A., F.S.A., *The Painted Glass of York*, S.P.C.K., London, 1927.

Harrison, Kenneth, *The Windows of King's College Chapel*, Cambridge University Press, Cambridge, 1952.

Journal of the British Society of Master Glass Painters, Heffer & Sons, 1924–1957.

Knowles, John A., *A History of the York School of Glass Painting*, S.P.C.K., London, 1936.

McKay, H., *The Tricks of Light and Colour*, Oxford Press, London, 1947.

Norris, Dom Charles, O.S.B., *Stained Glass Article in Buckfast Abbey Chronicle*, Vol. VI. No. 4, Dec. 1936.

Phillips, C. J., *Glass; The Miracle Maker*, Sir Isaac Pitman & Sons Ltd., London, 1941.

Phillips, L. March, *Form and Colour*, Duckworth & Co., London, 1915.

Read, Herbert, *English Stained Glass*, G. P. Putnam's Sons, London & New York, 1926.

Salzman, L. F., *Building in England Down to 1540*, Oxford University Press, Oxford, 1952.

Twining, E. W., *The Art and Craft of Stained Glass*, Sir Isaac Pitman & Sons, London, 1928.

Warrington, William, *History of Stained Glass*, London, 1848.

Weale, John, *Weale's Quarterly Papers on Architecture*, John Weale, London, 1845.

Webber, F. R., *Church Symbolism*, Jansen, Cleveland, U.S.A., 1927.

Werck, Alfred, *Stained Glass*, Nicholas L. Brown, New York, 1922.

Westlake, N. H. J., *A History of Design in Painted Glass*, James Parker & Co., London, 1881.

Whall, C. W., *Stained Glass Work*, John Hogg, London, 1931.

Willey, Basil, *Nineteenth Century Studies*, Chatto & Windus, London, 1949.

Winston, C., *Memoirs Illustrative of The Art of Glass Painting*, James Parker & Co., Oxford and London, 1847.

Woodforde, C., *English Stained and Painted Glass,* Clarendon Press, Oxford, 1954.

Woodforde, C., *The Stained Glass of New College, Oxford,* Oxford University Press, London, 1951.

Woodward, John, *A Treatise on Ecclesiastical Heraldry,* W. & A. K. Johnston, Edinburgh and London, 1894.

General Index

Index to Churches